BIZNOVATE

BIZNOVATE

CRACKING THE SECRETS OF BUSINESS INNOVATION

Authored By

Bob Philips

Disclaimer

Registered Office- 907-Sneh Nagar, Sapna Sangeeta Road,
Agrasen Square, Indore - 452001 (M.P.), India

Website: http://www.wingspublication.com

Email: mybook@wingspublication.com

First Published by WINGS PUBLICATION 2024

Title : Biznovate

Price : Rs. 999.99 | $ 14.99 | AED 49.99

ISBN : 978-93-6006-897-4

LIMITS OF LIABILITY/DISCLAIMER OF WARRANTY

"For my mom and dad
who have always believed in me."

Acknowledgment

This book would not have been possible without the constant support and encouragement of many wonderful people in my life.

First and foremost, I want to express my deepest gratitude to my family. To my mom, who is no longer with us, your love, guidance, and belief in me continue to inspire and drive me every day. To my dad, your steadfast support and wisdom have shaped who I am today. To my extended family, your affection, thoughts, and advice have been a source of strength and inspiration throughout this journey.

To my wife, thank you for your patience, understanding, and constant encouragement. Your love has been my anchor through every challenge.

To my friends, your companionship, fellowship, and wisdom have been invaluable. Our free time talks, casual meetings, and shared experiences have provided me with perspectives and insights that have enriched my understanding of the world.

I am profoundly grateful to my work colleagues. Your collaboration and dedication have been instrumental in every project we've undertaken together. Thank you for the late nights, the brainstorming sessions, and the relentless pursuit of excellence. Your commitment and passion inspire me every day.

To my clients, thank you for your trust and partnership. Through our collaborations, you have unknowingly taught me great lessons. Your challenges have pushed me to innovate and grow, and your successes have been my greatest rewards.

Finally, to everyone who has supported me in both good times and low times, your encouragement and belief in me have been my strength. Whether through words of wisdom, a listening ear, or a helping hand, you have all contributed to this journey.

This book is a reflection of the collective effort, wisdom, and support of all of you. I am deeply grateful for each and every one of you.

With heartfelt thanks,

Bob Philips

Preface

Welcome to this journey of innovation. This book was written to share the knowledge and experiences I've gathered over the years. As an innovator and leader, I've seen how creativity and resilience can drive change and progress. The goal of this book is to provide you with insights, tools, and confidence to start your own innovation journey.

This book covers the essential aspects of innovation, from developing the right mindset to implementing and sustaining new ideas. I've organized the content into a simple, effective framework to guide you through each stage of the innovation process. Throughout these pages, you'll find practical strategies, real-world examples, and personal stories to inspire and motivate you.

The eagle on the cover represents the incredible potential within each of us. Just as an eagle leaves its nest and takes flight, this book aims to help you explore new heights of creativity and innovation. The journey may be challenging, but the rewards are immense. With the right mindset, determination, and support, you can turn your ideas into reality and make a significant impact on the world around you.

Thank you for joining me on this adventure. I hope this book will be a valuable guide as you navigate the exciting world of innovation.

Best wishes,

Bob Philips

Team Innovation Readiness Assessment

Instructions: Consider each of the statements given below and indicate how frequently your team behaves in the manner indicated by the statement by entering the appropriate number from the rating scale in the blank beside the serial number.

Very frequently=4, Frequently=3, Sometimes=2, Rarely=1, Almost never=0

		MINDSET
	1	Our team embraces challenges and sees them as opportunities for growth.
	2	We regularly encourage creative thinking and new ideas.
	3	Team members are resilient and bounce back quickly from setbacks.
	4	We celebrate innovative efforts, even when they don't succeed.
		ANALYZE
	5	Our team consistently monitors market trends to identify new opportunities.
	6	We conduct thorough analyses of customer needs and preferences.
	7	We use data and insights to guide our decision-making process.
	8	Competitive intelligence is a regular part of our strategic planning.
		GENERATE
	9	Brainstorming sessions are a regular part of our team's activities.
	10	We use mind mapping and other visual tools to connect and develop ideas.
	11	Reverse thinking is employed to identify potential obstacles and solutions.
	12	Our team leverages diverse perspectives to generate innovative ideas.
		IMPLEMENT
	13	Our team follows a clear and detailed strategic plan for implementation.
	14	We regularly prototype and test our ideas before full-scale implementation.
	15	Feedback loops are in place to gather input and make necessary adjustments.
	16	We evaluate and adjust our strategies based on the results and feedback.
		CHANGE
	17	Leadership in our organization actively champions and supports innovation.
	18	We have embedded a culture of innovation into our daily operations.
	19	Our team is skilled at scaling innovations for broader impact.
	20	We have established metrics to measure the success of our innovation efforts.

Scoring

Add up your scores for each section:

Interpret your results:

80 - 64: Your team is highly innovative. Strengths include a strong collaborative culture, effective implementation of innovative ideas, and a clear vision for innovation. Continue to support and encourage these practices, and explore new opportunities to stay ahead.

63 - 48: Your team demonstrates good innovation potential with some areas needing improvement. Strengths include a proactive approach to generating ideas and adapting to change. Focus on improving areas such as resource allocation and continuous learning. Provide additional training and resources to bolster weaker areas.

47 - 32: Your team shows moderate alignment with innovation principles. Strengths include occasional successful implementations and some level of idea generation. Significant opportunities for growth exist in developing a consistent innovation mindset, enhancing collaboration, and refining implementation processes. Create an action plan to address these gaps.

31 - 16: Your team has significant opportunities for improvement in fostering innovation. Strengths may include isolated instances of creative thinking. Focus on building a foundational innovation culture, improving communication, and developing clear implementation strategies. Provide training and resources to build innovation capabilities within your team.

15 - 0: Your team struggles with innovation and may face considerable challenges in implementing innovative practices. Strengths may be minimal, with a need for comprehensive improvement across all areas. Consider a thorough review of team processes and culture. Engage with external experts or mentors to help build a foundation for innovation.

Use this assessment as a starting point to identify strengths and opportunities for growth in your team's innovation journey.

Personal Innovation Readiness Assessment

Instructions: Consider each of the statements given below and indicate how frequently your team behaves in the manner indicated by the statement by entering the appropriate number from the rating scale in the blank beside the serial number.

Very frequently=4, Frequently=3, Sometimes=2, Rarely=1, Almost never=0

		MINDSET
	1	I embrace challenges and see them as opportunities for growth.
	2	I regularly engage in creative thinking and generate new ideas.
	3	I am resilient and bounce back quickly from setbacks.
	4	I celebrate my innovative efforts, even when they don't succeed.
		ANALYZE
	5	I consistently monitor market trends to identify new opportunities.
	6	I conduct thorough analyses of customer needs and preferences.
	7	I use data and insights to guide our decision-making process.
	8	I regularly seek out competitive intelligence to inform my strategies.
		GENERATE
	9	I incorporate brainstorming sessions into my problem-solving process.
	10	I use mind mapping and other visual tools to connect and develop ideas.
	11	I employ reverse thinking to identify potential obstacles and solutions.
	12	I leverage diverse perspectives to generate innovative ideas.
		IMPLEMENT
	13	I follow a clear and detailed strategic plan for implementing my ideas.
	14	I regularly prototype and test my ideas before full-scale implementation.
	15	I gather feedback and make necessary adjustments to my plans.
	16	I evaluate and adjust my strategies based on results and feedback.
		CHANGE
	17	I actively champion and support innovation in my personal and professional life.
	18	I have embedded a culture of innovation into my daily routines.
	19	I am skilled at scaling my innovations for broader impact.
	20	I have established metrics to measure the success of my innovation efforts.

Scoring:

Add up your scores for each section:

Interpret your results:

80 - 64: You are highly innovative. Strengths include a strong creative mindset, effective implementation of ideas, and resilience in the face of challenges. Continue to nurture these strengths and seek new experiences to maintain your innovative edge.

63 - 48: You have a strong foundation for innovation with room for improvement. Strengths include the ability to generate ideas and adapt to change. Focus on enhancing areas such as detailed analysis and continuous learning. Seek feedback and engage in personal development activities.

47 - 32: You show moderate alignment with innovation principles. Strengths include occasional successful idea generation and implementation. Identify areas for growth, such as developing a consistent innovation mindset and improving resource management. Create a personal development plan to address these gaps.

31 - 16: You have significant opportunities for improvement in fostering innovation. Strengths may include sporadic instances of creative thinking. Conduct a self-assessment to identify key barriers and develop strategies to overcome them. Consider seeking mentorship or joining innovation-focused groups for support.

15 - 0: You may struggle with innovation and should consider a focused effort to build a more innovative mindset. Strengths may be minimal, requiring comprehensive improvement across all areas. Reflect on your current practices and mindset, and seek resources, training, and support to develop your innovation skills.

Use this assessment as a starting point to identify your strengths and opportunities for growth in your personal innovation journey.

Introduction: The Spark Behind The Magic

I'm excited that you're here. It's a true pleasure because it means you and I will have the opportunity to engage directly, just the two of us. There's something really close to my heart that I'm itching to share with you—innovation. It's this incredible force that's reshaped my entire world, and I've got this strong hunch that it's going to work wonders for you, too.

Let me take you back to where it all started for me. When I left the corporate world in 2009, I stepped into a role that required not just adaptation but a redefinition of how I viewed success and impact. As a consultant for global organizations, I quickly learned that innovation isn't just about new products or services—it's about seeing through the chaos and finding simplicity on the other side.

This book is an invitation to explore that process, to understand that innovation is more than a concept—it's a way of living. It's for the curious souls who look at the world and ask, "What could be?" It's for the brave, who see challenges not as barriers but as puzzles awaiting solutions. It's for you.

I'm writing because I've lived the struggle of translating a vision into reality. I've felt the thrill of a breakthrough and the crushing weight of a setback. Through it all, I've come to appreciate that the journey of innovation is as important as the destination. It's a path marked by resilience, creativity, and the relentless pursuit of something better.

This is not just my story—it's a testament to the collective spirit of innovators everywhere. It's a reflection of the countless hours spent in conversation with those who are shaping the future. It's the distilled essence of late-night brainstorming sessions and early-morning revelations. It's the product of collaboration and the result of facing down the fear of the unknown.

Why am I writing this book? Because I believe in the power of shared knowledge. I believe that the lessons we learn when we dare to innovate are too valuable to keep to ourselves. This book is my way of passing the torch to you so you can illuminate the corners of your own industry and maybe, just maybe, the world.

I write to connect with you, to share the principles that have guided me and to offer them as a compass for your own journey. I write in the hope that my experiences will resonate, inspire, and perhaps, make the road a bit clearer for someone else.

You know how sometimes; you stumble across something that just clicks? That "aha" moment that feels like a jigsaw piece falling right into place? That's what I want this book to be for you. My goal is to light that bulb over your head, to get you to say, "I've got it!"

I want this book to be the nudge you need to adopt innovation—not as a catchphrase, but as your new way of life. Think of it as your personal playbook for turning 'just another idea' into 'the idea that changed my life.' I'm talking about empowering you to take those wild, coffee-fueled dreams and give them legs. I'm here to help you navigate the maze of 'what-ifs' and come out on the other side with a 'here's how.'

What's in this book? From the garages where startups were incubated to the boardrooms where groundbreaking ideas were pitched, I've been there, right in the thick of it. I've also stood in countless boardrooms under the harsh glare of skeptical eyes, pitching ideas that felt too bold, too outlandish to be contained within those four walls. Yet, it was in those very rooms that imaginative ideas took flight, where a single, daring thought could pivot a company's destiny overnight.

Throughout my journey, I've had a front-row seat to the spectacle that is innovation. I've witnessed products that disrupt the market before the dawn breaks on their first day of release. I've been part of crafting strategies that didn't just play the game—they changed it entirely, rewriting the rules with a stroke of genius.

These aren't just moments; they're the brilliant points of light that create a constellation of innovation. It's this pattern, this framework of success against the odds, that I've come to call MAGIC. And within these pages, we'll delve deep into this blueprint, exploring its intricacies and discovering how you can apply it to your own ventures.

We won't just be talking theories here. You'll find real, tangible insights—lessons drawn from the front lines of business battles, strategies tested in the heat of market competition, and ideas that have bloomed in the fertile soil of creativity. This book is about taking that elusive concept of innovation and breaking it down into something you can hold, something you can use, something that can change the way you operate in your field.

I'll share with you the challenges that come with the territory of innovation—the roadblocks, the detours, and the pitfalls that many fall into. But more importantly, I'll share how to overcome them and how to navigate through the uncertainty with the grace of a seasoned traveler.

And then there's you. Beyond the strategies and the stories, this is about your journey of personal growth and renewal. It's about finding that place within you where the wellspring of innovation bubbles just beneath the surface, waiting for you to tap into it.

Finally, this conversation doesn't end with the last page. There lies the opportunity for a continued partnership. Through mentorship, we can take the seeds planted in this book and cultivate them, helping your ideas to flourish and grow into something beyond what you've imagined.

So, get ready. You're about to embark on a journey that will take you from where you are now to where you have the potential to be. It's time to dive into the pages of this book and discover the MAGIC within.

"Innovation is what drives progress; it's the quiet force behind every 'what if' and fuels our desire to try new things. When we innovate, we don't just create—we bring new ideas to life and shape the future with our imagination."

– Bob Philips –

Contents

Chapter 1

The Imperative Of Innovation

- **Why Innovation Matters.**
- **Risks Of Stagnation.**
- **The MAGIC Blueprint.**

The human mind is inherently curious and driven by a deep-seated need for discovery. This innate curiosity pushes us to seek out new experiences and solutions, fueling our relentless pursuit of improvement. According to a study by the University of California, Berkeley, this natural curiosity enhances learning and memory, proving that our brains are wired to explore and innovate.

From the moment early humans crafted their first tools, our desire to innovate has been the catalyst for progress. This drive has led to the monumental leaps we've seen throughout history, from the wheel's invention to the digital age's life-changing technologies. Our minds crave novelty and challenge, which explains why we are constantly striving to create, improve, and advance.

Innovation is an essential part of our human nature. It's what enables us to adapt to new challenges, solve complex problems, and push the boundaries of what's possible.

Why Innovation Matters

Innovation is the lifeblood of progress, the force that propels us forward and reshapes our world. It drives advancements in every field, from technology and healthcare to education and beyond. Imagine the leaps in medical treatments, the revolutionary gadgets we use daily, and the evolving methods of teaching—all fruits of relentless innovation.

For businesses, innovation is crucial. It's not just about survival; it's about thriving. In a rapidly changing market, innovation keeps companies ahead of the curve, allowing them to outpace competitors, satisfy shifting customer demands, and streamline operations for greater efficiency. Companies that innovate set themselves apart, creating unique value propositions that attract and retain customers.

On a personal level, innovation opens doors to growth and fulfillment. It encourages us to think creatively, solve problems effectively, and welcome new opportunities. By fostering an innovative mindset, we enhance our ability to adapt to change, overcome challenges, and achieve personal goals. This continuous improvement leads to a more engaging and rewarding life.

Innovation is more than just a business strategy or personal ambition—it's a fundamental human drive. It enables us to make a meaningful impact on our surroundings, improves the quality of our lives, and paves the way for a brighter, more dynamic future.

Let's start by looking at why innovation is crucial for business growth.

Business Growth Through Innovation

Staying Competitive:

In today's fast-paced market, standing still is a recipe for obsolescence. Competitors are always on the move, constantly finding fresh ways to attract customers and optimize operations. To stay in the game, businesses must pursue innovation. It's what keeps them relevant and ahead of the curve. By continually enhancing their products, services, and processes, businesses can carve out a unique identity that sets them apart. This continuous improvement not only helps retain existing customers but also attracts new ones, thereby maintaining and even expanding their market share. Innovation is the key to staying dynamic in a world that never stops evolving. It's about being proactive, anticipating changes, and turning challenges into opportunities. In a nutshell, innovation is the lifeline that keeps businesses vibrant and competitive in an ever-changing environment.

Meeting Customer Needs:

Customers' needs and preferences are in a constant state of flux. What was a hit yesterday might be obsolete tomorrow. This is where innovation steps in. It enables businesses to stay in sync with these evolving demands and adapt swiftly. By actively listening to their customers and anticipating future needs, companies can create solutions that genuinely resonate with their audience. This proactive approach ensures that businesses not only meet but exceed customer expectations. Innovation translates feedback into actionable insights, turning potential challenges into opportunities for growth. It's about staying relevant, being responsive, and delighting customers with products and services that feel tailor-made just for them. In a world where the customer is king, innovation is the key to building lasting relationships and ensuring continued success.

Driving Efficiency:

Innovation isn't just about flashy new products; it's about making everything run smoother and smarter. By streamlining processes, reducing waste, and boosting efficiency, businesses can make a big impact on their bottom line. Think of it as fine-tuning a machine—every little adjustment can lead to better performance. Innovative thinking helps companies find new, improved ways to operate, cutting down on time and resource wastage. This means not only doing things faster but also doing them better. The result? More time to focus on what really matters—delivering value to customers and growing the business. In a world where every second and penny counts, innovation is the key to staying lean, agile, and ahead of the competition.

Opening New Markets:

Innovation is a gateway to uncharted territories. Sometimes, it reveals entirely new markets just waiting to be tapped. By thinking outside the box, businesses can spot unmet needs and create products or services that perfectly address them. This isn't just about incremental improvements—it's about bold leaps into new arenas. When companies innovate, they unlock fresh revenue streams and broaden their horizons, reaching audiences they never thought possible. It's like finding a hidden treasure map in the everyday routine, guiding you to opportunities ripe for exploration. This proactive approach not only diversifies income sources but also positions the business as a trailblazer in the industry. In essence, innovation opens doors to new possibilities, ensuring sustained growth and long-term success.

Attracting and Retaining Talent:

Top talent is magnetically drawn to innovative companies. People are eager to work for organizations that are forward-thinking and dynamic, places where creativity and progress thrive. By fostering a culture of innovation, businesses become inspirations for passionate, driven individuals who want to make a difference. These employees are not just looking for a job; they're seeking an environment where their ideas are valued and their contributions matter. An innovative culture keeps them engaged, motivated, and loyal, significantly reducing turnover. When businesses prioritize innovation, they attract and retain the best minds, fueling continuous growth and success. It's a win-win: employees find fulfillment and purpose, while companies benefit from their talent and enthusiasm. In today's competitive world, an innovative workplace is the ultimate magnet for top-tier talent.

Personal Growth Through Innovation

Innovation isn't limited to businesses; it's equally important for personal growth. Here's why:

Enhancing Problem-Solving Skills:

Innovation sparks creative thinking and sharpens problem-solving skills. When you engage in innovative activities, you naturally develop these critical abilities. This isn't just useful in your professional life; it's a game-changer in everyday situations, too. Imagine being able to think on your feet, tackling challenges with fresh, creative solutions. Whether you're brainstorming a new project at work or figuring out a tricky situation at home, these skills are invaluable. They make you more adaptable, resourceful, and resilient. Embracing innovation means constantly pushing your mind to find better, smarter ways to solve problems, turning obstacles into opportunities. This growth mindset not only boosts your confidence but also prepares you to face any challenge life throws your way. Innovation, at its core, empowers you to navigate through life with ingenuity and confidence.

Fostering Adaptability:

The world is always changing, and those who can adapt are the ones who thrive. Innovation teaches you how to be adaptable. It encourages you to harness change, try new ideas, and pivot when needed. This kind of flexibility is crucial in a world where the only constant is change. By being innovative, you learn to navigate uncertainties with ease and confidence. You become more resilient, ready to face new challenges and seize opportunities as they come. Embracing innovation means you're always growing, always learning, and always ready for what's next. This adaptability not only helps you succeed in your career but also enriches your personal life, making you more dynamic and versatile. In a rapidly evolving world, the ability to adapt is your greatest strength, and innovation is the key to developing this vital skill.

Boosting Confidence:

Bringing an idea to life is incredibly empowering. Whether it's a new project at work or a personal endeavor, successfully innovating can significantly boost your confidence and self-esteem. It's a powerful reminder that you have the ability to make a difference and create something valuable. Every time you take a creative idea and turn it into reality, you're proving to yourself that you can overcome challenges and achieve your goals. This sense of accomplishment builds a positive cycle of confidence, motivating you to tackle even bigger and bolder projects. Innovation shows you that your contributions matter, and that you have the power to shape your world. With each success, your belief in your abilities grows, empowering you to continue pushing boundaries and striving for excellence.

Encouraging Lifelong Learning:

Innovation thrives on a willingness to learn. To innovate, you must stay curious, seek out new information, and continuously improve your skills. This mindset of lifelong learning keeps you open to new ideas and ready to adapt to change. It's about embracing every opportunity to grow and expand your knowledge. When you commit to lifelong learning, you unlock personal and professional growth. New doors open, and your horizons broaden. You become more versatile, adaptable, and equipped to face challenges head-on. This endless quest for knowledge not only fuels innovation but also enriches your life, making every day an adventure in discovery and improvement. Stay curious, keep learning, and let innovation guide you to new heights.

Creating Fulfillment:

At its heart, innovation is about making things better. This drive to improve can lead to a profound sense of fulfillment. Knowing that your efforts have made a positive impact—whether on a small scale or a grand one—brings incredible satisfaction. It infuses your work and life with purpose and meaning. When you see the results of your innovative ideas helping others, solving problems, or creating joy, it's deeply rewarding. It's a reminder that what you do matters. This sense of fulfillment motivates you to keep pushing boundaries and striving for excellence. Innovation not only redefines the world around you but also enriches your own life, giving you a lasting sense of achievement and purpose.

I would like to illustrate the importance of innovation. Let's look at a few real-world examples.

Apple:

I personally am inspired by Apple's relentless drive for innovation. From the first Macintosh computer to the revolutionary iPhone, Apple has consistently introduced groundbreaking products that have reshaped entire industries. Their journey is a testament to what can be achieved with vision and determination. As I write this book, Apple is still pushing the boundaries of technology. They're launching the Apple Vision Pro, a cutting-edge mixed-reality headset that promises to redefine how we interact with digital content. They're also making incredible advancements in AI-powered features across their devices. These innovations not only enhance user experiences but also set new standards for the tech industry. Apple's commitment to innovation is a powerful reminder of the impact creativity and vision can have on the world. It's stories like these that fuel my own passion for innovation and drive me to explore new possibilities.

Tesla:

I find Tesla's journey incredibly inspiring. Tesla has revolutionized the automotive industry with its electric vehicles, proving that cars can be both environmentally friendly and highly desirable. Their dedication to innovation goes beyond just making cars; it's about reimagining how we approach energy and transportation. Tesla continues to push the envelope with advancements in autonomous driving technology and sustainable energy solutions, like their solar panels and Powerwall battery storage systems. Tesla's approach is a brilliant example of how innovation can create products that not only meet but exceed customer expectations. Their relentless pursuit of better, greener solutions shows the power of visionary thinking. Tesla's success story encourages me to believe in the potential of innovative ideas to drive positive change in the world.

Amazon:

Amazon's story is a powerful source of inspiration for me. Starting as an online bookstore, Amazon has grown into a global e-commerce giant thanks to its unwavering commitment to innovation. Their success is rooted in their ability to constantly find new ways to add value for their customers. From developing sophisticated recommendation algorithms that personalize shopping experiences to introducing Amazon Prime, which revolutionized convenience with fast shipping and exclusive content, Amazon has continuously raised the bar. Amazon is still at the forefront of innovation, exploring advancements in AI, cloud computing, and even drone delivery. Their journey demonstrates how a relentless focus on innovation can evolve a simple idea into a world-changing enterprise. Amazon's innovative spirit inspires me to believe that with creativity and determination, any business can achieve remarkable growth and impact.

Netflix:

Netflix's journey is a major source of inspiration for me. What started as a DVD rental service has evolved into a powerhouse that reshaped the entertainment industry by embracing streaming. Netflix's willingness to innovate and take bold risks has kept them ahead of the competition and allowed them to adapt to changing consumer preferences. By investing in original content and using sophisticated algorithms to recommend shows and movies, Netflix has created a personalized viewing experience that millions love. Netflix continues to innovate, exploring new ways to deliver content and enhance the user experience. Their story shows how a commitment to innovation can lead to incredible growth and success. Netflix's journey motivates me to believe that embracing change and pushing boundaries can lead to groundbreaking results in any field.

Innovation is not a luxury; it's essential. For businesses, it's the key to staying competitive, meeting customer needs, driving efficiency, opening new markets, and attracting top talent. Companies that innovate thrive by continuously improving and adapting to the ever-changing marketplace. For individuals, innovation enhances problem-solving skills, fosters adaptability, boosts confidence, encourages lifelong learning, and creates a deep sense of fulfillment. Embracing innovation means constantly seeking better solutions and embracing new opportunities, both professionally and personally. It's about being proactive, creative, and resilient. Innovation drives growth and success, making it an imperative for anyone looking to make a meaningful impact in their field or life. As we explore further, you'll discover how to harness the power of innovation to achieve your goals and elevate your journey.

The Risks of Stagnation

I've seen firsthand how stagnation can be a silent killer for both businesses and individuals. Staying still in a rapidly changing world means more than just missing growth opportunities; it means falling behind, losing relevance, and risking failure. On the other hand, continuous innovation drives success and growth. I've learned from industry leaders and personal experience that embracing change and constantly seeking new ways to improve can open up incredible opportunities. Let's explore the risks of stagnation.

Loss of Competitive Edge

Failing to innovate can quickly cause businesses to lose their competitive edge. Competitors who adopt new technologies and methodologies leap ahead, capturing market share and customer attention. I've watched stagnant companies struggle, offering outdated products or services that no longer meet customer expectations. This leads to declining sales and a shrinking market presence. It's a harsh reality: if you're not moving forward, you're falling behind. Innovation is crucial to stay relevant and competitive. By continuously improving and adapting, businesses can meet evolving customer needs and maintain their place in the market.

Declining Customer Satisfaction

Have you noticed how quickly customer needs and preferences evolve? Companies that don't keep up with these changes risk losing their customers. Businesses that stagnate end up with dissatisfied customers who turn to competitors that better meet their evolving needs. In today's market, customer loyalty is hard-won and easily lost. Staying in tune with what customers want and continuously innovating to meet those needs is essential. When companies fail to adapt, they alienate their customer base, leading to a decline in satisfaction and loyalty. Keeping customers happy means constantly evolving and improving.

Reduced Efficiency

Have you seen how businesses that don't innovate can fall into the trap of relying on outdated processes and technologies? This leads to inefficiencies that can drive up costs, slow down response times, and decrease productivity. Over time, these inefficiencies can eat away at profit margins and make it tough to compete with more agile companies. Continuous innovation is key to staying efficient. By constantly improving and updating operations, businesses can stay lean, responsive, and competitive. It's all about finding better ways to do things and keeping up with the fast-paced changes in the market.

Inability to Attract and Retain Talent

I've seen how top talent gravitates towards dynamic, forward-thinking companies. When a business is perceived as stagnant, it struggles to attract and retain skilled employees. Talented professionals want to work where they can grow, learn, and contribute to exciting projects. Stagnation can lead to high turnover rates and a workforce lacking motivation and creativity. It's clear to me that fostering an innovative environment is key to keeping great employees. When companies drive innovation, they create a culture that inspires and retains top talent, ensuring a motivated and creative workforce.

Financial Instability

Stagnation can quickly lead to financial instability. When businesses fail to innovate, they often see declining revenue as customers migrate to more innovative competitors. This decline can create a vicious cycle where reduced revenue limits the ability to invest in new initiatives, further entrenching the company in its stagnant state. Over time, this financial instability can lead to layoffs, cutbacks, and even bankruptcy. Continuous innovation is crucial for financial health. By staying ahead of the curve and constantly improving, businesses can maintain steady revenue, invest in growth, and avoid the pitfalls of stagnation.

Erosion of Brand Reputation

Do you know how crucial a company's reputation is to its success? A brand's reputation is built on its ability to meet customer needs and stay relevant. When a company stagnates, it risks damaging its reputation, as customers and stakeholders start to see it as out-of-touch or unable to adapt. Once a good reputation is lost, it's incredibly hard to rebuild and can have long-lasting negative effects on the business. Continuous innovation is essential to maintaining a strong brand reputation. By staying relevant and responsive to customer needs, businesses can preserve their credibility and trustworthiness in the market.

Let me share a couple of real-world examples that highlight the impact of stagnation versus innovation.

Blockbuster vs. Netflix

Blockbuster was once a giant in the video rental industry but failed to innovate and adapt to changing consumer preferences. As streaming technology emerged, Blockbuster clung to its traditional rental model. Meanwhile, Netflix has embraced new technology, continuously innovating and changing the entertainment industry. Netflix's commitment to innovation led to its tremendous success, while Blockbuster's stagnation resulted in its downfall. This stark contrast shows how crucial it is to stay ahead and adapt to a rapidly evolving market.

Kodak vs. Digital Photography

Consider Kodak and the digital photography revolution. Kodak was a pioneer in photography and even invented the first digital camera. However, they failed to integrate the digital revolution, remaining focused on film. This hesitation to innovate allowed other companies, like Canon and Sony, to capitalize on digital photography. As a result, Kodak missed the opportunity to lead in this new era and eventually faced a significant decline.

This example clearly shows the risks of stagnation and the importance of embracing innovation to stay relevant and competitive in an ever-changing market.

Stagnation poses significant risks to both businesses and individuals, leading to a loss of competitiveness, customer dissatisfaction, inefficiency, talent drain, financial instability, and damaged reputations. Conversely, continuous innovation offers numerous benefits, including sustained competitive advantage, enhanced customer satisfaction, increased efficiency, talent attraction, financial growth, and a strong brand reputation.

Embracing continuous innovation is not just a strategy for survival—it's a pathway to thriving in a dynamic, ever-changing world. By fostering a culture of creativity, investing in research, encouraging collaboration, staying customer-centric, and being willing to adapt, businesses and individuals can harness the power of innovation to achieve remarkable success.

As you explore the principles and strategies in this book, I hope you'll be inspired to make continuous innovation a core part of your personal and professional journey. The rewards of embracing innovation are immense, leading to growth, fulfillment, and a lasting impact on the world around you. Let's move forward, innovate continuously, and shape a brighter future together.

Introducing the MAGIC Blueprint

Innovation can seem like an elusive concept, a spark of genius that appears out of nowhere. But through my journey, I've discovered that innovation isn't just a mysterious force; it's something that can be nurtured, developed, and harnessed. This realization led me to create the MAGIC Blueprint, my formula for fostering continuous innovation. It's a model that encapsulates the essence of what drives innovation and provides a structured approach to achieving it.

My Journey to Discovering MAGIC

Let me take you back to where this all started. As someone who has been deeply involved in both the corporate world and entrepreneurial ventures, I've always been fascinated by what makes some ideas soar while others fizzle out. I've seen firsthand the struggles and triumphs that come with trying to innovate. It's not always a smooth path, but it's one filled with moments of brilliance and breakthroughs.

I've worked with global organizations, helping them tackle complex problems and discover innovative solutions. Through this experience, I've learned that while the context and challenges may differ, the underlying principles of innovation remain consistent. I started to see patterns, common threads that wove through the success stories of groundbreaking companies and life-changing ideas.

These observations became the foundation of the MAGIC Blueprint. It's my way of distilling the vast, often chaotic world of innovation into a manageable, actionable framework. I'm thrilled to share this with you because I believe it can empower anyone to harness their creative potential and drive meaningful change.

The Essence of MAGIC

MAGIC stands for Mindset, Analyze, Generate, Implement, and Change. These five components form the core of the blueprint, each playing a crucial role in the innovation process. Think of it as a journey, where each step builds upon the last, guiding you from the initial spark of an idea to its full realization and beyond.

Mindset

The journey begins with cultivating the right mindset. Innovation starts within you. It's about fostering a mindset that absorbs creativity, curiosity, and resilience. I've seen how the right mindset can revolutionize not just individuals, but entire organizations. It's about believing that change is possible and that you can be the catalyst for that change.

Analyze

Once you have the mindset, the next step is to analyze. This involves understanding the ecosystem, identifying opportunities, and recognizing the challenges. It's about being a keen observer, spotting trends, and making sense of the data. Analysis provides the clarity needed to direct your innovative efforts effectively.

Generate

With a clear understanding of the ecosystem, it's time to generate ideas. This is where creativity comes into play. It's about brainstorming, thinking outside the box, and coming up with solutions that address the identified opportunities and challenges. Generating ideas is not just a one-time activity; it's an ongoing process of exploration and experimentation.

Implement

Ideas without action are just dreams. The next step is to implement those ideas. This involves planning, executing, and refining. It's about turning concepts into reality, testing them, and making necessary adjustments. Implementation is where the rubber meets the road, and it's often the most challenging part of the journey. But with the right approach, it's also the most rewarding.

Change

The final component is change. Innovation is not a one-time event; it's a continuous cycle. This means being open to feedback, learning from experiences, and being willing to pivot when necessary. It's about creating a culture of continuous improvement and adaptation. Change is both the outcome of successful innovation and the driving force for future innovation.

The Power of MAGIC

What excites me most about the MAGIC Blueprint is its versatility. It's not limited to any specific industry or type of innovation. Whether you're looking to improve business processes, develop new products, or even drive personal growth, MAGIC provides a structured yet flexible approach that can be tailored to your unique needs.

I've seen the MAGIC Blueprint in action across various settings. It has helped startups find their footing, enabled established companies to reinvent themselves, and inspired individuals to pursue their passions with renewed vigor. It's a model that grows with you, adapting to new challenges and opportunities as they arise.

The joy I feel in sharing the MAGIC Blueprint comes from knowing its potential to empower and change. It's a tool that can unlock your creative potential, guide you through the complexities of innovation, and help you achieve extraordinary results. Innovation doesn't have to be an intimidating concept; with the right approach, it can be a journey filled with discovery, growth, and fulfillment.

In the chapters that follow, we'll thoroughly examine each component of the MAGIC Blueprint. You'll gain insights, strategies, and practical tools that you can apply to your own innovation journey. My hope is that as you explore these concepts, you'll feel the same excitement and inspiration that I do.

Innovation is a journey, not a destination. It's about constantly pushing the boundaries, challenging the status quo, and striving for excellence. The MAGIC Blueprint is your guide on this journey, providing the structure and support you need to turn your ideas into reality.

Let's get going on this journey together. Embrace the MAGIC within you and discover the limitless possibilities that innovation can bring. I can't wait to see what you'll create.

"Innovation thrives where imagination meets persistence; it's not just about having great ideas, but about having the courage to bring them to life."

– Bob Philips –

Chapter 2

M - Mindset: Cultivating Innovation From Within

- **Importance Of Developing The Right Mindset For Innovation.**
- **Strategies For Fostering Creativity, Curiosity, And Resilience.**
- **How Mindset Prepares Individuals And Organizations For Successful Innovation Journeys.**

When I think about the foundation of innovation, one word always comes to mind: mindset. Over the years, I've learned that the right mindset is the key to unlocking creativity and progress. It's not just about having brilliant ideas; it's about cultivating a way of thinking that allows those ideas to flourish. A mindset geared toward innovation is open, curious, and resilient. It's about seeing possibilities where others see obstacles and being willing to experiment and learn from failures. This kind of mindset doesn't come naturally to everyone, but it can be developed and nurtured.

Why Mindset Matters

Let me start with a personal story. Early in my career, I worked with an insurance company that was struggling to stay relevant in a competitive market. Despite having skilled employees and ample resources, their claims department was lagging behind competitors. The team was working on streamlining the claims process, which had great potential, but progress was painfully slow. They were focused on following outdated procedures and were hesitant to try anything new.

I spent time observing their workflow and attending meetings. It became clear that the problem wasn't their technical ability—it was their mindset. The team was afraid to take risks or propose unconventional solutions, fearing failure and criticism. They were stuck in old ways of thinking, believing that sticking to familiar methods was safer.

I encouraged the team to shift their perspective and cultivate a growth mindset. We started by brainstorming sessions where no idea was too outlandish, and everyone was encouraged to think creatively. I shared stories of successful innovations in other companies that came from taking bold risks and learning from failures. Slowly, the team began to open up to new approaches.

One critical change was how they handled claims processing. Instead of sticking to a rigid, step-by-step procedure, they started implementing a more flexible, customer-centric approach. They also introduced new technologies, such as automated claim verification, which allowed them to process claims more quickly and accurately. The results were impressive—the claims process became faster and more efficient, leading to higher customer satisfaction.

This experience taught me that innovation starts from within. It begins with the way we think and approach problems. By fostering a mindset that welcomes change, creativity, and risk-taking, the team redefined their approach and achieved remarkable results.

A mindset geared towards innovation is open, curious, and resilient. It's about seeing possibilities where others see obstacles. It's about being willing to experiment, fail, and learn from those failures. This kind of mindset doesn't come naturally to everyone, but the good news is that it can be developed.

Embracing Curiosity

Curiosity is the fuel of innovation. When you're curious, you're always asking questions, seeking new knowledge, and exploring different perspectives. Think about children—they're naturally curious, always asking "why" and "how." As adults, we often lose that sense of wonder. To cultivate an innovative mindset, we need to reignite our curiosity.

Take, for example, the story of Steve Jobs. He was known for his insatiable curiosity. Jobs would immerse himself into subjects that interested him, from calligraphy to music, and these diverse interests often sparked new ideas. His curiosity led to the development of products that were not only functional but also beautifully designed. The Mac's typography options, for instance, were directly influenced by a calligraphy class Jobs attended.

This seemingly unrelated interest added a unique and valuable dimension to Apple's products.

Start by embracing your own curiosity. Read widely, explore new fields, and don't be afraid to ask questions. Curiosity opens your mind to new possibilities and can lead to unexpected breakthroughs. Think about the topics that fascinate you, even if they seem unrelated to your work. Dive into them, learn, and see how they might intersect with your projects and ideas.

Ask yourself questions daily. Challenge the status quo. Why do things work the way they do? How can they be improved? Surround yourself with curious people who inspire you to think differently and push boundaries. Remember, innovation often comes from connecting the dots between seemingly unrelated ideas. By reigniting your curiosity, you open the door to endless possibilities and pave the way for true innovation.

Embracing Risk and Failure

Innovation is inherently risky. When you try something new, there's always a chance it won't work out. But here's the thing: failure is not the end—it's part of the journey. Some of the most successful innovations have come from repeated failures and learning from those experiences.

Consider Thomas Edison, who famously said, "I have not failed. I've just found 10,000 ways that won't work." Edison's perseverance and willingness to accept failure led to the invention of the light bulb. His mindset was one of resilience and determination. Every unsuccessful attempt was a lesson that brought him closer to his goal.

To develop an innovative mindset, you need to shift your perspective on failure. Instead of seeing it as a setback, view it as a learning opportunity. Each failure brings you one step closer to success. Encourage yourself and your team to take calculated risks and learn from the outcomes.

Think of failure as a stepping stone rather than a stumbling block. Each misstep teaches you something valuable and provides insights that can guide your next attempt. Accept the uncertainty and the potential for mistakes as part of the creative process.

Create an environment where risk-taking is encouraged, and failures are seen as opportunities for growth. Celebrate the effort and the lessons learned, not just the successes. This approach will foster a culture of innovation where everyone feels empowered to experiment and push boundaries.

By embracing risk and failure, you open the door to greater creativity and innovation. It's through these experiences that breakthroughs are made and extraordinary ideas come to life. So, take that leap, learn from the falls, and keep pushing forward.

Staying Resilient

Resilience is the ability to bounce back from setbacks and keep moving forward. In the world of innovation, resilience is essential. There will be challenges, obstacles, and moments of doubt. But with a resilient mindset, you can overcome these hurdles and continue to pursue your goals.

I remember working on a project at Skills Cafe where we designed game-based content for behavioral competencies. We faced numerous setbacks, and each problem felt like a step backward. There were moments when it seemed easier to abandon the project altogether. But what kept us going was our resilience. We believed in our vision and were determined to find a way forward. Eventually, we succeeded, and the experience taught me the power of resilience. Seeing our game-based training programs come to life and positively impact our clients reaffirmed the importance of persistence.

Developing resilience starts with believing in yourself and your ideas. Surround yourself with supportive people who encourage you and provide constructive feedback. At Skills Cafe, our team's support and collective determination played a crucial role in overcoming obstacles. Practice self-care and stress management to maintain your mental and emotional well-being. This might mean taking breaks, engaging in activities you enjoy, or simply giving yourself time to recharge.

Resilience isn't about avoiding challenges; it's about facing them head-on and continuing to push forward. Each setback is an opportunity to learn and grow. By staying resilient, you build the strength to navigate the ups and downs of innovation, ultimately driving your projects to success. Confront the challenges, trust in your vision, and keep moving forward.

Fostering Creativity

Creativity is at the heart of innovation. It's the ability to see things differently, to connect seemingly unrelated ideas, and to come up with unique solutions. Cultivating a creative mindset involves nurturing your creativity and encouraging it in others.

One way to foster creativity is to create an environment that encourages it. Think about Google's approach to innovation. They provide their employees with creative spaces, flexible work hours, and the freedom to explore new ideas. This environment fosters creativity and has led to the development of some of the company's most successful products.

You can foster creativity by giving yourself time and space to think. Take breaks, engage in activities that inspire you, and allow your mind to wander. Sometimes, stepping away from a problem can lead to unexpected insights. Encourage brainstorming sessions where all ideas are welcome, no matter how unconventional they may seem. Remember, creativity often comes from thinking outside the box.

Value diverse perspectives and experiences, as they can provide fresh viewpoints and spark new ideas. By fostering a culture of creativity, you create a fertile ground for innovation to flourish. Let your imagination run free and see where it takes you. Nurturing creativity within yourself and your team can lead to remarkable breakthroughs and drive continuous innovation.

Cultivating a Growth Mindset

The concept of a growth mindset, introduced by psychologist Carol Dweck, is highly relevant to innovation. A growth mindset is the belief that abilities and intelligence can be developed through dedication and hard work. This contrasts with a fixed mindset, which assumes that talents are innate and unchangeable.

In an innovative mindset, a growth mindset is crucial. It allows you to see challenges as opportunities for growth, to persist in the face of setbacks, and to appreciate learning. When you believe that you can improve and develop, you're more likely to take on new challenges and push the boundaries of what's possible.

To cultivate a growth mindset, start by challenging your own beliefs about your abilities. Replace negative self-talk with positive affirmations and focus on your progress rather than your limitations. For instance, instead of thinking, "I can't do this," try, "I can't do this yet, but I'm learning."

Encourage a growth mindset in your team by celebrating effort and improvement, not just success. Acknowledge the hard work and learning process that goes into achieving results. This approach fosters an environment where people feel comfortable taking risks and experimenting, knowing that their efforts are valued.

Continuous learning and development are at the heart of a growth mindset. Seek out new knowledge, skills, and experiences. Leverage challenges as opportunities to grow and learn. By cultivating a growth mindset, you create a foundation for continuous innovation, both personally and within your team. This mindset shift can reshape how you approach problems and drive you toward greater achievements.

Emphasizing Collaboration

Innovation rarely happens in isolation. It's often the result of collaboration, where diverse perspectives come together to create something new. Developing a collaborative mindset involves recognizing the value of teamwork and actively seeking input from others.

Consider the example of the Wright brothers. Their innovative approach to flight was the result of continuous collaboration and shared insights. They combined their unique skills and knowledge to achieve a common goal. Their success in pioneering aviation wasn't just due to their individual talents but their ability to work together, share ideas, and build on each other's strengths.

To foster collaboration, create a culture of openness and trust. Encourage team members to share their ideas and respect different viewpoints. This means creating an environment where everyone feels safe to speak up and contribute. Collaboration is not just about working together; it's about creating a synergy where the whole is greater than the sum of its parts.

In practical terms, this could involve regular brainstorming sessions, cross-functional teams, and open forums for discussion. Make it a point to actively listen to others, valuing their input and considering their perspectives. Collaboration can lead to more creative solutions and a deeper understanding of the challenges at hand.

By emphasizing collaboration, you tap into the collective intelligence and creativity of your team. This collaborative mindset can drive innovation and lead to breakthroughs that might not have been possible through individual effort alone. Celebrate the power of teamwork and watch as new ideas flourish and grow.

Practicing Mindfulness

Mindfulness is the practice of being present and fully engaged in the moment. It's about paying attention to your thoughts, feelings, and surroundings without judgment. Mindfulness can enhance your ability to innovate by improving your focus, reducing stress, and increasing your awareness of new possibilities.

I've found that practicing mindfulness helps me stay centered and open to new ideas. Whether it's through meditation, deep breathing exercises, or simply taking a few moments to pause and reflect, mindfulness can be a powerful tool for cultivating an innovative mindset. When you're mindful, you're better able to notice the subtle connections and insights that can lead to breakthroughs.

Incorporate mindfulness into your daily routine. Take a few minutes each day to clear your mind, focus on your breath, and be present. This can be as simple as taking a few deep breaths before starting your day or setting aside a few minutes for meditation. Mindfulness helps you to stay grounded and calm, which is essential when facing the pressures and uncertainties of the innovation process.

By being fully present, you can approach problems with a fresh perspective and remain open to new ideas. Mindfulness allows you to engage deeply with your work and the people around you, fostering a more creative and collaborative environment. As you practice mindfulness, you'll find that it not only enhances your well-being but also unlocks your creative potential, enabling you to innovate more effectively.

Developing an innovative mindset isn't always straightforward. Along the journey, you'll encounter various *barriers and deception stages* that can cloud your thinking and hinder your progress. Understanding these barriers and learning how to navigate through deception stages are crucial steps toward fostering an extraordinary mindset. Here, I'll share insights into these challenges and provide strategies to overcome them, helping you cultivate a mindset primed for innovation.

There are some common barriers to an innovative mindset.

Fear of Failure

Fear of failure is one of the biggest barriers to innovation. It can paralyze you, making you reluctant to take risks or try new things. This fear often stems from past experiences or a desire for perfection. When you're afraid of failing, you might avoid challenges, overanalyze every decision, and shy away from opportunities that require stepping out of your comfort zone.

I recall a project where my fear of failure almost held me back. I was working on a new leadership learning module, and the pressure to make it perfect was intense. This fear was stopping me from experimenting and being creative. I became overly cautious, second-guessing every idea and decision. It wasn't until I accepted the possibility of failure that I began to find new and better ways to approach the project. Letting go of the need for perfection allowed me to take risks and innovate. It's important to see failure not as an end but as a stepping stone to success. Recognizing and addressing the symptoms of fear of failure—such as avoidance of challenges, over-analysis, and reluctance to take risks—can help you break free from its paralyzing grip and open the door to creativity and progress.

Fixed Mindset

A fixed mindset can significantly hinder your potential for growth and innovation. When you believe that your abilities and intelligence are static and unchangeable, you limit yourself from trying new things and improving. This mindset creates a fear of failure and discourages risk-taking, both of which are essential for innovation.

Symptoms of a fixed mindset include avoiding challenges, giving up easily when faced with obstacles, and viewing constructive criticism as a personal attack rather than a tool for growth. People with a fixed mindset often feel threatened by others' success, seeing it as a measure of their inadequacy instead of inspiration. They believe that talent is innate and cannot be developed through effort and practice.

For example, I once had a team member who avoided learning new software because they believed they were not "tech-savvy." This fixed mindset prevented them from gaining valuable skills that could have enhanced their performance and career. Recognizing and addressing these symptoms is crucial for shifting towards a growth mindset, where challenges are opportunities, persistence is valued, and feedback is a pathway to improvement.

Overwhelm and Stress

Overwhelm and stress can be significant barriers to innovation. The pressures of daily responsibilities and managing multiple tasks can cloud your thinking, making it difficult to focus on creative ideas. When you're overwhelmed, it's easy to feel stuck in survival mode, just trying to get through the day.

I've experienced times when the sheer volume of work left me feeling paralyzed. The constant juggling of tasks made it hard to concentrate on anything beyond immediate demands. Symptoms to watch out for include chronic fatigue, difficulty concentrating, and a sense of being perpetually behind. These feelings can stifle creativity and prevent you from exploring new possibilities.

Recognizing these symptoms is crucial. When I started prioritizing self-care and time management, I found that I could manage stress more effectively. Taking breaks, delegating tasks, and setting realistic goals helped clear my mind, allowing space for innovation. Addressing overwhelm and stress is essential for fostering an environment where new ideas can thrive.

Lack of Confidence

A lack of confidence can be a major barrier to innovation. When you doubt your abilities, you're less likely to explore new opportunities or take risks. This self-doubt often stems from negative self-talk or past failures, and it can be paralyzing.

Have you seen how a lack of confidence can hold people back? They might avoid speaking up in meetings, hesitate to share their ideas, or shy away from challenging projects. Symptoms to watch out for include excessive self-criticism, reluctance to take on new tasks, and a tendency to downplay achievements.

I remember a time when self-doubt almost stopped me from presenting a new concept. I kept telling myself it wasn't good enough. However, once I pushed through that doubt and shared my idea, it received positive feedback and opened up new opportunities. Building confidence involves acknowledging your achievements and focusing on growth. Overcoming self-doubt is key to unlocking your potential and driving innovation.

Comfort Zone

Staying within your comfort zone can significantly hinder innovation. When you're too comfortable, you're less likely to seek out new experiences or challenge the status quo. This complacency can stifle creativity and prevent growth.

I've seen how comfort zones can hold people back. They might stick to familiar routines, avoid taking risks, and resist change. Symptoms to watch out for include a reluctance to try new things, a lack of curiosity, and an aversion to feedback.

I recall a period when I was too comfortable in my role, avoiding new challenges. This stagnation left me feeling unfulfilled and uninspired. It wasn't until I intentionally pushed myself out of my comfort zone—by taking on new projects and embracing change—that I began to innovate and grow. Stepping out of your comfort zone is essential for sparking creativity and driving progress. Embracing discomfort can lead to new opportunities and breakthroughs.

I also want to remind you that apart from barriers, you need to be aware of the deception stages that you will go through. Deception stages are phases where false perceptions can mislead you, causing doubts about your ideas and abilities. These stages can make you question your progress and potential, often leading to unnecessary self-doubt. Recognizing these stages is crucial. By understanding that these doubts are temporary and part of the process, you can navigate through them more effectively. Acknowledging and pushing through these deception stages helps maintain focus and confidence, ensuring you stay on course toward innovation.

Initial Excitement

The initial excitement of a new idea can sometimes lead to overestimating its potential. This burst of enthusiasm can make you believe that success is inevitable and challenges will be minimal. However, this stage is often followed by a period of doubt when the reality of obstacles and complexities sets in. Symptoms to watch out for include overconfidence, rushing into implementation without thorough planning, and ignoring potential risks. Recognizing this deception stage is crucial. Understanding that initial excitement is just the beginning and not the guarantee of success helps you prepare for the challenges ahead. By maintaining a balanced perspective, you can channel your enthusiasm into sustainable progress and stay resilient when facing difficulties.

The Dip

After the initial excitement wanes, you may encounter significant obstacles that make progress difficult. This stage, known as the dip, can be particularly discouraging and might lead you to question the viability of your idea. Symptoms to watch out for include feelings of frustration, doubt, and a temptation to abandon the project. The dip can create a sense of stagnation where it feels like no matter what you do, progress is elusive. Recognizing this deception stage is crucial. Understanding that the dip is a normal part of the innovation process helps you stay resilient and focused. By pushing through this challenging phase, you can refine your ideas, overcome obstacles, and ultimately achieve your goals. Remember, perseverance during the dip often leads to the most rewarding breakthroughs.

False Peaks

You might experience moments where things seem to be improving, only to face setbacks again. These false peaks can create a rollercoaster of emotions, making it hard to stay focused. Symptoms to watch out for include a cycle of optimism followed by disappointment and fluctuating motivation levels. False peaks can lead you to prematurely celebrate progress, only to be caught off guard by subsequent challenges. Recognizing this deception stage is crucial. Understanding that progress can be uneven helps you maintain a steady and resilient mindset. By staying grounded and preparing for ups and downs, you can navigate false peaks more effectively, ensuring that each setback becomes a learning opportunity rather than a discouragement. This balanced approach keeps you on track towards your innovative goals.

Comparison Trap

Comparing your progress to others can lead to feelings of inadequacy. This stage can be particularly deceptive, as it might make you feel that you're not moving fast enough or achieving as much as others. Symptoms to watch out for include constant self-doubt, diminished motivation, and a tendency to undervalue your own achievements. The comparison trap can distract you from your unique journey and the progress you've made. Recognizing this deception stage is crucial. Understand that everyone's path is different, and comparing yourself to others can undermine your confidence. Focus on your own growth and milestones, and appreciate the unique value you bring to your projects. By maintaining a mindset centered on personal progress rather than external benchmarks, you can stay motivated and continue to innovate effectively.

How to navigate deception stages

Initial Excitement and The Dip: Recognize that initial excitement will naturally wane as challenges arise. When you hit the dip, remind yourself that this is a normal part of the process. Stay committed to your vision and push through the tough times.

False Peaks: Be prepared for setbacks and fluctuations in progress. Maintain a long-term perspective and stay focused on your overall goals. Celebrate small victories, but stay grounded and realistic about the journey ahead.

Comparison Trap: Avoid comparing your progress to others. Everyone's journey is unique, and comparing yourself to others can be misleading and discouraging. Focus on your own growth and the progress you're making.

Cultivating an Extraordinary Mindset

To cultivate an extraordinary mindset, integrate these strategies into your daily routine and mindset practices. Here are additional tips to help you stay on track:

Continuous Learning

Stay curious and committed to lifelong learning. Seek out new knowledge, skills, and experiences. Read widely, attend workshops, and engage with diverse perspectives. Continuous learning keeps your mind sharp and open to new possibilities.

Positive Environment

Create a positive environment that supports innovation. Surround yourself with people who inspire and challenge you. Foster a culture of collaboration, where ideas are shared freely and everyone feels valued.

Reflect and Adapt

Regularly reflect on your experiences and adapt your approach as needed. Take time to pause and assess what's working and what's not. Be willing to pivot and adjust your strategies based on what you learn.

Set Clear Intentions

Set clear, actionable goals and intentions for your innovation journey. Having a clear direction helps you stay focused and motivated. Break down your goals into smaller, manageable steps and track your progress.

Practice Gratitude

Cultivate a sense of gratitude for the opportunities and experiences you encounter. Gratitude can shift your focus from what's lacking to what's possible, fostering a positive and resilient mindset.

Stay Persistent

Persistence is key to overcoming barriers and deception stages. Stay committed to your vision and keep moving forward, even when the going gets tough. Remember that innovation is a journey, not a destination, and persistence will help you navigate the ups and downs.

Remember, the journey of innovation is filled with challenges and opportunities. By staying resilient, fostering creativity, emphasizing collaboration, and maintaining a growth mindset, you can navigate through obstacles and achieve remarkable results. Immerse yourself in the journey, trust in your abilities, and keep pushing forward. The potential for innovation is limitless when you cultivate the right mindset.

As you embark on this journey, remember that the innovative mindset starts from within. It's about changing the way you think and approach challenges. It's about believing in your ability to create and innovate.

Strategies for Fostering Creativity, Curiosity, and Resilience

Cultivating an innovative mindset requires a deliberate effort to foster creativity, curiosity, and resilience. These elements are the bedrock of a mindset that can drive continuous innovation and adaptation. Let me share strategies to help you develop these crucial traits, ensuring that your approach to innovation is both dynamic and sustainable.

Fostering Creativity

Creativity is the engine of innovation. It's the ability to see things differently, to make connections that others don't see, and to generate unique solutions to problems. Here are some strategies to foster creativity:

1. Create a Creative Environment

Your environment plays a significant role in your ability to think creatively. Design a workspace that inspires you and stimulates your imagination. This might include bright colors, art, or objects that spark joy and curiosity. Incorporate elements that reflect your personality and passions. Ensure that your environment is flexible, allowing for different types of work—from quiet, focused thinking to collaborative brainstorming sessions.

Consider the approach taken by Pixar, known for its highly creative workspaces. They have areas designed for quiet reflection as well as open spaces for collaboration, filled with playful and inspiring elements. This blend of environments encourages both individual creativity and team innovation. Surround yourself with things that make you happy and curious, and you'll find that your creativity flourishes. A well-designed space can ignite your imagination and help you generate new and exciting ideas.

2. Embrace Diverse Perspectives

Diversity is a powerful catalyst for creativity. Bringing together people with different backgrounds, experiences, and viewpoints generates a wealth of ideas. Encourage diverse teams and inclusive thinking to enhance your creative process.

For example, when working on a project, seek input from colleagues in different departments or even from outside your organization. This approach can provide fresh perspectives and spark new ideas that you might not have considered. Look at how IDEO, a global design company, blends designers, engineers, psychologists, and business strategists to foster innovation. By embracing diversity in your team, you can uncover groundbreaking solutions and achieve more innovative outcomes. It opens your mind to new possibilities and helps you see challenges from various angles, enriching the creative process. Diversity in thought leads to richer, more creative results.

3. Encourage Brainstorming Sessions

Brainstorming sessions are incredibly effective for generating creative ideas. Create a safe space where all ideas are welcome, no matter how unconventional they may seem. Use techniques like mind mapping or the "Yes, and…" approach from improv theater to build on each other's ideas without immediate criticism.

For example, think about how a local community theater group might brainstorm ideas for a new play. They gather actors, writers, and directors to freely share their thoughts, building on each other's suggestions to create a compelling story. By encouraging everyone to share their ideas openly, they often discover innovative concepts that might not have emerged in a more restrictive environment.

Creating a supportive atmosphere where everyone feels valued and heard can lead to breakthroughs and innovative solutions. Remember, the goal is to explore possibilities and foster creativity, making brainstorming an essential part of your innovation toolkit.

4. Allow Time for Creative Thinking

Innovation requires time. Schedule regular blocks of time for creative thinking and exploration. This might involve setting aside time each day for reading, reflecting, or working on side projects. Giving yourself permission to spend time on creative activities can lead to unexpected insights.

For instance, consider how renowned artists like Leonardo da Vinci dedicated time to explore various interests and ideas. By allowing himself the freedom to experiment and think creatively, da Vinci made groundbreaking discoveries in both art and science. Similarly, set aside time to delve into your passions and curiosity.

Whether it's a quiet morning spent journaling or an afternoon exploring new hobbies, dedicating time to creativity can unlock new perspectives and innovative solutions. Integrate this time as a vital part of your routine, and watch as fresh ideas and insights begin to flow, enhancing your overall creativity and innovation.

5. Break Out of Routine

Routine can stifle creativity. To stimulate new ways of thinking, it's important to break out of your regular patterns and routines. This could mean changing your work environment, taking a different route to work, or engaging in new activities outside of work.

Consider the story of J.K. Rowling, who found inspiration for Harry Potter while sitting on a delayed train. By stepping away from her usual writing environment and simply observing the world around her, she sparked the idea for one of the most beloved book series of all time.

Changing your physical environment or routine can provide fresh perspectives and inspire new ideas. Try working in a new location, picking up a new hobby, or simply altering your daily schedule. These small changes can open your mind to new possibilities and enhance your creativity, leading to innovative breakthroughs and fresh insights.

6. Use Creative Tools and Techniques

Leverage creative tools and techniques to facilitate the creative process. Techniques like SCAMPER (Substitute, Combine, Adapt, Modify, Put to another use, Eliminate, and Reverse) can help you look at problems from different angles and generate new solutions.

Consider how chefs often experiment with ingredients using a SCAMPER approach to create innovative dishes. They might substitute one ingredient for another, combine flavors in new ways, or modify cooking techniques to create a unique culinary experience.

Additionally, tools like design thinking provide a structured approach to creativity, helping you empathize with users, define problems, ideate, prototype, and test solutions in a creative and user-centered way. Think of how architects use design thinking to create buildings that are both functional and aesthetically pleasing, addressing user needs while pushing the boundaries of traditional design. Using these tools can unlock new ideas and drive innovation in your projects.

Cultivating Curiosity

Curiosity is the driving force behind discovery and innovation. It fuels your desire to learn, explore, and ask questions. Here's how you can cultivate curiosity:

1. Ask Questions Relentlessly

Adopt a mindset of relentless questioning. Don't take things at face value—ask why, how, and what if. Encourage yourself and your team to ask probing questions about everything, from daily operations to long-term strategies.

Think about how Richard Feynman, a renowned physicist, approached his work. He was known for his insatiable curiosity and his habit of questioning everything. This led to groundbreaking insights in quantum mechanics and other fields. By constantly asking questions, he was able to uncover new ideas and challenge established thinking.

Apply this approach in your own work. When faced with a problem or task, probe and explore every angle. Encourage your team to do the same, fostering a culture of curiosity and continuous learning. This relentless questioning can lead to deeper understanding and innovative solutions, driving progress and discovery in your field.

2. Embrace Lifelong Learning

Cultivate a habit of lifelong learning. Continuously seek out new knowledge and experiences. This could involve taking courses, attending workshops, reading widely, or exploring new hobbies. The more you learn, the more connections you can make between different pieces of information, which can lead to innovative ideas.

Consider the example of Benjamin Franklin. His insatiable curiosity and commitment to lifelong learning led him to excel in various fields, including science, politics, and literature. He constantly sought new knowledge and experiences, which fueled his many inventions and contributions to society.

Adopt a similar approach in your life. Make learning a daily habit, whether it's through reading a book, taking an online course, or trying something new. Embracing lifelong learning keeps your mind sharp and open to new possibilities, fostering a spirit of curiosity that drives innovation and personal growth.

3. Explore Different Fields

Expose yourself to different fields and disciplines. Cross-pollination of ideas from various domains can spark innovation. Attend conferences, join professional networks, and engage with communities outside your immediate field.

For example, the renowned Renaissance man Leonardo da Vinci drew inspiration from a wide range of disciplines, including anatomy, engineering, and art. His ability to integrate knowledge from different fields led to groundbreaking ideas and inventions that were ahead of his time.

By stepping outside your usual areas of expertise, you can gain fresh perspectives and new insights. Engage with professionals in different industries, read about subjects unrelated to your current work, and participate in interdisciplinary projects. This blending of diverse knowledge can lead to unique solutions and innovative thinking, enriching your own work and broadening your horizons. Embracing the richness of various fields fuels creativity and cultivates a mindset ready for innovation.

4. Encourage a Culture of Curiosity

Foster a culture of curiosity within your team or organization. Encourage open dialogue, exploration, and the pursuit of new ideas. Reward curiosity-driven initiatives and celebrate discoveries, even if they don't immediately lead to success.

Consider the approach taken by NASA. They encourage their scientists and engineers to pursue independent research projects, which has led to numerous breakthroughs in space exploration. By creating an environment where exploration and questioning are valued, NASA has been able to push the boundaries of what is possible.

You can do something similar by setting up "curiosity clubs" or innovation labs where team members can explore new ideas and technologies without the pressure of immediate results. This freedom to experiment and the support for curiosity can lead to unexpected innovations and foster a dynamic, creative work environment. Celebrating these efforts, regardless of their immediate outcomes, reinforces a culture where curiosity thrives.

5. Stay Open to New Experiences

Be open to new experiences and explore the unfamiliar. Travel, meet new people, and try new activities. These experiences can provide fresh perspectives and stimulate your curiosity.

Consider the example of Charles Darwin. His travels on the HMS Beagle exposed him to diverse ecosystems and species, which profoundly influenced his thinking and led to his groundbreaking work on evolution. By stepping out of his comfort zone and exploring the world, Darwin gained insights that would have been impossible to achieve otherwise.

You can do the same by seeking out new experiences. Attend a workshop on a topic you're unfamiliar with, visit new places, or engage in hobbies that challenge you. These activities broaden your horizons and fuel your curiosity, making you more open to innovative ideas and approaches. Embracing the new and unfamiliar can lead to unexpected discoveries and a richer, more creative mindset.

6. Reflect and Connect

Take time to reflect on your experiences and connect the dots. Journaling, mind mapping, or discussing your thoughts with others can help you see connections between seemingly unrelated ideas, leading to innovative insights.

Consider how Leonardo da Vinci used notebooks to jot down observations, sketches, and ideas. His practice of reflecting on his experiences and connecting diverse concepts led to remarkable innovations in art, science, and engineering. By documenting his thoughts, he could revisit and expand on his ideas, finding links that might have otherwise been missed.

You can adopt a similar practice by setting aside time each day to reflect. Write in a journal, create mind maps of your thoughts, or have thoughtful discussions with colleagues or friends. This reflection helps you synthesize information and see patterns, sparking creativity and innovation. Connecting the dots between different experiences and ideas can lead to breakthroughs and fresh perspectives.

Cultivating Resilience

Resilience is the ability to bounce back from setbacks and keep moving forward. It's essential for sustaining innovation, as the path to success is often fraught with challenges. Here's how to cultivate resilience:

1. Develop a Growth Mindset

A growth mindset, as introduced by psychologist Carol Dweck, is crucial for resilience. It's the belief that abilities and intelligence can be developed through effort and learning. Embrace challenges as opportunities for growth and view setbacks as learning experiences.

Think about how Winston Churchill approached his career. Despite numerous political failures early on, he saw each setback as a chance to learn and improve. His growth mindset enabled him to persevere and ultimately lead his country through World War II with determination and innovation.

To cultivate a growth mindset, start seeing difficulties as stepping stones rather than obstacles. Celebrate your efforts and improvements, not just the outcomes. When you encounter challenges, remind yourself that they are opportunities to develop new skills and insights. By adopting this perspective, you'll build the resilience needed to keep pushing forward, regardless of the hurdles you face.

2. Practice Self-Care

Taking care of your physical, mental, and emotional well-being is essential for resilience. Ensure you get enough rest, eat healthily, exercise regularly, and engage in activities that help you relax and recharge.

Consider how Oprah Winfrey incorporates self-care into her daily routine. Despite her busy schedule, she prioritizes meditation, exercise, and spending time in nature to maintain her well-being. This commitment to self-care has helped her sustain her energy and creativity over the years.

Incorporate self-care practices into your own life. Make sure to get adequate sleep, nourish your body with healthy foods, and find time for physical activities you enjoy. Engage in hobbies and activities that bring you joy and help you unwind. By taking care of yourself, you build the strength and resilience needed to face challenges and continue innovating effectively.

3. Build a Support Network

Surround yourself with supportive people who believe in you and your vision. Seek out mentors, peers, and friends who can provide encouragement, advice, and constructive feedback.

Think about how Nelson Mandela relied on his support network during his years of imprisonment. His friends, family, and fellow activists provided the emotional strength and motivation he needed to persevere. This support was crucial in maintaining his resilience and determination to fight for justice.

In your own life, build a network of people who uplift and challenge you. Whether it's a mentor who offers wisdom, a peer who shares your journey, or a friend who listens without judgment, these relationships can provide the strength you need to overcome obstacles. A strong support network helps you stay resilient, reminding you that you're not alone in your endeavors and that others believe in your potential.

4. Embrace Failure as Learning

Shift your perspective on failure and see it as a learning opportunity rather than a setback. Analyze what went wrong, identify lessons learned, and apply these insights to future efforts.

Consider how Michael Jordan, one of the greatest basketball players of all time, approached failure. Despite being cut from his high school basketball team, he used this setback as motivation to work harder and improve. Jordan famously said, "I've missed more than 9,000 shots in my career. I've lost almost 300 games. I've been trusted to take the game-winning shot and missed. I've failed over and over and over again in my life. And that is why I succeed."

In your own pursuits, treat each failure as a stepping stone to success. Reflect on your experiences, extract valuable lessons, and use them to refine your strategies. By embracing failure as a crucial part of the learning process, you build resilience and set the stage for future achievements.

5. Stay Adaptable

Innovation requires flexibility and adaptability. Be open to changing your approach when necessary. Stay agile and willing to pivot based on new information or changing circumstances.

Consider the example of Blockbuster. While Blockbuster clung to its traditional business model, a small startup called Netflix embraced the future of digital streaming, eventually revolutionizing the entertainment industry. The key difference was adaptability.

In your own endeavors, remember that clinging to one strategy can sometimes hinder progress. Instead, regularly assess your situation and be ready to make changes. Adaptability allows you to respond effectively to new challenges and opportunities. Whether it's altering your project plan, adopting new technologies, or shifting your focus entirely, staying adaptable ensures that you remain resilient and capable of thriving in a constantly evolving environment. Accept change as a necessary part of the innovation process and use it to your advantage.

6. Set Realistic Goals

Break down your long-term goals into smaller, manageable steps. Celebrate small victories along the way to maintain motivation and build momentum.

Consider how Mount Everest climbers approach their daunting goal. Reaching the summit seems overwhelming, but by setting incremental goals—such as reaching the base camp, then the next camp, and so on—they make steady progress. Celebrating each milestone keeps their spirits high and their determination strong.

In your own projects, set achievable short-term goals that lead toward your ultimate objective. Recognize and celebrate your progress, no matter how small. This approach not only keeps you motivated but also makes the larger goal feel more attainable. By focusing on one step at a time, you build resilience and maintain a steady course toward your vision. This method helps manage stress and prevents burnout, ensuring you stay committed and energized throughout your journey.

7. Reflect and Recharge

Regularly reflect on your experiences, celebrate your successes, and learn from your challenges. Taking time to recharge and renew your energy is essential for maintaining resilience and staying focused on your innovation journey.

Consider how athletes like Serena Williams approach their training and competition schedules. After intense periods of training and tournaments, they take time to rest, recover, and reflect on their performance. This balance helps them stay at the top of their game and come back stronger.

In your own life, set aside time for reflection and recharging. Whether it's a weekend retreat, daily meditation, or simply a quiet evening walk, these moments allow you to process your experiences, celebrate achievements, and learn from setbacks. By incorporating regular periods of rest and reflection, you maintain your energy and resilience, ensuring you stay motivated and ready to tackle new challenges with renewed vigor.

Cultivating an innovative mindset requires deliberate effort to foster creativity, curiosity, and resilience. By creating a supportive environment, embracing diverse perspectives, encouraging brainstorming, allowing time for creative thinking, breaking out of routines, and using creative tools and techniques, you can foster creativity. By asking questions relentlessly, embracing lifelong learning, exploring different fields, encouraging a culture of curiosity, staying open to new experiences, and reflecting and connecting, you can cultivate curiosity. By developing a growth mindset, practicing self-care, building a support network, embracing failure as learning, staying adaptable, setting realistic goals, and reflecting and recharging, you can cultivate resilience.

These strategies will help you develop a mindset that drives continuous innovation, allowing you to navigate challenges, seize opportunities, and achieve extraordinary results.

How Mindset Prepares Individuals and Organizations for Successful Innovation Journeys

As we wrap up our exploration of the importance of mindset in fostering innovation, it's essential to understand how the right mindset prepares both individuals and organizations for successful innovation journeys. A mindset attuned to innovation does more than just spark creative ideas—it lays the groundwork for sustainable progress, resilience, and adaptability. Here's how cultivating an innovative mindset can set the stage for long-term success.

Embracing a Visionary Outlook

An innovative mindset encourages a visionary outlook. This means looking beyond the immediate challenges and focusing on the broader possibilities. For individuals, this translates into setting ambitious goals and daring to dream big. For organizations, it involves creating a shared vision that inspires and motivates everyone to work towards a common goal. This visionary perspective helps in navigating through uncertainties and keeps the momentum going, even when the path forward is not entirely clear.

Take the example of the Wright brothers. Their vision of powered flight was far beyond the technological capabilities of their time. Yet, their unwavering belief in their vision kept them motivated through countless trials and errors. By maintaining a visionary outlook, they were able to achieve what many thought was impossible.

Fostering a Culture of Experimentation

A mindset geared towards innovation inherently values experimentation. It understands that not every idea will succeed, but each experiment brings valuable insights. For individuals, this means being willing to try new approaches and learn from mistakes. For organizations, it involves creating a culture where experimentation is encouraged, and failures are seen as learning opportunities rather than setbacks.

Consider how the early pioneers of the tech industry, like the developers of early computer software, embraced a culture of experimentation. They continuously tested new codes, faced numerous bugs and crashes, but each failure taught them something new. This relentless experimentation eventually led to the robust and sophisticated software we rely on today.

Building Emotional Resilience

An innovative mindset builds emotional resilience. It prepares individuals to handle the ups and downs of the innovation journey without losing hope or motivation. Resilience is crucial because the path to innovation is rarely smooth. There will be setbacks, rejections, and moments of doubt. A resilient mindset helps individuals bounce back from these challenges, learn from them, and continue moving forward.

Organizations, too, benefit from fostering resilience within their teams. By encouraging a resilient mindset, companies can ensure that their employees remain committed and engaged, even during tough times. This resilience is the backbone of sustained innovation and progress.

Encouraging Lifelong Learning

An innovative mindset is deeply rooted in the concept of lifelong learning. It recognizes that the world is constantly changing and that staying relevant requires continuous learning and adaptation. For individuals, this means being proactive in seeking new knowledge and skills. It involves staying curious, exploring new areas, and never settling for the status quo.

Organizations can foster a culture of lifelong learning by providing opportunities for professional development, encouraging knowledge sharing, and supporting continuous education. This commitment to learning keeps the organization agile and ready to adapt to new challenges and opportunities.

Enhancing Problem-Solving Skills

Cultivating an innovative mindset enhances problem-solving skills. It encourages individuals to approach problems creatively, think critically, and develop unique solutions. This problem-solving capability is essential for innovation, as it allows individuals to tackle challenges in novel ways and find solutions that others might overlook.

For organizations, promoting a problem-solving mindset means empowering employees to take ownership of challenges and explore innovative solutions. It involves creating an environment where questioning the status quo is encouraged and where creative solutions are valued.

Promoting Collaboration and Teamwork

An innovative mindset recognizes the power of collaboration and teamwork. It understands that diverse perspectives and collective intelligence lead to better outcomes. For individuals, this means being open to others' ideas, actively seeking input, and working effectively in teams.

Organizations can promote a collaborative mindset by fostering a culture of open communication, mutual respect, and shared goals. By encouraging teamwork, companies can harness the full potential of their workforce, driving innovation and achieving remarkable results.

Balancing Risk and Reward

An innovative mindset is adept at balancing risk and reward. It acknowledges that innovation involves taking risks but also understands the importance of calculated risks. For individuals, this means being willing to step out of their comfort zones and take on challenges that have the potential for high rewards.

Organizations can support this mindset by creating a safe environment for risk-taking. This involves encouraging employees to experiment and innovate without the fear of severe repercussions if things don't go as planned. By balancing risk and reward, organizations can foster a culture of innovation that leads to significant breakthroughs.

Instilling a Sense of Purpose

An innovative mindset instills a sense of purpose. It drives individuals to pursue innovation not just for the sake of novelty but to make a meaningful impact. This sense of purpose provides motivation and direction, helping individuals stay focused and driven.

For organizations, having a clear purpose aligned with innovation goals is crucial. It ensures that all efforts are directed towards creating value and making a difference. This sense of purpose can be a powerful motivator, driving the organization towards achieving its innovation objectives.

Leveraging Technology and Tools

An innovative mindset leverages technology and tools to enhance creativity and efficiency. For individuals, this means staying updated with the latest technological advancements and utilizing tools that can aid in the innovation process. It involves being tech-savvy and open to exploring new digital solutions.

Organizations can support this by providing access to cutting-edge tools and technologies. By integrating technology into their operations, companies can streamline processes, foster creativity, and accelerate innovation. This technological edge can be a significant advantage in today's fast-paced world.

Celebrating Successes and Learning from Failures

An innovative mindset celebrates successes and learns from failures. It understands that both are integral parts of the innovation journey. For individuals, this means taking the time to acknowledge achievements and reflecting on what worked well. It also involves analyzing failures to extract valuable lessons and applying these insights to future efforts.

Organizations can cultivate this mindset by recognizing and rewarding innovative efforts. Celebrating successes boosts morale and encourages further innovation, while learning from failures fosters a culture of continuous improvement.

Over the years, I've had the privilege of collaborating with industry leaders and engaging with some of the most innovative minds out there. Through these experiences, I've come to realize that mindset is absolutely crucial for anyone aiming to succeed in their innovation journey. It's not just about coming up with creative ideas; it's about developing the resilience, adaptability, and drive to bring those ideas to life.

For you as an individual, embracing an innovative mindset means taking on a visionary outlook, fostering a culture of experimentation, building emotional resilience, and committing to lifelong learning. It's about enhancing your problem-solving skills, promoting collaboration, balancing risk and reward, and instilling a sense of purpose. It involves leveraging technology and tools, celebrating your successes, and learning from your failures.

For organizations, it's about creating an environment that supports and nurtures these qualities. This means setting a clear vision, fostering a culture of collaboration and experimentation, and providing the resources and support needed to innovate. It's about valuing resilience, encouraging continuous learning, and recognizing the importance of both successes and failures in the innovation journey.

Ultimately, an innovative mindset is the foundation of sustained innovation and progress. It prepares both you and your organization to navigate challenges and seize opportunities that come with the pursuit of innovation. By cultivating this mindset, you can unlock your potential, drive meaningful change, and achieve extraordinary results.

"An innovative mindset sees beyond the ordinary, turning curiosity into creation and challenges into breakthroughs."

– Bob Philips –

Chapter 3

A - Analyze: Understanding The Innovation Ecosystem

- **Dive Into The Analysis Phase Of Innovation.**
- **Identifying Opportunities And Assessing The Competitive Landscape.**
- **The Role Of Thorough Analysis In Guiding Successful Innovation Strategies.**

Analyzing the innovation ecosystem is critical for turning ideas into successful innovations. This chapter will delve into the analysis phase, focusing on market trends, customer needs, and technological advancements. We'll explore methods for identifying opportunities and assessing the competitive landscape, and highlight the role of thorough analysis in guiding successful innovation strategies. By the end of this chapter, you should feel equipped to deeply analyze your innovation environment, identify key opportunities, and develop strategies that will set you apart.

Dive into the Analysis Phase of Innovation

Understanding the analysis phase of innovation is critical for laying a solid foundation for your ideas. It's where you gather the insights needed to guide your innovation journey. This involves digging deep into market trends, understanding customer needs, and staying updated with technological advancements. Let's break this down further.

Understanding Market Trends

Market trends are like the compass that guides your innovation journey. They signal where an industry is headed, helping you navigate the terrain and stay ahead of the curve. To maintain relevance and competitiveness, it's essential to continuously monitor these trends and understand their implications. By doing so, you can adapt your strategies, seize new opportunities, and avoid potential pitfalls. Let's explore how you can effectively understand and leverage market trends.

The Importance of Market Trends

Market trends are crucial for several reasons. They help you anticipate changes in customer behavior, identify new opportunities, and stay competitive. For example, during the rise of e-commerce, traditional retail businesses that noticed this trend early on and adapted, like Walmart, managed to stay relevant and competitive. Those who ignored the trend struggled to keep up.

By understanding market trends, you can:

1. *Anticipate Customer Needs:* Market trends provide insights into evolving customer preferences and behaviors, allowing you to tailor your offerings to meet their needs.
2. *Identifying Growth Opportunities:* Trends can highlight emerging markets, technologies, and business models that you can capitalize on.
3. *Mitigate Risks:* By staying informed about industry shifts, you can proactively address potential threats to your business.
4. *Drive Innovation:* Trends inspire new ideas and approaches, fueling your innovation efforts.

Key Steps to Understand Market Trends

To effectively understand market trends, you need to adopt a proactive and systematic approach. Here are some key steps to help you stay ahead:

1. ***Regularly Review Industry Reports***

Subscribing to industry publications and reports is a vital step in staying updated on market trends. These sources provide comprehensive analyses of current developments, future projections, and expert insights.

How to Utilize Industry Reports:

- *Identify Reliable Sources:* Look for reputable industry publications, market research firms, and trade associations that publish regular reports.

- *Set Up Alerts:* Subscribe to newsletters and set up email alerts for new publications and reports.
- *Analyze the Data:* Take the time to thoroughly read and analyze the reports. Look for patterns, emerging trends, and potential disruptions.

For instance, in the fashion industry, reports from organizations like the Business of Fashion and McKinsey & Company offer valuable insights into consumer behavior, technological advancements, and market dynamics. By regularly reviewing such reports, fashion brands can stay ahead of trends and make informed decisions.

2. ***Attend Industry Conferences and Seminars***

Industry conferences and seminars are excellent opportunities to gain real-time insights into market trends. These events bring together industry experts, thought leaders, and peers to share knowledge, discuss emerging trends, and network.

Benefits of Attending Conferences:

- *Networking:* Engage with industry professionals and build valuable connections.
- *Learning:* Attend sessions and workshops to learn about the latest developments and best practices.
- *Trend Spotting:* Listen to keynote speakers and panel discussions to identify emerging trends and technologies.

For example, the CES (Consumer Electronics Show) is a prominent event in the tech industry where companies showcase their latest innovations.

Attending such events helps participants gain a firsthand understanding of the direction the industry is headed and the technologies shaping the future.

3. ***Use Trend Analysis Tools***

Leveraging trend analysis tools can provide you with data-driven insights into market trends. These tools help you track and analyze changes in consumer behavior, search patterns, and social media activity.

Popular Trend Analysis Tools:

- *Google Trends:* This tool shows the popularity of search queries over time, helping you identify what people are interested in.
- *Social Media Analytics:* Platforms like Twitter, Instagram, and LinkedIn offer analytics tools to track trending topics, hashtags, and user engagement.
- *Market Research Tools:* Tools like Nielsen, Mintel, and Statista provide in-depth market research and trend analysis.

For instance, a food and beverage company can use Google Trends to monitor the rise in searches for plant-based diets. Social media analytics can further reveal how consumers are discussing and engaging with this trend. Armed with this information, the company can develop new products that align with consumer interests.

4. ***Engage with Customers***

Directly engaging with your customers is one of the most effective ways to understand market trends. Customer feedback provides real-world insights into their preferences, needs, and pain points.

Ways to Engage with Customers:

- *Surveys and Polls:* Regularly conduct surveys and polls to gather customer opinions and feedback.

- *Customer Reviews:* Analyze reviews and ratings on your products or services to identify common themes and areas for improvement.
- *Social Media Interactions:* Monitor and engage with customers on social media platforms to understand their sentiments and preferences.

For example, beauty brands often engage with their customers through social media to gather feedback on product launches. By listening to their customers, they can quickly adapt to emerging trends, such as the demand for clean and sustainable beauty products.

5. ***Monitor Competitors***

Keeping an eye on your competitors can provide valuable insights into market trends. By analyzing their strategies, product launches, and marketing campaigns, you can identify trends that are gaining traction in the industry.

How to Monitor Competitors:

- *Competitive Analysis:* Conduct regular analyses of your competitors' strengths, weaknesses, opportunities, and threats (SWOT).
- *Product Launches:* Track new product launches and updates from your competitors to see which innovations are resonating with customers.
- *Marketing Strategies:* Observe your competitors' marketing tactics, such as promotions, social media campaigns, and content marketing.

For instance, in the automotive industry, companies closely monitor each other's advancements in electric vehicles and autonomous driving technologies. By understanding what competitors are focusing on, companies can adjust their strategies to stay competitive.

6. ***Leverage Technology and Data Analytics***

Utilizing technology and data analytics can significantly enhance your ability to understand market trends. Advanced analytics tools can process large volumes of data to uncover patterns and insights that might not be immediately apparent.

Technologies to Leverage:

- *Big Data Analytics:* Use big data platforms to analyze large datasets and identify trends and correlations.
- *Artificial Intelligence (AI):* Implement AI-driven analytics to predict future trends based on historical data and current patterns.
- *Customer Relationship Management (CRM) Systems:* Utilize CRM systems to track customer interactions and preferences, providing valuable insights into market trends.

For example, retailers use big data analytics to analyze purchasing behavior across different demographics and regions. This helps them identify emerging trends and tailor their product offerings to meet customer demands.

Understanding market trends is a continuous and dynamic process. By regularly reviewing industry reports, attending conferences, using trend analysis tools, engaging with customers, monitoring competitors, and leveraging technology and data analytics, you can stay ahead of the curve. These steps will help you anticipate changes, identify new opportunities, and drive your innovation efforts effectively.

Staying informed and adaptable is key to maintaining a competitive edge in today's rapidly evolving market landscape. By making trend analysis a core part of your strategy, you can ensure that your innovation initiatives are aligned with market demands and poised for success.

Understanding Customer Needs

Innovation is meaningless if it doesn't meet customer needs. Therefore, understanding your customers is paramount. This means going beyond basic demographics and really getting into their pain points, desires, and behaviors. By deeply understanding your customers, you can create products and services that truly resonate with them, leading to greater satisfaction and loyalty. Here's how you can effectively understand and cater to your customers' needs.

The Importance of Understanding Customer Needs

Customer-centric innovation ensures that your efforts are aligned with what your customers truly want and need. This alignment can drive satisfaction, loyalty, and, ultimately, business success. By understanding customer needs, you can:

- *Enhance Product Development:* Create products that solve real problems and meet specific needs.
- *Improve Customer Experience:* Design seamless and enjoyable customer interactions.
- *Increase Customer Loyalty:* Foster a strong connection with your brand by consistently meeting customer expectations.
- *Identify Market Opportunities:* Spot gaps in the market that you can fill with innovative solutions.

Methods to Understand Customer Needs

To effectively understand customer needs, you need to use a variety of methods that provide both quantitative and qualitative insights. Let's explore some key techniques.

1. ***Customer Surveys and Feedback***

Regularly gathering feedback from your customers is a fundamental way to understand their needs and preferences. Surveys and direct interactions allow you to collect valuable information straight from the source.

How to Utilize Customer Surveys and Feedback:

- *Design Effective Surveys:* Create surveys that ask clear, concise questions about your customers' experiences, preferences, and pain points.
- *Use Multiple Channels:* Distribute surveys through various channels, such as email, social media, and your website, to reach a broad audience.
- *Analyze Feedback:* Carefully analyze the feedback to identify common themes and actionable insights.

For example, Netflix frequently uses customer surveys to gather feedback on its content and user experience. This feedback helps them understand what viewers enjoy and what improvements are needed, allowing them to tailor their offerings accordingly.

2. ***Customer Journey Mapping***

Customer journey mapping involves visualizing the steps your customers take when engaging with your product or service. This method helps you identify pain points and areas for improvement throughout the customer experience.

Steps to Create a Customer Journey Map:

- *Identify Key Stages:* Outline the key stages of the customer journey, from initial awareness to post-purchase support.
- *Gather Data:* Collect data on customer interactions at each stage

through surveys, interviews, and analytics.

- *Visualize the Journey:* Create a visual representation of the customer journey, highlighting touchpoints, pain points, and emotions.
- *Analyze and Improve:* Use the map to identify areas where the customer experience can be enhanced and develop strategies to address these issues.

For instance, a retail company might map out the customer journey from browsing their online store to receiving a purchase. By identifying pain points, such as a complicated checkout process or slow shipping times, they can make targeted improvements to enhance the overall experience.

3. ***Behavioral Data Analysis***

Behavioral data analysis involves using data analytics to understand how customers interact with your product or service. By analyzing patterns and behaviors, you can gain insights into preferences and issues that might not be apparent through direct feedback alone.

How to Conduct Behavioral Data Analysis:

- *Collect Data:* Gather data from various sources, such as website analytics, mobile app usage, and transaction records.
- *Analyze Patterns:* Look for patterns in the data that indicate customer preferences, common issues, and usage trends.
- *Identify Opportunities:* Use the insights to identify opportunities for improvement and innovation.

For example, Amazon uses behavioral data analysis to understand customer browsing and purchasing habits. By analyzing this data, they can recommend products that align with individual preferences, enhancing the shopping experience and driving sales.

4. ***Engaging with Customers Directly***

Direct engagement with customers can provide deep insights into their needs and preferences. This involves having conversations with your customers, whether through interviews, focus groups, or casual interactions.

Ways to Engage with Customers Directly:

- *Interviews:* Conduct one-on-one interviews with customers to explore their experiences and gather detailed feedback.
- *Focus Groups:* Organize focus groups to discuss specific topics and gather diverse perspectives.
- *Social Media Interaction:* Engage with customers on social media platforms, responding to their comments and queries to gain real-time insights.

For instance, a tech startup might hold focus groups with early adopters to understand their experiences with a new app. These discussions can reveal valuable insights into what features are most important and what challenges users face, guiding future development.

Understanding customer needs is a continuous and multifaceted process. By regularly gathering feedback through surveys, mapping out the customer journey, analyzing behavioral data, and engaging directly with customers, you can gain a comprehensive understanding of their needs and preferences. This deep understanding allows you to tailor your innovation efforts to create products and services that truly resonate with your customers, driving satisfaction and loyalty.

By making customer-centricity a core part of your innovation strategy, you can ensure that your efforts are aligned with what matters most to your customers. This alignment not only enhances the customer experience but also positions your business for long-term success in a competitive market.

Remember, the key to successful innovation lies in truly understanding and addressing the needs of your customers. By continuously seeking to understand and meet these needs, you can drive meaningful innovation that creates value for both your customers and your business.

Staying Updated with Technological Advancements

Technology evolves rapidly, and staying updated is crucial for innovation. Keeping an eye on technological advancements allows you to identify new tools and processes that can enhance your products or services. By integrating the latest technologies, you can maintain a competitive edge, improve operational efficiency, and meet the evolving needs of your customers. Let's explore various ways to stay updated with technological advancements and how you can leverage them for innovation.

The Importance of Staying Updated

In today's fast-paced world, technological advancements can quickly disrupt industries and change the way businesses operate. Staying updated with these changes is essential for several reasons:

1. *Competitive Advantage:* Early adoption of new technologies can give you a significant edge over competitors.
2. *Operational Efficiency:* New tools and processes can streamline operations, reduce costs, and improve productivity.
3. *Customer Satisfaction:* Leveraging the latest technologies can enhance the customer experience and meet their evolving needs.
4. *Innovation Opportunities:* Staying updated helps you spot emerging trends and technologies that can inspire new products and services.

Ways to Stay Updated

To effectively stay updated with technological advancements, you need to adopt a proactive and systematic approach. Here are some key methods to help you keep abreast of the latest developments.

1. *Follow Technology News and Blogs*

Technology news sources and blogs are invaluable resources for staying informed about the latest advancements. These platforms provide timely updates, expert analyses, and insights into emerging trends.

How to Utilize Technology News and Blogs:

- *Identify Reliable Sources:* Subscribe to reputable technology news websites, such as Wired, TechCrunch, and The Verge. These sources regularly publish articles on the latest technological developments and industry trends.
- *Set Up Alerts:* Use tools like Google Alerts to receive notifications about specific topics or keywords related to your industry. This ensures you stay updated on relevant advancements without having to constantly check for news.
- *Follow Influential Bloggers:* Many industry experts and tech enthusiasts maintain blogs where they share insights and analyses. Following these blogs can provide you with in-depth information and unique perspectives on technological trends.
- *Engage with Content:* Don't just read passively. Engage with the content by leaving comments, sharing articles, and participating in discussions. This active engagement can deepen your understanding and help you connect with other professionals interested in the same topics.

For example, staying updated through technology blogs helped Airbnb stay ahead of trends in the hospitality industry. By keeping a close eye on technological advancements and integrating them into their platform, Airbnb continuously improves the user experience and remains competitive.

2. *Join Tech Communities and Forums*

Engaging with tech communities and forums can provide you with valuable insights and firsthand experiences from professionals who are directly involved in technological advancements. These platforms foster a collaborative environment where ideas and knowledge are freely shared.

Benefits of Joining Tech Communities and Forums:

- *Networking:* Connect with like-minded professionals, industry experts, and innovators. Building these relationships can lead to collaborative opportunities and knowledge exchange.
- *Learning:* Participate in discussions, ask questions, and seek advice from experienced members. This can help you gain deeper insights into new technologies and their practical applications.
- *Staying Informed:* Tech communities and forums often share the latest news, research, and case studies, keeping you informed about current developments.
- *Problem-Solving:* Engage in problem-solving discussions where members share their challenges and solutions. This collective problem-solving can provide new perspectives and innovative ideas.

For instance, Stack Overflow and Reddit have active tech communities where professionals discuss a wide range of topics, from programming languages to the latest tech gadgets. By participating in these forums, you can stay updated on new developments and learn from the experiences of others.

3. *Collaborate with Tech Partners*

Partnering with technology firms can give you direct access to cutting-edge advancements. Collaboration with tech partners allows you to leverage their expertise, resources, and innovations to enhance your products or services.

How to Collaborate with Tech Partners:

- *Identify Potential Partners:* Look for technology firms that align with your business goals and can complement your capabilities. This could include startups, established tech companies, or research institutions.
- *Establish Relationships:* Build strong relationships with your tech partners through regular communication and mutual trust. Clearly define the objectives and expectations of the partnership.
- *Leverage Expertise:* Tap into the expertise of your tech partners to gain insights into new technologies and their potential applications. This collaboration can help you stay ahead of technological trends and incorporate them into your business.
- *Co-Develop Solutions:* Work together with your tech partners to co-develop innovative solutions. This collaborative approach can lead to the creation of unique products or services that give you a competitive edge.

For example, when Netflix shifted from a DVD rental service to a streaming service, it collaborated with tech partners to leverage advancements in internet speed and video compression technologies. This technological foresight allowed them to revolutionize the entertainment industry and set a new standard for content delivery.

4. *Attend Technology Conferences and Expos*

Technology conferences and expos are excellent opportunities to stay updated on the latest advancements and network with industry leaders. These events showcase cutting-edge technologies, provide insights from expert speakers, and offer hands-on experience with new tools and products.

Benefits of Attending Technology Conferences and Expos:

- *Exposure to New Technologies:* See firsthand the latest innovations and technologies that are shaping the industry.
- *Learning from Experts:* Attend keynote speeches, panel discussions, and workshops led by industry experts. These sessions provide valuable insights into current trends and future developments.
- *Networking Opportunities:* Meet and connect with industry professionals, potential partners, and thought leaders. These connections can lead to collaborative opportunities and knowledge sharing.
- *Hands-On Experience:* Participate in demonstrations and try out new tools and products. This hands-on experience helps you understand the practical applications and benefits of new technologies.

For instance, CES (Consumer Electronics Show) is a prominent tech event where companies showcase their latest innovations. By attending such events, businesses can stay informed about technological advancements and gain insights into how these technologies can be integrated into their operations.

5. *Engage in Continuous Learning and Development*

Continuous learning and development are crucial for staying updated with technological advancements. By regularly updating your skills and knowledge, you can better understand and leverage new technologies.

Ways to Engage in Continuous Learning:

- *Online Courses and Certifications:* Enroll in online courses and certifications offered by platforms like Coursera, Udacity, and edX. These courses cover a wide range of topics, from artificial intelligence to blockchain technology.
- *Workshops and Training Programs:* Participate in workshops and training programs that focus on emerging technologies and their applications. These programs provide hands-on experience and practical insights.
- *Webinars and Online Seminars:* Attend webinars and online seminars hosted by industry experts and organizations. These virtual events offer valuable information and allow you to stay updated from the comfort of your home or office.
- *Reading and Research:* Regularly read books, research papers, and articles on technological advancements. This helps you stay informed about the latest developments and theoretical foundations of new technologies.

For example, professionals in the healthcare industry often engage in continuous learning to stay updated on medical technologies and innovations. By keeping their skills and knowledge current, they can provide better patient care and contribute to advancements in the field.

Staying updated with technological advancements is essential for innovation and maintaining a competitive edge. By following technology news and blogs, joining tech communities and forums, collaborating with tech partners, attending technology conferences and expos, and engaging in continuous learning and development, you can keep abreast of the latest developments and leverage them to enhance your products or services.

In today's rapidly evolving technological landscape, proactive efforts to stay informed and adapt to new advancements are crucial. By making it a priority to stay updated, you can ensure that your innovation initiatives are aligned with current trends and poised for success. Embrace the opportunities that technological advancements offer, and use them to drive your business forward.

Identifying Opportunities and Assessing the Competitive Landscape

Identifying opportunities and assessing your competitive landscape are critical components of the analysis phase. These steps help you understand where you stand in the market and how you can leverage your strengths.

NEWT Analysis

In my journey through various industries and working with numerous organizations, I've discovered that having a structured approach to understanding your internal and external environment is crucial for innovation. To help guide you through this process, I've developed a technique called NEWT, which stands for Nurture, Eliminate, Win, and Threat. This method allows you to systematically assess your organization's capabilities and the market landscape to drive meaningful innovation and sustained success. Let's dive into how you can conduct a NEWT Analysis effectively.

Nurture: Identifying What You Do Well

The first step in the NEWT Analysis is to identify what your organization excels at. This involves recognizing your core strengths and capabilities that can be nurtured and leveraged to achieve your innovation goals.

Gathering Input from Stakeholders

Start by gathering input from various stakeholders within your organization. This includes employees at all levels, managers, and even customers. Use surveys, interviews, and brainstorming sessions to collect insights about what your organization does best.

Questions to Ask:

- What unique resources or capabilities do we have?
- What do our customers say we do better than others?
- What achievements are we most proud of?

By involving a diverse group of stakeholders, you ensure that you capture a comprehensive view of your organization's strengths.

Analyzing Internal Data

Next, review internal reports, performance metrics, and financial statements to identify areas where your organization excels. Look for patterns and trends that highlight your strengths.

Metrics to Consider:

- Financial performance indicators like profit margins and return on investment.
- Operational efficiency metrics such as production costs and time-to-market.
- Customer satisfaction scores and loyalty metrics.

For instance, a retail company might discover that its strength lies in efficient supply chain management, which allows it to offer competitive pricing and maintain high customer satisfaction levels.

Compiling and Prioritizing Strengths

Once you have gathered input and analyzed data, compile a list of strengths and prioritize them based on their impact on your business. Focus on those that align with your strategic goals and provide a competitive advantage.

By understanding and nurturing these strengths, you can build a solid foundation for your innovation efforts.

Eliminate: Addressing Areas for Improvement

The next step in the NEWT Analysis is to identify and address areas where your organization needs improvement. This involves acknowledging your weaknesses and developing strategies to eliminate them.

Gathering Honest Feedback

Encourage employees, managers, and customers to provide honest feedback about the areas where your organization can improve. Create a safe environment where stakeholders feel comfortable sharing their thoughts.

Questions to Ask:

- What challenges do we face in our operations?
- What do our customers frequently complain about?
- Where do we fall short compared to our competitors?

By gathering candid feedback, you can gain valuable insights into the areas that need attention.

Analyzing Internal Data for Weaknesses

Review internal reports, performance metrics, and financial statements to identify areas where performance is lacking or where costs are disproportionately high.

Metrics to Consider:

- Areas with consistently high operational costs.
- Departments with low productivity or efficiency.
- Customer service metrics indicate high complaint rates or low satisfaction scores.

For example, a manufacturing company might identify inefficiencies in its production process that lead to high defect rates and increased production costs.

Developing Action Plans to Address Weaknesses

Once you have identified and prioritized areas for improvement, develop action plans to address them. This might involve investing in new technology, providing additional training for employees, or reevaluating your business processes.

By eliminating these weaknesses, you can enhance your overall performance and create a more robust platform for innovation.

Win: Identifying and Capitalizing on Opportunities

The third step in the NEWT Analysis is to identify and capitalize on external opportunities that can help your organization win in the marketplace.

Conducting Market Research

Conduct thorough market research to identify external opportunities. This includes analyzing industry trends, customer behavior, and technological advancements. Use both primary and secondary research methods to gather data.

Questions to Ask:

- What emerging trends could we capitalize on?

- Are there gaps in the market that we can fill?
- How can new technologies enhance our offerings?

For instance, during the rise of mobile technology, many companies identified the opportunity to develop mobile apps to complement their services. Uber, for example, leveraged this trend to revolutionize the transportation industry.

Analyzing Competitors

Study your competitors to identify opportunities they might be overlooking. Look for areas where they are weak or where they are not fully addressing customer needs.

Questions to Ask:

- What customer needs are our competitors not addressing?
- Are there markets or segments our competitors are not serving?
- How can we differentiate ourselves from our competitors?

For example, a small coffee shop might notice that larger chains are not catering to customers who prefer organic, locally sourced products. By focusing on this niche, the shop can attract a dedicated customer base.

Leveraging Technological Advancements

Stay updated on technological advancements that can create new opportunities for your business. This includes advancements in artificial intelligence, automation, data analytics, and more.

Example:

A marketing firm might leverage advancements in data analytics to offer personalized marketing solutions, providing more value to clients and gaining a competitive edge.

Exploring Strategic Partnerships

Identify potential partnerships that can help you capitalize on new opportunities. This could involve collaborating with other businesses, joining industry associations, or forming alliances with technology providers.

Example:

A fitness brand might partner with a health tech company to develop a new line of wearable fitness devices, combining expertise to create innovative products that meet customer needs.

Developing a Plan to Exploit Opportunities

Once you have identified and prioritized your opportunities, develop a strategic plan to exploit them. This might involve launching new products, entering new markets, or adopting new business models.

Example:

A home automation company might identify the growing trend of smart home devices and develop a range of connected home products that integrate with popular smart home ecosystems.

By proactively identifying and capitalizing on opportunities, you can position your organization for success and drive continuous innovation.

Threat: Mitigating External Challenges

The final step in the NEWT Analysis is to recognize and mitigate external challenges that could hinder your progress. This involves identifying potential threats and developing strategies to address them.

Conducting a SCAN Analysis

To identify external challenges, I use an approach called SCAN, which stands for Social, Competitive, Analytical, and Navigational. This framework helps you systematically assess the external environment and identify potential threats to your business.

Social Factors:

Consider social trends and shifts in consumer behavior that could impact your business. This includes changes in demographics, lifestyle preferences, and cultural attitudes.

For example, a shift towards eco-friendly products can pose a threat to companies that rely heavily on non-sustainable practices.

Competitive Factors:

Analyze your competitive landscape to identify potential threats from existing and new competitors. Look at their strengths, weaknesses, and market strategies.

For instance, a new entrant in your market with a disruptive business model can significantly impact your market share.

Analytical Factors:

Use data analytics to monitor market conditions and identify potential threats. This includes economic indicators, industry reports, and market forecasts.

For example, an economic downturn can pose a threat to discretionary spending industries like luxury goods and travel.

Navigational Factors:

Assess technological advancements and regulatory changes that could impact your business. This includes new regulations, technological disruptions, and changes in industry standards.

For example, new data privacy regulations can pose a threat to companies that rely heavily on data-driven marketing strategies.

Keep a close eye on your competitors to identify potential threats. This includes new product launches, strategic alliances, and market expansion efforts.

Questions to Ask:

- Are our competitors developing new products that could threaten our market share?
- Have our competitors formed strategic partnerships that give them an advantage?
- Are our competitors expanding into new markets that we serve?

Example:

A small retail chain might view the expansion of a large competitor into its local market as a significant threat.

Develop strategies to mitigate identified threats. This might involve diversifying your product offerings, investing in new technology, or developing contingency plans.

Example:

A financial services company might develop a plan to mitigate the threat of cybersecurity breaches by investing in advanced security technologies and conducting regular security audits.

By identifying and addressing potential threats, you can protect your organization from external challenges and ensure continued success.

Conducting a NEWT Analysis is an essential part of understanding your organization's internal and external environment. This structured planning method helps you identify areas to nurture, elements to eliminate, opportunities to win, and threats to mitigate. By thoroughly analyzing these aspects, you can develop strategies that drive innovation and ensure long-term success.

To effectively conduct a NEWT Analysis, involve key stakeholders, gather comprehensive data, and use this information to make informed decisions. Remember, the goal is to build on your strengths, address your weaknesses, capitalize on opportunities, and mitigate threats. This proactive approach to strategic planning will help you stay competitive and agile in an ever-changing business landscape. Adopt the NEWT Analysis as a tool for continuous improvement and innovation, ensuring your organization is well-equipped to navigate future challenges and seize new opportunities.

Using Porter's Five Forces

Porter's Five Forces is a powerful tool that helps you analyze the competitive forces in your industry. Developed by Michael E. Porter, this framework allows you to understand the intensity of competition and the profitability potential of your market. By assessing these forces, you can develop strategies to enhance your competitive position and drive sustainable success. Let's delve into the components of Porter's Five Forces and how they can be applied effectively.

Competitive Rivalry: Assessing the Number and Strength of Competitors

The first force, competitive rivalry, examines the level of competition within your industry. Highly competitive rivalry can limit profitability and growth, as companies must continually invest in marketing, innovation, and price adjustments to stay ahead.

Factors to Consider:

- *Number of Competitors:* A large number of competitors typically increases the intensity of rivalry. In contrast, industries with fewer competitors may experience less intense competition.

- *Industry Growth Rate:* Slow-growing industries often have higher rivalry as companies vie for a limited customer base. Conversely, high-growth industries may experience less rivalry as expanding markets provide opportunities for all players.
- *Product Differentiation:* When products are similar, competition tends to focus on price, increasing rivalry. Differentiated products, on the other hand, reduce direct competition as companies focus on unique value propositions.
- *Fixed Costs:* Industries with high fixed costs, such as manufacturing, tend to have an intense rivalry as companies strive to maximize capacity utilization to spread fixed costs over more units.
- *Exit Barriers:* High exit barriers, such as significant investment in specialized assets, can increase rivalry as companies stay in the market despite low profitability.

Example:

Consider the airline industry, which is characterized by intense competitive rivalry. Numerous airlines compete for the same customer base, leading to price wars and continuous investment in marketing and service enhancements. Companies like Southwest Airlines have differentiated themselves by focusing on low-cost travel and exceptional customer service, allowing them to thrive in a highly competitive environment.

Threat of New Entrants: Evaluating Market Entry Barriers

The second force, the threat of new entrants, examines how easy or difficult it is for new competitors to enter your market. High entry barriers protect established companies by limiting the number of new entrants.

Factors to Consider:

- *Capital Requirements:* High initial investments, such as for manufacturing facilities or technology development, can deter new entrants.

- *Economies of Scale:* Established companies often benefit from economies of scale, making it difficult for new entrants to compete on cost.
- *Regulatory Barriers:* Industries with strict regulations and compliance requirements can have high entry barriers, reducing the threat of new entrants.
- *Brand Loyalty:* Strong brand loyalty among customers can make it challenging for new entrants to gain market share.
- *Access to Distribution Channels:* Established companies often have well-developed distribution networks, making it harder for new entrants to access the market.

Example:

The pharmaceutical industry has high entry barriers due to the significant capital required for research and development, regulatory approval processes, and the need for specialized expertise. These barriers protect established companies and limit the number of new entrants.

Bargaining Power of Suppliers: Determining Supplier Influence

The third force, the bargaining power of suppliers, assesses the influence suppliers have over your business. Strong supplier power can impact costs, quality, and availability of inputs, affecting your overall competitiveness.

Factors to Consider:

- *Number of Suppliers:* A limited number of suppliers increases their bargaining power, as companies have fewer alternatives.

- *Supplier Differentiation:* Unique or highly differentiated inputs can increase supplier power, as companies rely on specific suppliers for critical components.
- *Switching Costs:* High switching costs make it difficult for companies to change suppliers, increasing supplier power.
- *Supplier Concentration:* Industries with a high concentration of suppliers can experience greater supplier power.

Example:

In the technology industry, companies like Apple rely on specialized components from a limited number of suppliers. These suppliers have significant bargaining power, influencing the cost and availability of critical inputs like microprocessors and display screens.

Bargaining Power of Customers: Analyzing Customer Influence

The fourth force, the bargaining power of customers, evaluates the influence customers have over your business. Strong customer power can drive prices down and demand higher quality or better service.

Factors to Consider:

- *Number of Customers:* A small number of large customers can wield significant power, as losing a single customer could have a substantial impact on your business.
- *Product Differentiation:* Standardized or undifferentiated products increase customer power, as customers can easily switch between suppliers.

- *Price Sensitivity:* Price-sensitive customers are more likely to exert pressure on companies to lower prices.
- *Customer Loyalty:* High customer loyalty can reduce customer power, as customers are less likely to switch suppliers.

Example:

In the retail industry, large retailers like Walmart have significant bargaining power over their suppliers. Their ability to buy in bulk and their influence on consumer preferences allow them to negotiate favorable terms and prices.

Threat of Substitutes: Identifying Alternative Products or Services

The fifth force, the threat of substitutes, examines the presence of alternative products or services that can meet the same customer needs. The availability of substitutes can limit profitability by capping prices and reducing demand for your products.

Factors to Consider:

- *Availability of Substitutes:* A high number of substitutes increases the threat, as customers can easily switch to alternative products.
- *Switching Costs:* Low switching costs make it easier for customers to choose substitutes, increasing the threat.
- *Relative Price and Performance:* Substitutes that offer a better price-performance ratio can attract customers away from your products.

Example:

In the beverage industry, the threat of substitutes is high due to the availability of various alternatives like water, juices, and energy drinks. Companies like Coca-Cola continuously innovate and diversify their product offerings to mitigate this threat.

Applying Porter's Five Forces: A Practical Approach

Understanding and applying Porter's Five Forces can provide valuable insights into your competitive landscape and help you develop strategies to enhance your position. Here's how you can effectively use this framework:

Step 1: Define Your Industry

Clearly define the industry you are analyzing. This ensures that your assessment is focused and relevant. For example, if you are a software company, you might define your industry as enterprise software or consumer software, depending on your market focus.

Step 2: Analyze Each Force

Conduct a detailed analysis of each force, considering the specific factors that apply to your industry. Gather data from reliable sources, such as industry reports, market research, and expert opinions.

Competitive Rivalry:

- Assess the number and strength of your competitors.
- Evaluate market growth rates and product differentiation.

Threat of New Entrants:

- Identify barriers to entry in your industry.
- Consider capital requirements, economies of scale, and regulatory barriers.

Bargaining Power of Suppliers:

- Determine the number and concentration of suppliers.
- Assess the uniqueness of inputs and switching costs.

Bargaining Power of Customers:

- Analyze the number of customers and their buying power.

- Consider product differentiation and customer loyalty.

Threat of Substitutes:

- Identify alternative products or services.
- Evaluate switching costs and the relative price-performance ratio.

Step 3: Identify Strategic Implications

Based on your analysis, identify the strategic implications for your business. Consider how each force impacts your competitive position and profitability.

Examples:

- If competitive rivalry is high, focus on differentiating your products and enhancing customer loyalty.
- If the threat of new entrants is low, capitalize on your established market position to expand and innovate.
- If supplier power is strong, explore alternative suppliers or negotiate long-term contracts to secure favorable terms.

Step 4: Develop Strategic Responses

Develop strategic responses to address the findings from your analysis. This involves creating action plans to enhance your strengths, mitigate weaknesses, capitalize on opportunities, and defend against threats.

Examples:

- To counter highly competitive rivalry, invest in R&D to innovate and differentiate your products.
- To reduce the threat of new entrants, strengthen your brand and customer loyalty through marketing and superior customer service.
- To manage strong supplier power, diversify your supplier base and establish strong relationships with key suppliers.

- To handle high customer power, enhance your value proposition and focus on building long-term customer relationships.
- To address the threat of substitutes, continuously innovate and adapt your products to meet changing customer needs and preferences.

Step 5: Monitor and Adapt

The competitive landscape is dynamic, and the forces affecting your industry can change over time. Regularly monitor these forces and adapt your strategies accordingly. Stay informed about industry trends, competitor activities, and technological advancements to ensure that your strategic responses remain effective.

Porter's Five Forces is a comprehensive tool that helps you understand the competitive dynamics of your industry. By analyzing competitive rivalry, the threat of new entrants, the bargaining power of suppliers, the bargaining power of customers, and the threat of substitutes, you can gain valuable insights into the factors that influence your market position and profitability.

Applying this framework allows you to develop informed and effective strategies that enhance your competitive advantage. By continuously monitoring and adapting to these forces, you can navigate the complexities of your industry and drive sustainable success. Use Porter's Five Forces as a guiding tool to stay ahead of the competition, identify new opportunities, and build a resilient and innovative business.

Gathering Competitive Intelligence

Staying ahead of your competitors is essential for sustained success. Competitive intelligence involves gathering and analyzing information about your competitors to understand their strategies, strengths, and weaknesses. This proactive approach helps you anticipate market shifts, identify opportunities, and develop strategies to outperform your rivals. Here's how you can effectively gather and utilize competitive intelligence.

The Importance of Competitive Intelligence

Competitive intelligence is not just about spying on your competitors; it's about understanding the market dynamics and positioning your business for success. By knowing what your competitors are up to, you can make informed decisions, avoid potential pitfalls, and seize new opportunities.

Benefits of Competitive Intelligence:

1. *Strategic Planning:* Gain insights into competitor strategies to inform your own strategic planning.
2. *Market Positioning:* Understand your competitors' strengths and weaknesses to better position your products or services.
3. *Innovation:* Identify gaps in the market that your competitors are not addressing, sparking innovative ideas for new products or services.
4. *Risk Management:* Anticipate competitive moves and market changes to mitigate risks.

Methods to Gather Competitive Intelligence

There are several methods you can use to gather competitive intelligence. Each method offers unique insights and can be used in combination to provide a comprehensive view of your competitive landscape.

1. Market Research Reports

Market research reports are valuable resources that provide detailed insights into competitor activities, market trends, and industry dynamics. These reports are often compiled by research firms and include data on market share, growth rates, product performance, and more.

How to Utilize Market Research Reports:

- *Identify Key Competitors:* Use market research reports to identify who your main competitors are and what market share they hold.
- *Analyze Market Trends:* Look for trends in the market that could impact your business. This includes changes in consumer behavior, technological advancements, and economic factors.
- *Benchmark Performance:* Compare your performance against competitors in areas such as sales, growth, and customer satisfaction.

Example:

For instance, a technology company might use a market research report to analyze the competitive landscape in the smartphone market. By understanding the market share and growth rates of competitors like Apple and Huawei, the company can identify opportunities to differentiate its products and capture market share.

2. Social Media Monitoring

Social media platforms are a goldmine of information about your competitors. By monitoring their social media activities, you can gain insights into their marketing strategies, customer engagement, and public perception.

How to Monitor Social Media:

- *Follow Competitors:* Follow your competitors' official social media accounts on platforms like Facebook, Twitter, LinkedIn, and Instagram.
- *Analyze Content:* Pay attention to the type of content they post, the frequency of posts, and the engagement they receive. Look for

patterns in their messaging and campaigns.

- *Monitor Customer Interactions:* Observe how competitors interact with their customers. This can provide insights into their customer service practices and the issues their customers face.

Example:

Samsung has excelled at using social media monitoring to keep an eye on Apple's product launches and marketing strategies. By analyzing the buzz around Apple's announcements, Samsung can quickly adapt its own strategies and develop competitive products that address gaps in Apple's offerings.

3. Customer Feedback

Customers are often the best source of information about how your products stack up against competitors. By gathering and analyzing customer feedback, you can identify areas where you excel and areas that need improvement.

How to Gather Customer Feedback:

- *Surveys and Questionnaires:* Conduct surveys and questionnaires to gather feedback from your customers. Include questions that compare your products with those of your competitors.
- *Review Analysis:* Analyze customer reviews on platforms like Amazon, Google, and Yelp. Look for recurring themes and comparisons to competitors.
- *Customer Interviews:* Conduct in-depth interviews with customers to gain deeper insights into their experiences and preferences.

Example:

A software company might find through customer feedback that its product lacks certain features that competitors offer. By addressing these gaps, the company can improve its product and better meet customer needs, ultimately gaining a competitive edge.

4. Public Records and Filings

Public records and regulatory filings can provide valuable information about your competitors' financial health, strategic moves, and operational practices. These documents are often available through government databases, industry associations, and financial institutions.

How to Use Public Records:

- *Financial Statements:* Analyze competitors' financial statements to understand their revenue, profitability, and investment areas.
- *Patent Filings:* Monitor patent filings to stay updated on competitors' innovations and technological advancements.
- *Regulatory Filings:* Review regulatory filings to learn about new market entries, product approvals, and compliance issues.

Example:

A pharmaceutical company might track patent filings to monitor competitors' research and development activities. By understanding what new drug competitors are developing, the company can adjust its own R&D strategy to stay ahead.

5. Competitive Benchmarking

Competitive benchmarking involves comparing your business processes, performance metrics, and practices against those of your competitors. This method helps you identify best practices and areas for improvement.

How to Conduct Competitive Benchmarking:

- *Identify Key Metrics:* Determine which metrics are most relevant to your business, such as cost efficiency, customer satisfaction, or innovation rate.

- *Collect Data:* Gather data on these metrics from both your organization and your competitors. Use a combination of primary research, market reports, and public data.
- *Analyze and Compare:* Analyze the data to identify performance gaps and areas where you can improve.

Example:

A retail chain might benchmark its customer service practices against those of a leading competitor. By identifying best practices in customer service, the chain can implement similar strategies to enhance its own customer experience.

Implementing Competitive Intelligence Insights

Once you have gathered and analyzed competitive intelligence, the next step is to implement the insights into your business strategy. Here's how you can do that effectively:

Develop Strategic Responses

Use the intelligence you've gathered to develop strategic responses to competitive threats and opportunities. This might involve launching new products, adjusting pricing strategies, or enhancing customer service.

Example:

If you discover that a competitor is planning to enter a new market, you can expedite your own market entry plans or strengthen your presence in that market to defend your position.

Enhance Product Development

Incorporate competitive insights into your product development process. Identify features or services that your competitors offer and consider how you can improve or differentiate your offerings.

Example:

If customer feedback indicates that competitors offer superior user interfaces, invest in improving your product's user experience to match or exceed that of your competitors.

Improve Marketing Strategies

Adjust your marketing strategies based on what you learn about your competitors' tactics. This might involve adopting new channels, refining your messaging, or targeting different customer segments.

Example:

If social media monitoring reveals that a competitor's campaign is resonating well with customers, analyze what aspects of the campaign are effective and consider how you can apply similar strategies to your own marketing efforts.

Strengthen Customer Relationships

Use competitive intelligence to identify gaps in your customer relationship management and find ways to enhance customer loyalty. This might involve offering personalized services, loyalty programs, or improved customer support.

Example:

If customer feedback suggests that a competitor's customer support is more responsive, invest in training your support team and implementing new tools to enhance your customer service capabilities.

Gathering competitive intelligence is a critical component of staying ahead in today's competitive business environment. By using methods such as market research reports, social media monitoring, customer feedback, public records, and competitive benchmarking, you can gain valuable insights into your competitors' strategies, strengths, and weaknesses.

Implementing these insights into your strategic planning, product development, marketing, and customer relationship management can help you position your business for success. By staying informed and proactive, you can anticipate market shifts, identify opportunities, and navigate the competitive landscape with confidence. Embrace competitive intelligence as a continuous process to ensure that your business remains agile, innovative, and ahead of the competition.

The Role of Thorough Analysis in Guiding Innovation Strategies

Thorough analysis is essential for developing effective innovation strategies. This involves using your findings to craft strategic plans, allocate resources effectively, and create a roadmap for innovation.

Developing Strategic Plans

Strategic planning is the cornerstone of any successful innovation journey. It involves setting long-term goals and determining the actions needed to achieve them. The analysis phase you've completed provides the data needed to make informed decisions and set realistic objectives. This process ensures that your efforts are aligned with your vision and that you have a roadmap to guide your actions.

Steps to Develop Strategic Plans

Set Clear Goals

The first step in developing a strategic plan is to set clear and achievable goals. These goals should be specific, measurable, attainable, relevant, and time-bound (SMART). Clear goals provide direction and a sense of purpose, helping you stay focused on what you want to achieve.

How to Set Clear Goals

Define Your Vision: Start with a broad vision of what you want to accomplish. This vision should align with your overall mission and values.

Break Down the Vision: Divide your vision into specific goals. These goals should be detailed and clearly articulated, outlining what success looks like.

Prioritize Goals: Not all goals can be pursued simultaneously. Prioritize them based on their impact and feasibility. Focus on the most critical objectives first.

Example:

When Tesla planned to enter the automotive market, they set clear goals such as developing cutting-edge electric vehicle technology, building a strong brand, and creating a robust manufacturing process. These goals provided a clear direction for their innovation efforts.

Identify Key Actions

Once you have set your goals, the next step is to identify the specific actions needed to achieve them. This involves breaking down each goal into actionable steps and determining the best approach to take.

How to Identify Key Actions

- *Outline the Steps:* For each goal, list the steps required to achieve it. Be as detailed as possible, considering all the necessary tasks and milestones.
- *Assign Responsibilities:* Determine who will be responsible for each action. Assign tasks to individuals or teams with the appropriate skills and expertise.
- *Create a Timeline:* Develop a timeline for each action, setting

deadlines for completion. This helps keep the project on track and ensures timely progress.

Example:

To achieve its goal of developing electric vehicle technology, Tesla identified key actions such as researching battery technologies, designing prototype vehicles, and testing performance. Each action was assigned to specific teams, and they were given a timeline for completion.

Allocate Resources

Successful strategic planning requires adequate resources. This includes not only financial resources but also time, personnel, and technology. Proper allocation of resources ensures that your team has everything they need to execute the plan effectively.

How to Allocate Resources:

- *Assess Resource Needs:* Determine the resources required for each action. This includes budget, personnel, equipment, and technology.
- *Allocate Budget:* Distribute the budget across different actions and departments. Ensure that critical areas receive sufficient funding.
- *Manage Personnel:* Assign the right people to the right tasks. Consider their skills, experience, and workload. Ensure that your team is well-equipped to handle their responsibilities.
- *Invest in Technology:* Identify the tools and technologies needed to support your actions. Invest in the necessary software, hardware, and infrastructure.

Example:

Tesla allocated significant resources to research and development, hiring top engineers and scientists, investing in advanced manufacturing facilities, and securing funding for their projects. This comprehensive resource allocation was crucial to their success.

Monitor Progress

Regularly monitoring your progress is essential to ensure that you stay on track and make necessary adjustments. Continuous evaluation helps identify any issues early on and allows you to adapt your plan as needed.

How to Monitor Progress:

- *Set Milestones:* Establish key milestones to track progress. These milestones should be specific, measurable, and time-bound.
- *Review Regularly:* Conduct regular reviews of your progress. This can be done through team meetings, progress reports, and performance reviews.
- *Adjust as Needed:* Be flexible and willing to adjust your plan based on the insights gained from your reviews. If something isn't working, find out why and make the necessary changes.

Example:

Tesla continuously monitored the progress of its projects, holding regular meetings to review performance and address any challenges. This proactive approach allowed them to stay agile and make adjustments to their strategy as needed.

Example of a Strategic Plan in Action

To illustrate how strategic planning works in practice, let's take a closer look at Tesla's entry into the automotive market.

1. ***Set Clear Goals:***

   - *Develop Electric Vehicle Technology:* Focus on creating efficient, high-performance electric vehicles.

- *Build a Strong Brand:* Establish Tesla as a leader in the electric vehicle market.
- *Create a Robust Manufacturing Process:* Develop efficient manufacturing processes to produce vehicles at scale.

2. **Identify Key Actions:**

- *Research and Development:* Invest in battery technology research, design prototype vehicles, and conduct performance testing.
- *Brand Building:* Launch marketing campaigns, participate in industry events, and build a strong online presence.
- *Manufacturing:* Construct manufacturing facilities, streamline production processes, and ensure quality control.

3. Allocate Resources:

- *Budget:* Secure funding from investors and allocate it to R&D, marketing, and manufacturing.
- *Personnel:* Hire top engineers, scientists, marketing professionals, and manufacturing experts.
- *Technology:* Invest in advanced manufacturing equipment, design software, and battery technology.

4. Monitor Progress:

- *Milestones:* Set specific milestones for R&D breakthroughs, marketing campaign launches, and manufacturing output.
- *Reviews:* Hold regular team meetings to review progress, address challenges, and make necessary adjustments.
- *Adaptation:* Adjust the strategy based on market feedback, technological advancements, and competitive actions.

Strategic Planning for Innovation

Strategic planning is essential for guiding your innovation efforts and ensuring that they align with your long-term goals. Here's how you can tailor your strategic planning process specifically for innovation:

Foster a Culture of Innovation

Creating an environment that encourages creativity and experimentation is crucial for successful innovation. This involves promoting a culture where new ideas are welcomed, risks are taken, and failures are seen as learning opportunities.

How to Foster a Culture of Innovation:

- *Encourage Idea Generation:* Create channels for employees to share their ideas. This can include brainstorming sessions, innovation workshops, and suggestion boxes.
- *Celebrate Innovation:* Recognize and reward innovative thinking and successful projects. This encourages a culture of continuous improvement and creativity.
- *Accept Failure:* Encourage a mindset where failure is seen as a step towards success. Provide support for teams to learn from their mistakes and iterate on their ideas.

Example:

Companies like 3M have built a strong culture of innovation by allowing employees to spend a portion of their time on personal projects. This approach has led to the development of numerous successful products, including Post-it Notes.

Align Innovation with Business Strategy

Ensure that your innovation efforts align with your overall business strategy.

This alignment helps ensure that your innovation initiatives support your long-term goals and provide value to the organization.

How to Align Innovation with Business Strategy:

- *Identify Strategic Priorities:* Determine the areas where innovation can have the greatest impact on your business goals. Focus your efforts on these areas.
- *Integrate Innovation into Planning:* Include innovation initiatives in your strategic planning process. Ensure that innovation is a key component of your business strategy.
- *Measure Impact:* Develop metrics to measure the impact of your innovation efforts on your business goals. Use these metrics to assess the effectiveness of your initiatives.

Example:

Tesla's focus on electric vehicle technology aligns with its strategic goal of becoming a leader in sustainable transportation. By prioritizing innovation in this area, Tesla has been able to achieve significant success and drive industry change.

Invest in Innovation Resources

Investing in the necessary resources is crucial for supporting your innovation initiatives. This includes providing funding, tools, and training to enable your teams to innovate effectively.

How to Invest in Innovation Resources:

- *Funding:* Allocate a portion of your budget specifically for innovation projects. This funding can be used for research, prototyping, and testing.
- *Tools and Technology:* Provide access to the latest tools and technology

to support innovation. This can include software, hardware, and other resources.

- *Training and Development:* Offer training programs to develop the skills and knowledge needed for innovation. This can include workshops, courses, and mentorship programs.

Example:

Google invests heavily in innovation resources by providing its employees with access to advanced technology, funding for personal projects, and opportunities for continuous learning. This investment has led to the development of numerous groundbreaking products and services.

Developing strategic plans is a critical step in guiding your innovation efforts and achieving your long-term goals. By setting clear goals, identifying key actions, allocating resources, and monitoring progress, you can ensure that your innovation initiatives are aligned with your business strategy and positioned for success.

Remember to foster a culture of innovation, align your efforts with your strategic priorities, and invest in the necessary resources to support your teams. By doing so, you can drive meaningful innovation, create value for your organization, and achieve sustained success in a competitive market. Embrace strategic planning as a dynamic and continuous process, and use it to navigate the challenges and opportunities of the ever-evolving business landscape.

Allocating Resources Effectively

Resource allocation is a critical component of executing your innovation strategy. It involves distributing your available resources—financial, human, and technological—in a way that maximizes efficiency and effectiveness. Proper resource allocation ensures that your projects have the support they need to succeed and that your organization can achieve its strategic goals.

How to Allocate Resources

Allocating resources effectively requires a structured approach. Here are key steps to ensure that your resources are deployed in the best possible way:

A. Prioritize Projects

Not all projects are created equal. To make the most of your resources, you need to prioritize projects that align with your strategic goals and offer the highest potential return on investment.

How to Prioritize Projects:

- *Evaluate Strategic Alignment:* Assess how each project aligns with your organization's long-term goals and vision. Projects that closely align with your strategic priorities should be given higher priority.
- *Analyze Potential Return:* Consider the potential return on investment for each project. Projects with higher potential returns, whether in terms of revenue, market share, or customer satisfaction, should be prioritized.
- *Assess Risk:* Evaluate the risks associated with each project. High-risk projects might offer high rewards, but they should be balanced with more stable, low-risk initiatives.
- *Consider Resource Availability:* Ensure that you have the necessary resources to support high-priority projects. Projects that require resources you don't currently have access to might need to be deprioritized until those resources become available.

Example:

In the tech industry, a company might prioritize the development of a new software platform that aligns with its strategic goal of expanding into cloud computing. This project might offer a high potential return and aligns with the company's vision for growth.

B. Manage Budgets

Effective financial resource management is crucial for ensuring that each project has the necessary funding to succeed. This involves careful planning and ongoing management of project budgets.

How to Manage Budgets:

- *Create Detailed Budgets:* Develop detailed budgets for each project, outlining all anticipated costs. This includes personnel, materials, technology, and any other expenses.
- *Allocate Funds Wisely:* Distribute financial resources based on the priority and needs of each project. Ensure that high-priority projects receive sufficient funding.
- *Monitor Spending:* Regularly track spending against the budget. Use financial reports and analytics to identify any variances and address them promptly.
- *Adjust as Needed:* Be flexible and willing to adjust budgets as projects evolve. If a project requires more funding than initially anticipated, reallocate resources from lower-priority projects if possible.

Example:

A healthcare company might allocate a significant portion of its budget to developing a new medical device, ensuring that it has the funding necessary for research, development, clinical trials, and regulatory approval.

C. Deploy Talent

Human resources are one of your most valuable assets. Ensuring that the right people with the right skills are assigned to each project is essential for successful execution.

How to Deploy Talent:

- *Identify Required Skills:* Determine the specific skills and expertise needed for each project. This includes technical skills, industry knowledge, and project management capabilities.
- *Assign Roles:* Assign roles and responsibilities based on team members' strengths and expertise. Ensure that each team member understands their role and how it contributes to the project's success.
- *Provide Training:* Offer training and development opportunities to fill any skill gaps. Continuous learning helps your team stay current with industry trends and best practices.
- *Foster Collaboration*: Encourage collaboration and communication among team members. Effective teamwork can enhance creativity and problem-solving.

Example:

An automotive company might assign its top engineers and designers to a project developing a new electric vehicle. By leveraging their expertise, the company can ensure high-quality outcomes and innovation.

D. Track Utilization

Monitoring how resources are being used is crucial for avoiding waste and maximizing impact. Regular tracking allows you to make adjustments as needed to ensure resources are used efficiently.

How to Track Utilization:

- *Implement Tracking Systems:* Use project management software and tools to track resource utilization. This includes time tracking, budget monitoring, and task management systems.
- *Conduct Regular Reviews:* Hold regular review meetings to assess

progress and resource utilization. Identify any areas where resources are being underutilized or over-utilized.

- *Make Data-Driven Decisions:* Use data and analytics to inform decision-making. This helps you understand where resources are being used effectively and where adjustments are needed.
- *Optimize Resource Allocation:* Continuously optimize resource allocation based on insights from tracking and reviews. Reallocate resources from underperforming projects to those that are delivering high value.

Example:

A retail company might use project management software to track the time and budget spent on various marketing campaigns. By analyzing this data, the company can identify which campaigns are delivering the best return on investment and adjust its resource allocation accordingly.

Benefits of Effective Resource Allocation

Allocating resources effectively offers several benefits, including:

1. *Increased Efficiency:* Proper allocation ensures that resources are used where they are needed most, reducing waste and increasing overall efficiency.
2. *Enhanced Innovation:* By prioritizing high-impact projects and ensuring they have the necessary resources, you can drive innovation and stay ahead of the competition.
3. *Improved Performance:* Effective resource allocation leads to better project outcomes, higher productivity, and improved organizational performance.
4. *Risk Mitigation*: By carefully managing budgets and monitoring

resource utilization, you can identify and address potential issues before they become significant problems.

5. *Employee Satisfaction:* When team members are assigned to projects that match their skills and interests, they are more likely to be engaged and satisfied with their work.

Real-World Example: Amazon Web Services (AWS)

Amazon's allocation of resources to develop Amazon Web Services (AWS) is a prime example of effective resource allocation. In the early 2000s, Amazon recognized the potential of cloud computing and decided to invest heavily in this area. Here's how they did it:

Prioritizing Projects

Amazon's strategic decision to prioritize the development of AWS was rooted in its goal to diversify revenue streams and capitalize on its existing infrastructure. Recognizing the burgeoning potential of cloud computing, Amazon identified a significant opportunity to enter a market with high growth potential and strong demand for scalable, reliable cloud services. The decision was not made lightly; it involved thorough market research, analysis of industry trends, and a clear understanding of the competitive landscape.

By focusing on AWS, Amazon aligned this initiative with its broader strategic objectives. The company aimed to reduce dependency on retail sales by creating a new, high-margin business unit that could leverage Amazon's robust IT infrastructure. This prioritization meant that AWS received the necessary attention and resources to ensure its development and eventual success. The commitment to AWS was evident in the dedicated efforts to build a robust, scalable platform that could meet the needs of diverse customers, from startups to large enterprises. Amazon's foresight in prioritizing AWS paid off, as it now dominates the cloud services market, contributing significantly to Amazon's overall revenue and profitability.

Managing Budgets

Effective budget management was crucial for the successful development of AWS. Amazon allocated substantial financial resources to ensure that AWS had the funding necessary for extensive research, development, and scaling activities. This allocation wasn't arbitrary; it was based on a detailed financial plan that considered both the immediate and long-term needs of the project. The company invested heavily in state-of-the-art technology, recognizing that cutting-edge infrastructure was essential for providing reliable and efficient cloud services.

Furthermore, Amazon was strategic in its budget allocation, ensuring that each phase of AWS development was adequately funded. This included initial investments in infrastructure, such as data centers and networking equipment, as well as ongoing expenses for maintenance, upgrades, and scaling efforts. The careful management of these financial resources allowed Amazon to maintain a steady pace of development without encountering significant financial bottlenecks. By prioritizing expenditures that directly contributed to the platform's robustness and scalability, Amazon was able to build a competitive edge in the cloud computing market. This meticulous budget management ensured that AWS could sustain its growth path and continually improve its offerings, reinforcing its market leadership.

Deploying Talent

Amazon's deployment of talent was another critical factor in the success of AWS. The company assigned some of its best engineers and IT professionals to the project, leveraging their expertise to develop a high-quality product. These individuals brought a wealth of knowledge and experience in software development, network engineering, and systems architecture, which were essential for creating a reliable and scalable cloud platform. Amazon also recognized the need for specialized skills in cloud computing and data management, leading to the recruitment of new talent with expertise in these areas.

The team was not just technically proficient; they were also innovative and forward-thinking, capable of anticipating and addressing the evolving needs of cloud computing customers. By fostering a collaborative environment, Amazon encouraged its talent to experiment, innovate, and push the boundaries of what was possible with cloud technology. This approach led to the development of unique features and services that set AWS apart from its competitors. Additionally, Amazon invested in ongoing training and professional development to ensure that its team remained at the forefront of technological advancements. This continuous investment in talent ensured that AWS was not only built on solid technical foundations but also remained adaptable and responsive to market changes.

Tracking Utilization

To ensure the efficient use of resources and the smooth progression of AWS development, Amazon implemented advanced tracking systems. These systems allowed the company to monitor various aspects of the project, including resource allocation, budget spending, and project milestones. By having real-time visibility into these metrics, Amazon could quickly identify any issues or bottlenecks and take corrective action as needed. Regular reviews and updates ensured that the project stayed on track and that any deviations from the plan were promptly addressed.

Data-driven insights played a crucial role in optimizing resource allocation. By analyzing performance data, Amazon could determine which areas required more attention and resources and which were performing well with the current allocation. This dynamic approach to resource management allowed Amazon to be agile and responsive, reallocating resources to where they were most needed to maximize impact. Additionally, these tracking systems facilitated transparent communication among team members and stakeholders, fostering a culture of accountability and continuous improvement. The ability to track utilization effectively ensured that AWS development was not only efficient but also aligned with the strategic objectives of the company, paving the way for its long-term success and market dominance.

Effective resource allocation is essential for executing your innovation strategy and achieving your long-term goals. By prioritizing projects, managing budgets, deploying talent, and tracking utilization, you can ensure that your resources are used efficiently and effectively. This approach not only enhances your ability to innovate but also improves overall organizational performance and employee satisfaction.

Remember, resource allocation is not a one-time task. It requires continuous monitoring and adjustment to respond to changing circumstances and ensure that your projects remain on track.

Creating a Roadmap for Innovation

Creating a roadmap for innovation is a crucial step in achieving your strategic goals. A well-crafted roadmap provides a clear timeline, sets measurable milestones, identifies task dependencies, and allows for necessary adjustments. This structured approach helps you stay on track, measure progress, and ensure that your innovation efforts are aligned with your overall vision.

Elements of an Innovation Roadmap

An effective innovation roadmap comprises several key elements that guide your journey from concept to execution. Let's delve into each element in detail:

1. Timeline

The timeline is the backbone of your innovation roadmap. It defines the timeframes for each phase of your innovation projects, helping you manage time effectively and stay focused on your goals.

How to Define the Timeline:

- *Phases*: Break down your project into distinct phases, such as ideation, development, testing, and launch. Assign a specific timeframe to each phase based on the scope and complexity of the tasks involved.
- *Start and End Dates:* Clearly mark the start and end dates for each phase. This helps you plan your activities and allocate resources accordingly.
- *Key Dates:* Highlight important dates, such as project kick-off, major reviews, and final delivery. These dates serve as checkpoints to ensure that you are on track.

Example:

A software company might define a timeline for developing a new application, with phases such as market research (Q1), design (Q2), development (Q3-Q4), and beta testing (Q1 next year). By setting clear timeframes, the company can manage its efforts efficiently and meet deadlines.

2. Milestones

Milestones are specific, measurable goals that mark significant points in your project. They help you track progress, celebrate achievements, and identify any delays or issues early on.

How to Set Milestones:

- *SMART Goals:* Ensure that each milestone is Specific, Measurable, Achievable, Relevant, and Time-bound. This clarity helps in precise tracking and assessment.

- *Major Deliverables*: Identify key deliverables or outputs for each phase. These could include prototypes, completed modules, or validated concepts.
- *Review Points:* Include regular review points where progress is assessed and decisions are made about the next steps. These reviews keep the project aligned with its goals.

Example:

For a new marketing campaign, milestones might include completing market analysis (Month 1), finalizing campaign strategy (Month 2), launching initial ads (Month 3), and analyzing campaign performance (Month 4). These milestones help the team stay focused and measure the campaign's success at each stage.

3. Dependencies

Dependencies are the relationships between tasks that determine the sequence of activities. Identifying and managing dependencies is crucial for ensuring a smooth project flow and avoiding bottlenecks.

How to Identify Dependencies:

- *Task Relationships:* Determine which tasks depend on the completion of others. Use project management tools to visualize these relationships.
- *Critical Path:* Identify the critical path—the sequence of tasks that directly impact the project timeline. Any delay in these tasks will affect the overall project.
- *Resource Allocation:* Ensure that resources are allocated in a way that supports the dependencies. Avoid overloading team members with dependent tasks simultaneously.

Example:

In a product development project, the design phase might depend on the completion of the market research phase. Recognizing this dependency ensures that the design team is prepared to start work as soon as the research is complete, preventing delays.

4. Adjustments

Flexibility is key to successful innovation. Be prepared to adapt your roadmap as new information and challenges arise. This requires a proactive approach to monitoring progress and making adjustments when necessary.

How to Make Adjustments:

- *Regular Reviews*: Conduct regular project reviews to assess progress and identify any issues. Use these reviews to make informed decisions about adjustments.
- *Feedback Loops:* Establish feedback loops with stakeholders to gather input and make necessary changes. This ensures that the project remains aligned with its goals and stakeholder expectations.
- *Contingency Planning:* Develop contingency plans for potential risks and uncertainties. Having a plan B helps you respond quickly to unforeseen challenges.

Example:

If a new regulatory requirement emerges during a pharmaceutical development project, the team might need to adjust the timeline and add new tasks to ensure compliance. Regular reviews and feedback loops help the team stay agile and responsive to changes.

Example of an Innovation Roadmap in Action

To illustrate how an innovation roadmap works in practice, let's consider SpaceX's approach to planning its space missions.

1. Timeline

SpaceX defines a detailed timeline for each mission, from initial planning to launch and beyond. This timeline includes phases such as mission concept, design, testing, launch preparations, and post-launch analysis.

Example Timeline:

- Mission Concept: Q1-Q2
- Design Phase: Q3-Q4
- Testing and Validation: Q1-Q2 (next year)
- Launch Preparations: Q3 (next year)
- Launch: Q4 (next year)
- Post-Launch Analysis: Q1-Q2 (following year)

2. Milestones

SpaceX sets clear milestones to track progress and ensure that each phase of the mission is on track. These milestones include key deliverables and review points.

Example Milestones:

- Concept Approval: End of Q2
- Design Review: End of Q4
- Prototype Testing Complete: End of Q2 (next year)
- Launch Readiness Review: End of Q3 (next year)
- Successful Launch: Q4 (next year)

- Mission Report: End of Q2 (following year)

3. Dependencies

SpaceX carefully manages dependencies to ensure a smooth workflow. For example, the design phase cannot start until the mission concept is approved, and testing cannot begin until the design phase is complete.

Example Dependencies:

- Design Phase Depends on Concept Approval: Design cannot start until the mission concept is approved.
- Testing Depends on Design Completion: Testing can only begin once the design is finalized.
- Launch Preparations Depend on Successful Testing: Launch preparations proceed only after successful prototype testing.

4. Adjustments

SpaceX's roadmap includes provisions for adjustments based on new information and challenges. Regular reviews and feedback loops help the team stay agile and make necessary changes.

Example Adjustments:

- Regulatory Changes: If new regulations are introduced, the team adjusts the timeline and tasks to ensure compliance.
- Technical Challenges: If testing reveals technical issues, the team revises the design and testing phases to address these challenges.
- Stakeholder Feedback: Regular feedback from stakeholders, such as NASA or commercial clients, informs adjustments to ensure the mission meets all requirements.

Benefits of an Innovation Roadmap

Creating a roadmap for innovation offers several benefits:

- Clarity and Focus: A roadmap provides a clear plan of action, helping you stay focused on your goals and avoid distractions.
- Alignment: It ensures that all team members are aligned with the project's objectives and timelines, promoting collaboration and cohesion.
- Progress Tracking: Regular milestones and reviews allow you to track progress and make data-driven decisions.
- Risk Management: Identifying dependencies and potential risks helps you develop contingency plans and respond proactively to challenges.
- Flexibility: A roadmap allows for adjustments, helping you stay agile and responsive to new information and changing circumstances.

Creating a roadmap for innovation is essential for guiding your projects from concept to execution. By defining a clear timeline, setting measurable milestones, identifying task dependencies, and allowing for adjustments, you can ensure that your innovation efforts are structured, efficient, and aligned with your strategic goals.

Use the principles outlined in this section to develop your own innovation roadmap. This structured approach will help you stay on track, measure progress, and achieve your innovation objectives. Embrace the roadmap as a dynamic tool that evolves with your project, and use it to navigate the complexities of the innovation journey with confidence and clarity.

Overcoming Common Barriers and Setbacks in the Analysis Phase

As you navigate the analysis phase, you will undoubtedly encounter barriers and setbacks. Being aware of these potential challenges and knowing how to overcome them can make a significant difference in your innovation journey. Let's explore some common obstacles and strategies to address them.

Dealing with Information Overload

In the age of information, it's easy to become overwhelmed by the sheer volume of data available. Information overload can lead to analysis paralysis, where decision-making becomes difficult due to an excess of information.

Strategies to Overcome Information Overload

Prioritize Information

The first step in managing information overload is to prioritize the information you consume. Not all data is equally important, and focusing on the most relevant information can help you stay on track.

- *Identify Key Data Sources:* Determine which sources of information are most relevant to your innovation goals. This could include industry reports, customer feedback, or specific research studies.
- *Filter Unnecessary Data*: Use filters to exclude irrelevant information. Focus on data that directly impacts your strategic objectives and ignore the rest.
- *Rank Information by Importance:* Assign a level of importance to different pieces of information. Prioritize high-impact data that can influence critical decisions over less significant details.

Use Analytical Tools

Leveraging analytical tools can greatly enhance your ability to process and organize large volumes of data efficiently. These tools can help you filter, sort, and analyze data, turning raw information into actionable insights.

- *Data Analysis Software:* Employ software solutions like Excel, Tableau, or Power BI to visualize and analyze data. These tools can help you identify trends, patterns, and key insights without getting bogged down by details.
- *Automated Filters and Alerts:* Set up automated filters and alerts to notify you of important data changes or trends. This helps you stay updated without having to manually sift through all the information.
- *Custom Dashboards:* Create custom dashboards that aggregate and display only the most relevant data. This ensures that you have a clear overview of essential metrics and can make informed decisions quickly.

Set Clear Objectives

Having clear objectives helps you stay focused on gathering and analyzing only the necessary information. When you know what you need to achieve and why, it becomes easier to filter out extraneous data.

- *Define Your Goals:* Clearly outline your innovation goals and the specific information you need to achieve them. This focus helps you avoid getting sidetracked by irrelevant data.
- *Ask Specific Questions:* Formulate precise questions that your data needs to answer. This narrows down your information search and ensures that you are only collecting data that serves a specific purpose.

- *Review Regularly:* Periodically review your information needs and objectives. As your project progresses, adjust your focus to ensure that you are always gathering the most pertinent data.

By streamlining your information intake, you can make more informed and timely decisions.

Managing Resistance to Change

Resistance to change is a common barrier in any innovation process. This resistance can come from within the organization or from external stakeholders who are hesitant to adopt new ideas or technologies.

Strategies to Manage Resistance:

Communicate Clearly

Clear communication is the foundation for managing resistance to change. People need to understand why change is necessary and how it will benefit them and the organization.

- *Explain the Benefits:* Clearly articulate the advantages of the proposed changes. Highlight how the changes will improve processes, increase efficiency, or enhance outcomes. When people see the tangible benefits, they are more likely to support the change.
- *Align with Vision:* Ensure that the proposed changes are aligned with the organization's overall vision and strategic goals. Communicate how the changes will help achieve long-term objectives, creating a sense of purpose and direction.
- *Transparency:* Be transparent about the reasons for the change, the steps involved, and the expected outcomes. Transparency builds trust and reduces uncertainty.

Involve Stakeholders

Involving key stakeholders in the innovation process can significantly reduce resistance. When people feel included and heard, they are more likely to support the changes.

- *Engage Early:* Engage stakeholders early in the process. Seek their input and feedback on proposed changes. Early involvement fosters a sense of ownership and collaboration.
- *Build Consensus:* Work towards building a consensus among stakeholders. Address their concerns and incorporate their suggestions where feasible. Consensus-building helps create a unified approach to change.
- *Empower Champions:* Identify and empower change champions within the organization. These individuals can advocate for change, influence their peers, and help drive the initiative forward.

Provide Training

Training is essential for helping stakeholders understand and adapt to new technologies or processes. Adequate training can alleviate fears and build confidence in the new system.

- *Skill Development:* Offer training sessions to develop the necessary skills for adapting to the new changes. This could include hands-on workshops, online courses, or one-on-one coaching.
- *Continuous Support:* Provide ongoing support and resources to help stakeholders navigate the transition. This could involve setting up a helpdesk, creating user manuals, or offering follow-up training sessions.
- *Address Knowledge Gaps:* Identify any knowledge gaps that may exist and tailor training programs to address these areas. Customized

training ensures that all stakeholders are adequately prepared for the change.

Address Concerns and Demonstrate Value

Addressing concerns and demonstrating the value of innovation is crucial for overcoming resistance. People need to see that their concerns are being taken seriously and that the changes will bring real benefits.

- *Listen Actively:* Actively listen to the concerns of stakeholders. Show empathy and understanding, and acknowledge the challenges they may face during the transition.
- *Provide Evidence:* Use case studies, pilot projects, or testimonials to provide evidence of the positive impact of similar changes. Real-world examples can help stakeholders visualize the benefits.
- *Celebrate Successes:* Celebrate small wins and successes throughout the implementation process. Recognize and reward efforts that contribute to the successful adoption of the change.

By addressing concerns and demonstrating the value of innovation, you can reduce resistance and foster a more supportive environment.

Navigating Uncertainty

Innovation inherently involves navigating uncertainty. This uncertainty can stem from market dynamics, technological changes, or evolving customer preferences. Uncertainty can make it challenging to plan and execute innovation strategies effectively.

Strategies to Navigate Uncertainty:

Adopt Agile Methodologies

Agile methodologies are designed to help teams stay flexible and adapt quickly to changes. By breaking projects into smaller, manageable increments and continuously reassessing priorities, agile practices enable organizations to respond promptly to new information and shifting conditions.

- *Iterative Development:* Implement iterative development cycles where you build, test, and refine products or solutions in short timeframes. This approach allows for constant feedback and adjustments.
- *Cross-Functional Teams:* Form cross-functional teams that bring together diverse expertise. This collaboration enhances problem-solving and fosters innovation.
- *Regular Stand-Ups:* Hold regular stand-up meetings to review progress, address obstacles, and adjust plans as needed. These meetings keep the team aligned and focused on immediate priorities.

Conduct Scenario Planning

Scenario planning involves preparing for different potential outcomes by considering various scenarios and their implications. This proactive approach helps you anticipate changes and develop strategies to address them.

- *Identify Key Drivers:* Determine the key drivers of change in your industry, such as economic factors, regulatory changes, or technological advancements.
- *Develop Scenarios:* Create multiple scenarios based on these drivers, ranging from best-case to worst-case outcomes. Consider how each scenario could impact your business.
- *Plan Responses:* Develop strategic responses for each scenario. This

includes identifying opportunities, mitigating risks, and allocating resources appropriately.

Stay Informed

Staying informed about market trends, technological advancements, and customer feedback is essential for navigating uncertainty. Continuous monitoring allows you to identify emerging opportunities and threats early, enabling timely and informed decision-making.

- *Market Research:* Regularly conduct market research to understand industry trends, competitor activities, and customer preferences. Use this information to guide your innovation efforts.
- *Technology Watch:* Keep an eye on technological advancements that could impact your business. Subscribe to industry journals, attend conferences, and network with tech experts to stay updated.
- *Customer Feedback:* Gather and analyze customer feedback through surveys, focus groups, and social media. This direct input helps you stay attuned to customer needs and expectations.

Embracing uncertainty as part of the innovation process allows you to remain agile and responsive to new developments.

By understanding these common barriers and implementing strategies to overcome them, you can ensure a smoother and more effective analysis phase. This preparation will enable you to gather the insights needed to drive successful innovation strategies.

"Welcoming change with an innovative mindset allows the seeds of progress to grow into remarkable achievements."

– Bob Philips –

Chapter 4

G - Generate: Ideation And Concept Development

- **Outline Techniques For Generating, Evaluating, And Refining Ideas.**
- **Stress The Importance Of Collaboration And Diverse Perspectives In The Ideation Process.**
- **Present Frameworks And Tools That Aid In Creating Innovative Solutions.**

Innovation begins with generating ideas and developing them into viable concepts. This chapter will analyze the processes and techniques that can help you unleash your creative potential and mold initial sparks into well-rounded, actionable concepts. We will explore techniques for generating, evaluating, and refining ideas, emphasize the importance of collaboration and diverse perspectives, and present frameworks and tools that aid in creating innovative solutions.

Techniques for Generating, Evaluating, and Refining Ideas

Generating ideas is where the magic of innovation begins. Think of it as the spark that ignites the flame of creativity. We will dive into different techniques that I've found incredibly helpful in stimulating my creativity and refining those ideas into solid, actionable concepts. Whether you're brainstorming solo or with a team, visualizing your thoughts, or seeking feedback, these methods will guide you through the ideation process effectively. Let's explore these techniques together and set the stage for your innovation journey.

Brainstorming Sessions:

Brainstorming sessions are one of the most effective ways to unleash creativity and generate a wide range of ideas. Over the years, I've found that the key to successful brainstorming lies in creating an environment that encourages free thinking and maintains a non-judgmental atmosphere. Let's take a closer look at how you can make the most of your brainstorming sessions.

Unleashing Creativity

The magic of brainstorming lies in its ability to spark creativity. When done right, it can lead to a plethora of innovative ideas that you might not have considered otherwise. The goal is to create a space where ideas can flow freely without the fear of criticism or judgment. Here's how to set the stage for a successful brainstorming session:

Create a Safe Environment

- *Encourage Openness:* Let everyone know that all ideas are welcome, no matter how unconventional they may seem. This openness can inspire participants to think outside the box and share their most creative thoughts.
- *No Judgments:* Make it clear that there will be no criticism during the brainstorming phase. The purpose is to generate as many ideas as possible, not to evaluate them. Judgment can stifle creativity, so it's important to maintain a positive and encouraging atmosphere.

Set the Tone

- *Positive Energy:* Start the session with positive energy and enthusiasm. This can be contagious and help participants feel more comfortable and excited about contributing.
- *Encouraging Participation:* Actively encourage everyone to participate. Sometimes, the best ideas come from those who might be quieter or less confident in sharing their thoughts.

Structured vs. Unstructured Sessions

Deciding whether to have a structured or unstructured brainstorming session depends on your goals and the nature of the problem you're tackling. Both approaches have their benefits, and you might find that a combination of the two works best for your team.

Structured Brainstorming:

- *Clear Objectives:* Structured sessions have specific goals and objectives. This can help keep the discussion focused and productive.
- *Guided Techniques:* Use guided techniques like the "6-3-5 Brainwriting" method, where six participants write down three ideas in five minutes and then pass their paper to the next person to build on those ideas. This ensures that everyone contributes and builds on each other's thoughts. You may choose to increase the time here.
- *Time Management:* Set time limits for each part of the session. This helps keep the discussion on track and ensures that all topics are covered.

Unstructured Brainstorming:

- *Free Flow of Ideas:* Unstructured sessions allow for a more free-flowing exchange of ideas. There are no strict guidelines or limits, which can lead to unexpected and creative outcomes.
- *Flexibility:* This approach is more flexible and can adapt to the natural flow of the conversation. It can be particularly useful when exploring new or complex problems without predefined constraints.
- *Encouraging Creativity:* Without the pressure of structure, participants might feel more relaxed and open to sharing unconventional ideas.

Maximizing the Effectiveness of Brainstorming Sessions

Regardless of whether you choose a structured or unstructured approach, there are several strategies you can use to maximize the effectiveness of your brainstorming sessions.

1. ***Define the Problem Clearly:***

- *Clarity:* Start by clearly defining the problem or challenge you are trying to address. This ensures that everyone is on the same page and understands the context of the discussion. Check for the audience's understanding.
- *Focus:* A well-defined problem helps focus the brainstorming session and prevents it from veering off track.

2. ***Use Creative Prompts:***

- *Stimulate Thinking*: Use creative prompts or questions to stimulate thinking. For example, ask, "What if we had unlimited resources?" or "How would a child approach this problem?" These prompts can help participants think in new and innovative ways.
- *Challenge Assumptions:* Encourage participants to challenge existing assumptions and consider alternative perspectives.

3. ***Record All Ideas:***

- *Documentation:* Record all ideas generated during the session. This can be done on a whiteboard, flip chart, or digital tool. The goal is to capture every thought, no matter how small or incomplete it may seem.
- *Visual Representation:* Visual representation of ideas can help participants see connections and build on each other's thoughts.

4. ***Encourage Building on Ideas:***

- *Yes, and...:* Use the "Yes, and..." technique from improv theater to build on each other's ideas. This approach fosters collaboration and continuous improvement of concepts.
- *Combine Ideas:* Encourage participants to combine multiple ideas to create more robust and innovative solutions.

5. Allow Time for Reflection:

- *Silent Reflection:* Give participants time for silent reflection before or during the session. This can help them gather their thoughts and come up with more considered ideas.
- *Breaks:* Incorporate short breaks to allow participants to recharge and return to the discussion with fresh perspectives.

6. Follow Up:

- *Next Steps:* After the brainstorming session, review the ideas and identify the most promising ones. Develop a plan for further exploration and implementation.
- *Feedback:* Provide feedback to participants and keep them informed about the progress of their ideas. This can motivate them to continue contributing in the future.

Creating a Brainstorming Culture

Building a culture that embraces brainstorming and creative thinking can have a lasting impact on your organization. Here are some tips to foster a brainstorming culture:

1. Regular Sessions:

- *Routine:* Schedule regular brainstorming sessions to keep the creative momentum going. This can be a weekly or monthly practice that everyone looks forward to.
- *Variety:* Vary the format and focus of the sessions to keep things fresh and engaging.

2. Inclusive Participation:

- *Diverse Teams:* Encourage participation from diverse teams across the organization. Different perspectives can lead to more innovative ideas.

- *Inclusivity:* Ensure that everyone, regardless of their role or level, feels welcome and valued in brainstorming sessions.

3. Celebrate Creativity:

- *Recognition:* Recognize and celebrate creative ideas and contributions. This can be through awards, shout-outs in meetings, or other forms of acknowledgment.
- *Incentives:* Consider providing incentives for particularly innovative ideas that are implemented successfully.

4. Continuous Improvement:

- *Learning:* Continuously seek ways to improve your brainstorming process. Gather feedback from participants and be open to experimenting with new techniques.
- *Adaptability:* Be adaptable and willing to change your approach based on what works best for your team.

Overcoming Common Challenges

While brainstorming sessions can be incredibly productive, they can also present certain challenges. Here's how to overcome some common obstacles:

1. Groupthink:

- *Encourage Diversity:* Actively seek out diverse perspectives and encourage independent thinking to avoid groupthink.
- *Devil's Advocate:* Assign a "devil's advocate" role to challenge ideas and promote critical thinking.

2. Dominant Voices:

- *Equal Participation:* Ensure that everyone has an equal opportunity to speak. Use techniques like round-robin or passing the "talking stick" to give everyone a chance to share.
- *Facilitation:* A skilled facilitator can help manage the discussion and ensure that no single voice dominates the session.

3. Idea Fatigue:

- *Breaks:* Incorporate short breaks to prevent fatigue and maintain high energy levels.
- *Fresh Perspectives:* Occasionally bring in external facilitators or guest speakers to provide fresh perspectives and inspire new ideas.

4. Lack of Follow-Through:

- *Action Plan*: Develop a clear action plan to follow up on the ideas generated. Assign responsibilities and set deadlines for the next steps.
- *Accountability:* Hold regular check-ins to ensure that the ideas are being pursued and progress is being made.

Brainstorming sessions are a powerful tool for generating a wide range of ideas and unleashing creativity. By creating a safe and encouraging environment, choosing the right format, and employing effective techniques, you can maximize the potential of your brainstorming sessions. Remember, the goal is not just to come up with ideas but to refine and develop them into actionable concepts. Embrace the process, encourage participation, and continuously seek ways to improve your approach. With the right mindset and strategies, you can turn your brainstorming sessions into a driving force for innovation and success.

Mind Mapping:

Mind mapping is a powerful technique for visualizing ideas and connecting different thoughts. It helps you see the bigger picture and explore various angles, making it an invaluable tool in the innovation process. When done effectively, mind mapping can expand your thought process, uncover new connections, and lead to more comprehensive and creative solutions.

Visualizing Ideas

Mind mapping starts with visualizing your ideas. This process involves creating a diagram that represents your thoughts, making it easier to see how different concepts are interconnected. Here's how to get started with visualizing your ideas through mind mapping:

Start with a Central Concept

- *Identify the Core Idea:* Begin with a central concept or question that you want to explore. This will be the focal point of your mind map. Write it down in the center of a blank page or digital canvas.
- *Use Visual Elements:* Enhance your central concept with visual elements like shapes, colors, and images. These elements make your mind map more engaging and easier to understand at a glance.

Branch Out

- *Create Branches:* From the central concept, draw branches to represent related ideas or subtopics. Each branch represents a different aspect or component of the main idea.
- *Label Branches:* Clearly label each branch with keywords or short phrases that describe the related ideas. This helps to quickly identify and categorize different thoughts.

Add Details

- *Sub-Branches:* Expand on each branch by adding sub-branches that delve deeper into specific details. This hierarchical structure allows you to break down complex ideas into manageable parts.
- *Use Keywords:* Use keywords and short phrases rather than full sentences. This keeps your mind map concise and focused, making it easier to navigate and understand.

Incorporate Visuals

- *Icons and Images:* Use icons, images, and symbols to represent different ideas visually. Visuals can make your mind map more memorable and easier to recall.
- *Color Coding:* Use different colors to distinguish between branches and sub-branches. Color coding can help highlight relationships and categorize information.

Expanding Ideas

Mind mapping is not just about visualizing existing ideas; it's also a tool for expanding your thought process and discovering new connections. Here's how to use mind mapping to broaden your thinking:

Brainstorm Freely

- *Unrestricted Thinking:* Allow yourself to brainstorm freely without worrying about structure or organization initially. Write down all ideas that come to mind, even if they seem unrelated or far-fetched.
- *No Judgments:* Avoid judging or evaluating ideas during the brainstorming phase. The goal is to generate as many ideas as possible, no matter how unconventional they may seem.

Explore Connections

- *Look for Relationships:* Once you have a broad range of ideas, look for relationships and connections between them. Draw lines or arrows to show how different ideas are linked.
- *Combine Concepts:* Combine different ideas to create new and innovative solutions. Sometimes, the most creative ideas come from merging seemingly unrelated concepts.

Expand Branches

- *Deep Dive:* Take each branch of your mind map and expand it further. Ask questions like "What if?" and "How?" to delve deeper into each subtopic.
- *Iterative Process:* Mind mapping is an iterative process. Continuously add to and refine your mind map as new ideas emerge and connections become apparent.

Engage Others

- *Collaborative Mind Mapping:* Engage colleagues, team members, or friends in the mind-mapping process. Different perspectives can lead to new insights and expand the range of ideas.
- *Feedback and Refinement:* Seek feedback on your mind map and use it to refine and improve your ideas. Collaboration can enhance creativity and lead to more comprehensive solutions.

Practical Applications of Mind Mapping

Mind mapping can be applied in various contexts to enhance creativity and problem-solving. Here are some practical applications:

Project Planning

- *Outline Tasks:* Use mind mapping to outline the tasks and activities involved in a project. This helps visualize the project's scope and identify dependencies.
- *Resource Allocation:* Plan resource allocation by mapping out the team members, tools, and materials needed for each task.

Product Development

- *Feature Mapping:* Map out the features and functionalities of a new product. This helps visualize the product's design and identify potential improvements.
- *User Experience:* Use mind mapping to explore different aspects of the user experience. Consider factors like usability, accessibility, and customer feedback.

Problem-Solving

- *Root Cause Analysis:* Use mind mapping to conduct a root cause analysis of a problem. Identify the main issue and branch out to explore underlying causes and contributing factors.
- *Solution Generation:* Brainstorm potential solutions and map out their pros and cons. This helps in evaluating different options and selecting the most effective solution.

Strategic Planning

- *Vision and Goals:* Map out your organization's vision, goals, and strategic initiatives. This helps in aligning efforts and ensuring that everyone is working towards the same objectives.
- *NEWT Analysis:* Conduct a NEWT analysis using mind mapping. Identify areas to nurture, eliminate, win, and threats, and explore their interrelationships.

Tips for Effective Mind Mapping

To make the most of mind mapping, consider the following tips:

1. Keep It Simple:

- *Avoid Complexity:* Keep your mind map simple and focused. Avoid adding too many details that can make it cluttered and difficult to navigate.
- *Focus on Key Ideas:* Highlight the key ideas and concepts that are most important. Use sub-branches to add details without overwhelming the main branches.

2. Use Digital Tools:

- *Mind Mapping Software:* Use digital tools like MindMeister, XMind, or Lucidchart to create and organize your mind maps. These tools offer features like easy editing, collaboration, and sharing.
- *Templates and Themes:* Take advantage of templates and themes available in mind mapping software to save time and ensure a professional look.

3. Review and Revise:

- *Regular Updates:* Regularly review and update your mind map as new information becomes available or as your project progresses.
- *Refinement:* Refine your mind map by removing outdated or irrelevant information and adding new insights. This keeps it current and useful.

4. Encourage Creativity:

- *Incorporate Fun Elements:* Incorporate fun elements like drawings, doodles, or inspirational quotes to keep the mind mapping process enjoyable and engaging.

- *Creative Prompts:* Use creative prompts or challenges to stimulate thinking and encourage participants to explore new ideas.

5. Practice Regularly:

- *Consistent Use:* Make mind mapping a regular practice in your problem-solving and brainstorming activities. The more you use it, the more proficient you'll become.
- *Experiment:* Experiment with different styles and approaches to find what works best for you and your team.

Mind mapping is a versatile and powerful tool for generating, visualizing, and expanding ideas. By creating a visual representation of your thoughts, you can see the bigger picture, explore various angles, and uncover new connections. Whether you're planning a project, developing a product, solving a problem, or strategizing for the future, mind mapping can help you organize your ideas, enhance creativity, and drive innovation.

Embrace mind mapping as a regular part of your creative process. Use it to brainstorm freely, explore connections, and collaborate with others. With practice and continuous refinement, you'll find that mind mapping becomes an indispensable tool for unlocking your creative potential and achieving your innovation goals.

Reverse Thinking:

Reverse thinking, also known as reverse engineering or backward thinking, is a powerful technique for generating innovative solutions by flipping the perspective. Instead of starting with the goal and figuring out how to achieve it, you consider what could prevent the goal from being achieved and work backward to develop solutions. This approach can reveal hidden obstacles and spark creative thinking, leading to unexpected and effective solutions.

Flipping the Perspective

Traditional problem-solving often starts with defining the goal and brainstorming ways to achieve it. Reverse thinking, on the other hand, starts by considering the barriers and challenges that could prevent success. By flipping the perspective, you can uncover new insights and opportunities for innovation.

How to Implement Reverse Thinking

Start with the End in Mind:

- *Define the Goal:* Clearly define the goal or outcome you want to achieve. This gives you a reference point to work backward from.
- *Visualize Success:* Imagine that you have already achieved the goal. What does success look like? What are the key elements that contributed to this success?

Identify Potential Obstacles:

- *Brainstorm Barriers:* Make a list of all the possible obstacles, challenges, and risks that could prevent you from achieving the goal. Think broadly and consider both internal and external factors.
- *Consider Worst-Case Scenarios:* Imagine the worst-case scenarios. What could go wrong? What are the most significant threats to success?

Reverse Engineer Solutions:

- *Work Backward:* Start with the identified obstacles, work backward to develop solutions. Ask yourself, "If this is the problem, what could have caused it? How can we prevent it?"
- *Think Creatively:* Use creative thinking to come up with innovative solutions. Consider unconventional approaches and challenge existing assumptions.

Identifying Obstacles

One of the key benefits of reverse thinking is its ability to identify potential obstacles early in the process. By proactively considering what could go wrong, you can develop strategies to mitigate risks and increase the likelihood of success.

Techniques for Identifying Obstacles:

NEWT Analysis:

- *Nurture and Eliminate:* Focus on identifying the strengths that you need to nurture. These are the positive attributes, resources, and capabilities within your organization that can help you achieve your goal. Pinpoint the weaknesses or areas that could hinder your progress. These are internal factors that need to be addressed or eliminated to ensure success.
- *Win and Threat:* Look for opportunities in the external environment that you can capitalize on. These are the factors that could provide a competitive advantage or open up new avenues for growth. Recognize potential threats from the external environment that could impede your success. These could be competitive actions, regulatory changes, or economic shifts.

Stakeholder Analysis:

- *Engage Stakeholders:* Involve stakeholders in identifying obstacles. Different perspectives can reveal new insights and potential challenges that you might not have considered.
- *Map Influences:* Create a stakeholder map to understand the influence and interests of different stakeholders. This helps in anticipating resistance or support.

Risk Assessment:

- *Identify Risks:* Conduct a thorough risk assessment to identify potential risks. Consider factors such as market changes, technological advancements, regulatory requirements, and competitive pressures.
- *Evaluate Impact:* Assess the impact and likelihood of each risk. This helps prioritize risks and focus on the most significant ones.

Overcoming Obstacles with Reverse Thinking

Once you've identified the potential obstacles, the next step is to develop strategies to overcome them. Reverse thinking helps you approach these challenges creatively and find effective solutions.

Developing Solutions

Brainstorming Sessions:

- *Encourage Creativity:* Conduct brainstorming sessions specifically focused on overcoming identified obstacles. Encourage participants to think creatively and propose innovative solutions.
- *Diverse Perspectives:* Involve people from different backgrounds and departments to bring diverse perspectives and ideas.

Scenario Planning:

- *Prepare for Different Scenarios:* Use scenario planning to prepare for different potential outcomes. Develop strategies for each scenario to ensure you're ready to adapt to changes.
- *Flexible Plans:* Keep your plans flexible and adaptable. This allows you to pivot quickly if circumstances change.

Prototyping and Testing:

- *Build Prototypes:* Develop prototypes or pilot projects to test your solutions. This helps in identifying any issues early and making necessary adjustments.
- *Iterative Process:* Use an iterative process to refine your solutions. Continuously test, gather feedback, and improve.

Collaborative Problem-Solving:

- *Engage Teams:* Engage teams in collaborative problem-solving. Work together to develop and implement solutions, leveraging the collective expertise and creativity of the group.
- *Shared Ownership:* Foster a sense of shared ownership and responsibility for overcoming obstacles. This encourages commitment and accountability.

Practical Applications of Reverse Thinking

Reverse thinking can be applied in various contexts to drive innovation and problem-solving. Here are some practical applications.

Product Development:

- *User Experience:* Consider what could prevent users from having a positive experience with your product. Work backward to address these issues and enhance usability.
- *Market Fit:* Identify factors that could prevent your product from fitting well in the market. Develop strategies to align your product with market needs and preferences.

Project Management:

- *Timeline Risks:* Identify potential risks to your project timeline. Work backward to develop contingency plans and ensure timely delivery.
- *Resource Allocation:* Consider what could prevent optimal resource allocation. Develop strategies to manage resources effectively and avoid bottlenecks.

Strategic Planning:

- *Goal Achievement:* Identify obstacles that could prevent achieving strategic goals. Develop reverse-engineered solutions to address these challenges.
- *Competitive Advantage:* Consider what could erode your competitive advantage. Develop strategies to strengthen your market position and stay ahead of competitors.

Change Management:

- *Resistance to Change:* Identify factors that could cause resistance to change within the organization. Develop strategies to manage resistance and foster a positive change culture.
- *Communication:* Consider what could hinder effective communication during the change process. Develop strategies to ensure clear, transparent, and consistent communication.

Tips for Effective Reverse Thinking

To make the most of reverse thinking, consider the following tips:

1. Embrace a Growth Mindset:

- *Openness to Learning:* Cultivate a growth mindset that values learning and improvement. Be open to new ideas and perspectives.

- *Adaptability:* Be willing to adapt and change your approach based on new information and insights.

2. Encourage Diverse Perspectives:

- *Inclusive Environment:* Create an inclusive environment where diverse perspectives are valued and encouraged.
- *Cross-Functional Teams:* Involve cross-functional teams in the reverse thinking process to bring different viewpoints and expertise.

3. Use Visual Tools:

- *Diagrams and Charts:* Use visual tools like diagrams, charts, and mind maps to organize and visualize your thoughts. This helps in seeing connections and relationships.
- *Storyboard:* Create a storyboard to map out the reverse thinking process. This provides a clear visual representation of the steps involved.

4. Practice Regularly:

- *Consistent Use:* Make reverse thinking a regular part of your problem-solving and brainstorming activities. The more you use it, the more proficient you'll become.
- *Experiment:* Experiment with different techniques and approaches to find what works best for you and your team.

5. Foster a Culture of Innovation:

- *Encourage Risk-Taking:* Foster a culture that encourages risk-taking and experimentation. Emphasize the value of learning from failure.
- *Recognize and Reward:* Recognize and reward innovative thinking

and creative problem-solving. This motivates and inspires others to embrace reverse thinking.

Reverse thinking is a powerful technique for generating innovative solutions by flipping the perspective and identifying potential obstacles. By considering what could prevent success and working backward to develop solutions, you can uncover hidden insights and opportunities for innovation. Embrace reverse thinking as a regular part of your creative process, and use it to expand your thought process, enhance problem-solving, and drive meaningful change.

Incorporate the strategies and tips outlined in this section to make the most of reverse thinking. Whether you're developing a new product, managing a project, planning strategically, or leading change, reverse thinking can help you navigate challenges and achieve your goals with creativity and confidence. With practice and continuous refinement, you'll find that reverse thinking becomes an indispensable tool for unlocking your innovative potential and driving success.

IMAGINE Technique:

I would like to introduce you to one of the techniques that I have used. The IMAGINE technique is a powerful method to challenge and refine ideas, helping you explore new dimensions and possibilities for innovation. Each component of IMAGINE represents a different approach to enhancing and refining your ideas.

Integrate

Think about how you can integrate different elements, processes, or ideas to create something new. Integration involves combining separate parts to form a cohesive whole that offers improved functionality or a novel solution.

- *Integrate Different Technologies:* Combine various technologies to enhance the performance or capabilities of your product.
- *Merge Features:* Integrate multiple features or services into one comprehensive offering to provide more value to your customers.

Modify

Modification involves altering your existing ideas to improve them or make them more suitable for a different context. This can include changing certain aspects, tweaking designs, or adjusting functionalities.

- *Adjust Design:* Modify the design of your product to improve usability or aesthetics.
- *Change Process:* Modify your workflow or processes to increase efficiency or reduce costs.

Amplify

Amplification means enhancing certain aspects of your idea to make them more impactful. This can involve scaling up features, increasing capabilities, or intensifying the user experience.

- *Enhance Features*: Amplify the key features of your product to make them more powerful and appealing.
- *Increase Capacity*: Amplify the capacity or scale of your operations to meet higher demand.

Generate

Generating involves coming up with entirely new ideas or variations. This is about brainstorming and creating new concepts that can be added to or combined with your original idea.

- *New Concepts:* Generate new concepts that complement your existing product or service.

- *Innovative Solutions:* Generate innovative solutions to existing problems by thinking outside the box.

Innovate

Innovation is about implementing creative ideas that add value. This step involves taking bold steps to convert your original idea into something groundbreaking.

- *New Technologies:* Innovate by incorporating cutting-edge technologies that differentiate your product from competitors.
- *Unique Business Models:* Develop unique business models that offer new value propositions to your customers.

Neutralize

Neutralizing involves identifying and addressing any negative aspects or potential obstacles related to your idea. This step is about mitigating risks and eliminating weaknesses.

- *Reduce Risks:* Neutralize risks by implementing safety measures or backup plans.
- *Eliminate Weaknesses:* Address and eliminate weaknesses in your product or service to strengthen its overall offering.

Expand

Expansion involves extending your idea to new markets, applications, or user groups. This step is about thinking broadly and considering how your idea can be applied in different contexts.

- *New Markets:* Expand into new markets to reach a broader audience.
- *Additional Uses:* Find additional uses for your product or service to increase its utility and value.

Practical Application of IMAGINE

Let's see how to apply each element of IMAGINE to an initial idea to refine and improve it.

Example: Developing a New Educational App

Integrate:

- *Combine Learning Methods:* Integrate video tutorials, interactive quizzes, and gamified elements into the app to create a comprehensive learning experience.
- *Social Features:* Integrate social features that allow students to collaborate and share their progress.

Modify:

- *Adjust Interface:* Modify the user interface to make it more intuitive and user-friendly.
- *Update Content:* Regularly update the content to keep it relevant and engaging for users.

Amplify:

- *Enhance Features:* Amplify the app's features by adding advanced analytics that track student progress and provide personalized feedback.
- *Scale Up:* Increase the app's capacity to handle more users simultaneously without compromising performance.

Generate:

- *New Subjects:* Generate new content for different subjects to expand the app's offerings.
- *Interactive Elements:* Generate innovative interactive elements that make learning more engaging.

Innovate:

- *AI Integration:* Innovate by incorporating AI to provide personalized learning paths based on user performance.
- *Unique Gamification:* Develop unique gamification techniques that reward students for their achievements.

Neutralize:

- *Address Security:* Neutralize security risks by implementing robust data protection measures.
- *Reduce Distractions:* Eliminate unnecessary features that could distract users from their learning goals.

Expand:

- *New Languages:* Expand the app's reach by offering content in multiple languages.
- *Corporate Training:* Find additional uses for the app by adapting it for corporate training programs.

The IMAGINE technique provides a structured yet flexible approach to challenging and refining your ideas. By integrating, modifying, amplifying, generating, innovating, neutralizing, and expanding, you can morph initial concepts into powerful and innovative solutions. Embrace each step of the IMAGINE technique to push the boundaries of creativity and drive successful innovation in your projects.

Six Thinking Hats:

Edward de Bono's Six Thinking Hats is a powerful technique for exploring ideas from multiple perspectives, ensuring a comprehensive and balanced evaluation. By metaphorically putting on different hats, you can systematically approach problems and opportunities from various angles—

logical, emotional, creative, and more. This method helps you avoid cognitive biases, fosters creativity, and leads to well-rounded decision-making. Let's dive into how you can effectively use the Six Thinking Hats technique.

Different Perspectives

The essence of the Six Thinking Hats technique lies in its ability to make you think in diverse ways. Each hat represents a different perspective, allowing you to focus on one aspect of the problem at a time. Here's a breakdown of each hat and how to use it:

White Hat: Objective and Analytical

- *Focus on Facts:* When wearing the White Hat, you concentrate on the available data and information. It's about being objective and analytical.
- *Ask Questions:* What information do we have? What information do we need? Where can we get it?
- *Avoid Emotions:* This hat is all about logic and facts, leaving emotions and opinions aside.

***Red Hat:* Emotions and Intuition**

- *Express Feelings:* The Red Hat allows you to express your emotions and intuition about the situation. It's about gut feelings and instincts.
- *Honest Emotions:* What are your immediate reactions? How do you feel about this idea or problem?
- *No Justification:* There's no need to justify your feelings. It's about acknowledging the emotional aspect.

Black Hat: Critical and Cautious

- *Identify Risks:* The Black Hat focuses on critical thinking and identifying potential risks and drawbacks. It's about being cautious and realistic.

- *Play Devil's Advocate:* What could go wrong? What are the weaknesses? What obstacles might we face?
- *Constructive Criticism:* Use this hat to provide constructive criticism to improve the idea.

Yellow Hat: Positive and Optimistic

- *Highlight Benefits:* The Yellow Hat is all about optimism and positivity. It focuses on the benefits and opportunities.
- *Think Positively:* What are the strengths? What positive outcomes can we expect?
- *Encourage Optimism:* Use this hat to motivate and inspire, emphasizing the positive aspects.

Green Hat: Creativity and Growth

- *Generate Ideas:* The Green Hat is for creativity and innovation. It encourages you to think outside the box.
- *Explore Possibilities:* What new ideas can we generate? How can we improve or innovate?
- *Foster Creativity:* Use this hat to explore alternatives and encourage creative thinking.

Blue Hat: Process and Control

- *Organize Thoughts:* The Blue Hat focuses on process and control. It's about managing the thinking process.
- *Facilitate Discussion:* How will we organize our thinking? What's the next step? How do we move forward?

- *Guide Thinking:* Use this hat to ensure that all perspectives are considered and the process stays on track.

Balanced Evaluation

Using the Six Thinking Hats technique ensures a balanced evaluation of ideas, considering all possible angles. This method helps you avoid cognitive biases and ensures that decisions are well-rounded and thoroughly thought out.

Structured Approach:

- *Sequential Thinking*: Use each hat sequentially to guide your thinking process. Start with the White Hat to gather facts, move to the Red Hat to express emotions, and so on.
- *Comprehensive View*: This structured approach ensures that all aspects of the problem are considered, leading to a comprehensive view.

Diverse Perspectives:

- *Incorporate All Views*: The technique forces you to consider diverse perspectives, which can reveal insights you might have missed.
- *Inclusive Process*: It's an inclusive process that values logical analysis, emotional responses, creative ideas, and critical thinking equally.

Practical Applications of Six Thinking Hats

The Six Thinking Hats technique can be applied in various contexts to enhance decision-making and problem-solving. Here are some practical applications:

Team Meetings:

- *Structured Discussions:* Use the Six Thinking Hats in team meetings to structure discussions and ensure that all perspectives are considered.
- *Balanced Input:* Encourage balanced input from all team members, fostering a culture of open and inclusive communication.

Project Planning:

- *Comprehensive Planning:* Apply the technique to project planning to evaluate risks, opportunities, and stakeholder emotions comprehensively.
- *Detailed Analysis:* Ensure that all aspects of the project are analyzed in detail, leading to more robust planning.

Problem Solving:

- *Thorough Evaluation:* Use the Six Thinking Hats to solve complex problems by thoroughly evaluating all possible solutions and their implications.
- *Creative Solutions:* Encourage creative problem-solving by exploring unconventional ideas with the Green Hat.

Strategic Decision-Making:

- *Informed Decisions:* Apply the technique to strategic decision-making to ensure that decisions are well-informed and balanced.
- *Risk Management:* Identify and manage risks effectively by critically evaluating potential drawbacks with the Black Hat.

Tips for Effective Use of Six Thinking Hats

To make the most of the Six Thinking Hats technique, consider the following tips:

1. Clearly Define the Problem:

- *Specific Focus:* Clearly define the problem or decision at hand. This helps in keeping the discussion focused and relevant.
- *Shared Understanding:* Ensure that all participants have a shared understanding of the issue.

2. Assign Hats Deliberately:

- *Role Assignment:* Assign hats to participants deliberately. This can help in balancing input and ensuring that all perspectives are considered.
- *Rotate Hats:* Consider rotating hats among participants to encourage diverse thinking and prevent dominance by any single perspective.

3. Use Visual Aids:

- *Colored Hats:* Use physical colored hats or visual aids to represent each thinking hat. This can make the process more engaging and memorable.
- *Visual Representation:* Create visual representations of the ideas and insights generated under each hat.

4. Encourage Participation:

- *Inclusive Environment:* Create an inclusive environment where all participants feel comfortable expressing their thoughts and ideas.
- *Active Engagement:* Encourage active engagement from all participants, ensuring that all perspectives are heard.

5. Summarize and Reflect:

- *Summarize Insights:* At the end of the session, summarize the key insights and ideas generated under each hat.
- *Reflect on Process:* Reflect on the process and consider what worked well and what could be improved for future sessions.

The Six Thinking Hats technique is a versatile and powerful tool for exploring ideas from multiple perspectives. By systematically wearing different hats, you can ensure a balanced evaluation of ideas, avoiding cognitive biases and fostering creativity. This method helps you make well-rounded decisions, considering all possible angles and insights.

Embrace the Six Thinking Hats technique as a regular part of your problem-solving and decision-making processes. Use it in team meetings, project planning, strategic decision-making, and more. With practice and continuous refinement, you'll find that the Six Thinking Hats technique becomes an indispensable tool for driving innovation and achieving your goals. By adopting this structured approach to thinking, you can unlock new perspectives, enhance creativity, and make more informed and balanced decisions.

Idea Journals:

Keeping an idea journal is a simple yet profoundly effective way to capture your thoughts and foster creativity. Over the years, I've found that maintaining a journal to jot down ideas as they come can lead to unexpected insights and connections. This practice not only helps in recording fleeting thoughts but also provides a valuable resource for continuous reflection and development.

Recording Thoughts

The first step in leveraging an idea journal is to get into the habit of recording your thoughts. Inspiration can strike at any time—whether you're in a meeting, on a walk, or just before falling asleep. Having a dedicated space to capture these moments ensures that no idea is lost.

Why Record Your Thoughts?

- *Capture Fleeting Ideas*: Our minds are constantly generating ideas, but they can be fleeting. An idea journal helps capture these thoughts before they slip away.
- *Organized Creativity*: Recording ideas helps organize your creative process. It provides a structured way to keep track of thoughts, making it easier to revisit and build upon them later.
- *Immediate Access*: With a journal, you have immediate access to your ideas. This can be particularly useful during brainstorming sessions or when you need a burst of inspiration.

How to Start an Idea Journal:

- *Choose Your Medium:* Decide whether you prefer a physical notebook or a digital journal. Both have their advantages—physical notebooks can be more tactile and satisfying, while digital journals offer searchability and easy editing.
- *Consistency:* Make it a habit to carry your journal with you or have easy access to your digital journal. Consistency is key to capturing ideas as they come.
- *Date Entries:* Always date your entries. This helps track the evolution of your ideas over time and provides context for when and how you thought of them.

What to Include:

- *Ideas and Concepts:* Write down any ideas or concepts that come to mind, no matter how incomplete or unpolished they may seem.
- *Observations:* Note observations from your surroundings, conversations, or experiences that spark thoughts or could lead to new ideas.
- *Questions:* Record any questions that arise. Questions can be powerful prompts for further exploration and ideation.
- *Sketches and Diagrams:* Don't limit yourself to words. Sketches, diagrams, and doodles can help visualize ideas and make connections that words alone might not convey.

Continuous Reflection

The real power of an idea journal lies in continuous reflection. Regularly revisiting and reflecting on your notes can spark further insights and help refine and develop your ideas. Here's how to make the most of this process:

Regular Review:

- *Set Aside Time:* Schedule regular review sessions to go through your journal entries. This could be daily, weekly, or monthly, depending on your workflow and preference.
- *Pattern Recognition:* Look for patterns and recurring themes in your entries. These patterns can highlight areas of interest or potential breakthroughs.
- *Evaluate Progress:* Assess the progress of your ideas. Identify which ones have evolved, which need further exploration, and which might be set aside for now.

Deep Dive into Entries:

- *Expand on Ideas:* Take time to expand on the ideas you've jotted down. Flesh out the details, consider different angles, and think about how they might be implemented.
- *Connect the Dots:* Look for connections between different entries. Sometimes, combining two or more ideas can lead to innovative solutions that you might not have considered before.
- *Refine Concepts:* Refine your concepts by critically evaluating them. What works? What doesn't? How can the idea be improved or made more practical?

Incorporating Feedback:

- *Seek Input:* Share selected entries with trusted colleagues, mentors, or friends to get their input and perspectives.
- *Iterative Improvement:* Use the feedback to iteratively improve your ideas. This collaborative approach can lead to more robust and well-rounded concepts.

Practical Applications of Idea Journals

Idea journals can be incredibly versatile and beneficial in various contexts. Here are some practical applications:

Personal Development:

- *Goal Setting:* Use your journal to set personal goals and track your progress. Reflect on your achievements and areas for improvement.
- *Skill Building:* Document your learning journey as you acquire new skills. Jot down insights, challenges, and breakthroughs.

Professional Projects:

- *Project Planning:* Capture ideas and plans for professional projects. Regularly review and refine these plans to keep them on track.
- *Innovation Tracking:* Keep a record of innovative ideas and solutions related to your field. This can be a valuable resource for future projects or initiatives.

Creative Pursuits:

- *Artistic Endeavors:* Whether you're a writer, artist, or musician, use your journal to capture creative ideas, plot points, sketches, or lyrics.
- *Inspiration Log:* Document sources of inspiration—books, movies, conversations, or experiences—that spark creative ideas.

Problem Solving:

- *Idea Generation:* Use your journal to brainstorm solutions to problems you encounter. Revisit these entries to see if new insights or solutions emerge.
- *Decision Making:* Reflect on significant decisions, noting the factors considered and the outcomes. This can help improve your decision-making process over time.

Tips for Effective Idea Journaling

To maximize the benefits of an idea journal, consider the following tips:

1. Be Consistent:

- *Regular Entries:* Make journaling a regular habit. The more consistently you record your ideas, the more valuable your journal will become.

- *Daily Routine:* Incorporate journaling into your daily routine. This could be a morning or evening ritual, or a few minutes dedicated to jotting down thoughts during breaks.

2. Embrace Imperfection:

- *Unfiltered Thoughts:* Don't worry about making your entries perfect. The goal is to capture your thoughts as they come, without self-editing or judgment.
- *Raw Ideas:* Embrace raw, unpolished ideas. They don't have to be fully formed to be valuable.

3. Use Prompts:

- *Creative Prompts:* Use creative prompts to stimulate thinking. Questions like "What if…?" or "How might we…?" can help generate new ideas.
- *Reflective Prompts:* Reflective prompts such as "What did I learn today?" or "What challenges did I face?" can provide valuable insights.

4. Mix Mediums:

- *Visual Elements:* Incorporate visual elements like sketches, diagrams, and mind maps into your journal. These can help visualize and explore ideas in different ways.
- *Multimedia:* If you're using a digital journal, consider adding photos, videos, or audio recordings to capture ideas in various formats.

5. Experiment with Formats:

- *Different Styles:* Experiment with different journaling styles and formats. Bullet points, freeform writing, and structured templates can all be effective.

- *Flexibility:* Be flexible and adapt your journaling style to what works best for you.

Overcoming Common Challenges

While idea journaling is a valuable practice, it can come with challenges. Here's how to overcome some common obstacles:

***1. Writer's Block*:**

- *Prompt Yourself:* Use prompts to kickstart your thinking. Reflect on recent experiences, current challenges, or future aspirations.
- *Free Writing*: Engage in free writing, where you write continuously without stopping to edit or censor yourself. This can help you overcome mental blocks and get your creative juices flowing.

2. Consistency:

- *Set Reminders*: Set reminders or alarms to prompt you to journal regularly. Consistency is key to building a valuable idea journal.
- *Accountability Partner:* Consider partnering with a friend or colleague who also keeps an idea journal. Check-in with each other regularly to stay accountable.

3. Perfectionism:

- *Embrace Imperfection:* Remind yourself that your journal is a space for exploration and creativity, not perfection. Allow yourself to jot down incomplete or messy ideas.
- *Reframe Mistakes:* View mistakes or rough entries as part of the creative process. They can provide valuable insights and lead to new directions.

4. Lack of Time:

- *Short Entries:* Even short entries can be valuable. If you're pressed for time, jot down a quick thought or observation rather than skipping the practice entirely.
- *Integrate into Routine:* Find small pockets of time in your routine where you can incorporate journaling, such as during your commute or lunch break.

Maintaining an idea journal is a powerful tool for capturing thoughts, fostering creativity, and driving innovation. By recording your ideas as they come and regularly reflecting on them, you can uncover new insights, develop your concepts, and continuously refine your thinking. An idea journal not only helps in organizing your creative process but also serves as a valuable resource for personal and professional growth.

Embrace the practice of idea journaling with consistency and an open mind. Use it to capture fleeting thoughts, explore connections, and expand on your ideas. With time and dedication, your journal will become a rich repository of creative potential, ready to inspire and guide you on your innovation journey. Whether you're solving problems, planning projects, or pursuing creative endeavors, an idea journal can be your companion in unlocking new possibilities and achieving your goals.

Prototyping:

Prototyping is an essential step in the innovation process, bridging the gap between conceptual ideas and tangible solutions. By creating physical or digital models of your ideas, you can visualize and test them, gaining valuable insights that drive iterative improvement. Prototyping allows you to experiment, learn, and refine your concepts in a practical and hands-on way.

Building Models

Creating prototypes is all about bringing your ideas to life in a form that can be explored and tested. Whether physical or digital, prototypes provide a concrete representation of your concepts, allowing you to evaluate their feasibility and functionality.

Types of Prototypes

Physical Prototypes:

- *Materials and Tools:* Use materials like cardboard, clay, wood, or 3D printing to build physical models. Choose materials based on the complexity and requirements of your prototype.
- *Mock-Ups:* Start with simple mock-ups to visualize the basic structure and design. These do not need to be fully functional but should represent the overall concept.
- *Functional Models:* As you refine your ideas, create more detailed and functional models. These prototypes should closely mimic the final product in terms of functionality and user experience.

Digital Prototypes:

- *Wireframes:* For digital products, start with wireframes to outline the basic layout and structure. Tools like Sketch, Figma, or Adobe XD can be used to create wireframes quickly.
- *Interactive Prototypes*: Develop interactive prototypes that allow users to navigate through the product. This helps in testing the user interface and user experience.
- *High-Fidelity Prototypes:* Create high-fidelity prototypes that resemble the final product in terms of design and functionality. These prototypes can be used for detailed testing and feedback.

Benefits of Prototyping

Visualization:

- *Concrete Representation:* Prototypes provide a tangible representation of your ideas, making them easier to understand and evaluate.
- *Communication:* They serve as a visual tool to communicate your concepts to stakeholders, team members, and potential users.

Testing and Validation:

- *Functionality:* Prototypes allow you to test the functionality of your ideas in a real-world context. This helps identify any issues or areas for improvement.
- *User Feedback:* By sharing prototypes with users, you can gather valuable feedback on usability, design, and overall experience.

Experimentation:

- *Creative Exploration:* Prototyping encourages experimentation and creative exploration. You can try out different approaches and solutions without committing to a final design.
- *Iterative Development:* It supports iterative development, allowing you to refine and improve your ideas based on testing and feedback.

Iterative Improvement

Prototyping is an iterative process where each version of the prototype is improved based on feedback and testing. This cycle of iteration helps in refining your concepts and moving closer to a final, viable solution.

Steps in the Iterative Prototyping Process:

1. Initial Prototype:

- *Start Simple:* Begin with a simple, low-fidelity prototype that captures the core idea. The goal is to create a basic model that can be quickly tested and evaluated.
- *Focus on Key Features:* Identify the key features or components that need to be tested. This helps in narrowing down the focus and making the initial prototype manageable.

2. Testing and Feedback:

- *User Testing:* Conduct user testing to gather feedback on the initial prototype. Observe how users interact with the model and note any issues or areas of confusion.
- *Gather Insights:* Collect feedback from stakeholders, team members, and potential users. This feedback provides valuable insights into the strengths and weaknesses of the prototype.

3. Analysis and Refinement:

- *Evaluate Feedback:* Analyze the feedback to identify common themes and areas for improvement. Prioritize the issues that need to be addressed in the next iteration.
- *Refine Design:* Make the necessary changes to the prototype based on the feedback. This could involve redesigning certain features, improving functionality, or addressing usability issues.

4. Iterate and Improve:

- *Develop Next Version:* Build a new version of the prototype that incorporates the improvements and refinements. Each iteration should move closer to the final product, adding more detail and functionality.

- *Repeat the Cycle:* Repeat the testing, feedback, and refinement cycle multiple times. Each iteration helps in honing the concept, ensuring that it meets user needs and performs as expected.

5. Final Prototype:

- *High-Fidelity Model:* Create a high-fidelity prototype that closely resembles the final product in terms of design, functionality, and user experience. This prototype should be thoroughly tested and refined.
- *Validation:* Use the final prototype for comprehensive validation, ensuring that it meets all requirements and performs well in real-world scenarios.

Practical Applications of Prototyping

Prototyping is a versatile tool that can be applied in various contexts, from product development to service design. Here are some practical applications:

Product Development:

- *Hardware Products:* For hardware products, create physical prototypes to test functionality, ergonomics, and design. Use materials like plastic, metal, or wood, depending on the product requirements.
- *Software Products:* For software products, develop digital prototypes to test user interfaces, user experiences, and functionality. Tools like InVision, Axure, or Balsamiq can be used for this purpose.

Service Design:

- *Service Blueprints:* Create service blueprints to visualize and test service processes. This helps identify potential bottlenecks and improve service delivery.

- *Role-Playing:* Use role-playing techniques to simulate service interactions and gather feedback from participants. This can provide valuable insights into user experiences and service improvements.

Architectural Design:

- *Scale Models:* Build scale models of architectural designs to visualize the structure and layout. This helps in assessing the design's aesthetics and functionality.
- *Virtual Reality:* Use virtual reality (VR) to create immersive experiences of architectural designs. This allows clients and stakeholders to explore the design in a virtual environment and provide feedback.

Education and Training:

- *Educational Tools:* Develop prototypes of educational tools and resources to test their effectiveness and usability. This helps in refining the tools and ensuring they meet educational goals.
- *Training Programs:* Create prototypes of training programs and materials to gather feedback from participants. Use this feedback to improve the content and delivery methods.

Tips for Effective Prototyping

To maximize the benefits of prototyping, consider the following tips:

1. Start with Low-Fidelity Prototypes:

- *Keep It Simple:* Begin with low-fidelity prototypes that capture the basic idea. This allows for quick testing and iteration without significant investment.

- *Focus on Core Features:* Concentrate on the core features or components that need to be tested. Avoid getting bogged down in details initially.

2. *Involve Stakeholders Early:*

- *Collaborative Approach*: Involve stakeholders, team members, and potential users early in the prototyping process. Their input can provide valuable insights and help shape the development.
- *Open Feedback Channels:* Create open channels for feedback and encourage constructive criticism. This fosters a collaborative environment and enhances the quality of the prototype.

3. *Embrace Iteration:*

- *Iterative Mindset*: Embrace the iterative nature of prototyping. Be prepared to make multiple versions of the prototype, each improving on the previous one.
- *Learn from Failures:* View each iteration as a learning opportunity. Failures and setbacks are part of the process and can lead to valuable insights.

4. *Test in Real-World Conditions:*

- *Realistic Testing:* Test your prototypes in real-world conditions to gather accurate feedback. This helps identify practical issues and areas for improvement.
- *User Scenarios:* Create user scenarios and test the prototype in different contexts. This provides a comprehensive understanding of its performance and usability.

5. *Document the Process:*

- *Keep Records:* Document each iteration of the prototype, including the changes made and the feedback received. This creates a valuable record of the development process.

- *Visual Documentation:* Use photos, videos, and sketches to visually document the prototypes. This can be useful for presentations and future reference.

6. Stay Flexible:

- *Adapt and Adjust:* Stay flexible and open to changes. Be willing to pivot and adjust your approach based on feedback and new insights.
- *Avoid Perfectionism:* Avoid the trap of perfectionism. The goal is to create a functional and testable prototype, not a flawless final product.

Overcoming Common Challenges

Prototyping can come with challenges, but with the right approach, these can be effectively managed. Here's how to overcome some common obstacles:

1. Resource Constraints:

- *Use Affordable Materials:* Use affordable and readily available materials for low-fidelity prototypes. This reduces costs and allows for quick iterations.
- *Leverage Digital Tools*: For digital prototypes, use free or low-cost software tools. Many tools offer robust features at a fraction of the cost.

2. Time Limitations:

- *Prioritize Key Features:* Focus on the key features that need to be tested. This helps in making the most of limited time and ensures that critical aspects are addressed.
- *Set Clear Milestones:* Set clear milestones and deadlines for each

iteration. This helps in managing time effectively and keeping the project on track.

3. Feedback Fatigue:

- *Structured Feedback Sessions:* Schedule structured feedback sessions to gather input efficiently. This prevents feedback fatigue and ensures that all voices are heard.
- *Selective Testing*: Be selective about which iterations require extensive feedback. Not every version needs to undergo comprehensive testing.

4. Managing Expectations:

- *Communicate Clearly:* Clearly communicate the purpose and scope of the prototype to stakeholders. This helps manage expectations and ensures that everyone understands the iterative nature of the process.
- *Set Realistic Goals:* Set realistic goals for each iteration. Understand that not all issues can be addressed in a single version.

Prototyping is a vital part of the innovation process, translating abstract ideas into tangible models that can be tested and refined. By building physical or digital prototypes, you can visualize your concepts, gather valuable feedback, and iteratively improve your designs. This hands-on approach fosters creativity, encourages experimentation, and drives practical innovation.

Embrace prototyping as a regular practice in your creative process. Use it to explore new ideas, test functionality, and refine your concepts. With each iteration, you'll move closer to a final product that meets user needs and performs exceptionally well. Whether you're developing a new product, designing a service, or creating educational tools, prototyping can help you navigate the complexities of innovation and achieve your goals with confidence and creativity.

Feedback Loops:

Feedback loops are a crucial part of the innovation process, enabling continuous improvement and refinement of your ideas. By regularly seeking input from peers, mentors, and potential users, you can gather valuable insights that help shape and enhance your concepts. This iterative refinement ensures that your ideas evolve to meet the needs and expectations of your target audience, ultimately leading to more successful outcomes.

Seeking Input

The first step in creating effective feedback loops is to actively seek input from a diverse range of sources. This involves reaching out to peers, mentors, and potential users to gather their perspectives and insights.

Why Seek Feedback?

- *Diverse Perspectives:* Different people bring different perspectives, experiences, and expertise to the table. By seeking feedback from a variety of sources, you can gain a more comprehensive understanding of your idea's strengths and weaknesses.
- *Uncover Blind Spots:* It's easy to become blind to the flaws or limitations of your own ideas. Feedback from others can help uncover blind spots and areas that need improvement.
- *Validate Assumptions:* Seeking feedback allows you to validate your assumptions and ensure that your ideas are aligned with the needs and expectations of your target audience.

How to Seek Feedback:

Engage Peers:

- *Peer Reviews:* Organize peer review sessions where colleagues can evaluate your ideas and provide constructive feedback. This can be done through informal discussions, structured meetings, or dedicated feedback sessions.

- *Collaborative Workshops:* Hold collaborative workshops to brainstorm and refine ideas with your peers. This encourages active participation and collective problem-solving.

Consult Mentors:

- *Mentorship Sessions*: Schedule regular mentorship sessions to discuss your ideas and seek guidance from experienced mentors. Their expertise and insights can provide valuable direction and support.
- *Advisory Boards*: Form advisory boards comprising industry experts and thought leaders who can offer strategic advice and feedback on your concepts.

Engage Potential Users:

- *User Interviews:* Conduct interviews with potential users to understand their needs, preferences, and pain points. This direct interaction provides first-hand insights into how your idea will be received.
- *Focus Groups:* Organize focus groups to gather feedback from a representative sample of your target audience. This helps in identifying common themes and areas for improvement.
- *Surveys and Questionnaires*: Use surveys and questionnaires to collect feedback from a larger audience. This quantitative approach can complement qualitative insights from interviews and focus groups.

Create Feedback Channels:

- *Online Platforms:* Utilize online platforms and tools to create feedback channels. Platforms like Slack, Microsoft Teams, or dedicated feedback portals can facilitate continuous input from stakeholders.

- *Anonymous Feedback:* Provide options for anonymous feedback to encourage honest and candid responses. This can help uncover critical insights that might not be shared openly.

Iterative Refinement

Once you have gathered feedback, the next step is to use this input to iteratively refine and improve your concepts. This process involves analyzing the feedback, identifying areas for improvement, and making the necessary changes to enhance your ideas.

Steps in Iterative Refinement:

1. Analyze Feedback:

- *Categorize Input:* Organize the feedback into categories such as strengths, weaknesses, opportunities, and threats. This helps identify common themes and prioritize areas for improvement.
- *Identify Patterns:* Look for patterns and recurring comments in the feedback. These patterns can highlight critical issues that need to be addressed.

2. Prioritize Changes:

- *Critical Improvements:* Identify the most critical improvements that need to be made based on the feedback. Focus on changes that will have the most significant impact on the overall success of your idea.
- *Feasibility and Impact:* Consider the feasibility and impact of each suggested change. Prioritize changes that are both feasible to implement and likely to have a positive impact.

3. Implement Changes:

- *Action Plan:* Develop an action plan for implementing the prioritized changes. Define clear steps, assign responsibilities, and set timelines for each task.
- *Iterative Updates:* Make iterative updates to your idea based on the action plan. Implement changes incrementally and test their impact.

***4. Test and Validate*:**

- *User Testing:* Conduct user testing to validate the changes and gather additional feedback. This helps in ensuring that the changes meet user needs and improve the overall experience.
- *Continuous Monitoring:* Continuously monitor the performance and reception of your idea. Gather ongoing feedback to identify any new issues or areas for further improvement.

5. Reflect and Adjust:

- *Reflection Sessions:* Hold reflection sessions to review the feedback and changes made. Discuss what worked well, what didn't, and what can be improved in the next iteration.
- *Adjust Strategy*: Adjust your strategy based on the reflections and insights gained. This iterative approach ensures that your idea continues to evolve and improve over time.

Practical Applications of Feedback Loops

Feedback loops can be applied in various contexts to drive innovation and improvement. Here are some practical applications:

Product Development:

- *Prototype Testing:* Use feedback loops to test and refine product prototypes. Gather input from users, engineers, and designers to iteratively improve the product's design, functionality, and usability.

- *Feature Development:* Continuously gather feedback on product features and updates. Use this input to prioritize feature development and ensure that the product meets user needs.

Service Design:

- *Service Prototyping:* Develop and test service prototypes with potential users. Gather feedback on the service experience and make iterative improvements based on user input.
- *Customer Experience:* Use feedback loops to continuously improve the customer experience. Gather feedback from customers at different touchpoints and use this input to enhance service delivery.

Marketing and Branding:

- *Campaign Testing:* Test marketing campaigns with a small audience before launching them widely. Gather feedback on the campaign's message, visuals, and effectiveness, and refine the campaign based on this input.
- *Brand Perception*: Continuously gather feedback on brand perception from customers and stakeholders. Use this input to adjust branding strategies and ensure alignment with audience expectations.

Education and Training:

- *Curriculum Development:* Use feedback loops to develop and refine educational curricula. Gather input from students, educators, and industry professionals to ensure that the curriculum is relevant and effective.
- *Training Programs:* Continuously gather feedback on training

programs and materials. Use this input to improve the content, delivery methods, and overall effectiveness of the training.

Tips for Effective Feedback Loops

To maximize the benefits of feedback loops, consider the following tips:

1. Be Open to Feedback:

- *Receptive Attitude:* Approach feedback with an open and receptive attitude. Be willing to listen to different perspectives and consider all input, even if it's critical.
- *No Defensiveness:* Avoid being defensive when receiving feedback. View criticism as an opportunity for growth and improvement.

2. Encourage Constructive Feedback:

- *Specific and Actionable:* Encourage feedback that is specific and actionable. General comments can be less helpful than detailed, concrete suggestions.
- *Positive and Negative:* Encourage both positive and negative feedback. Positive feedback reinforces what's working well, while negative feedback highlights areas for improvement.

3. Foster a Feedback Culture:

- *Regular Feedback Sessions*: Schedule regular feedback sessions to gather input from stakeholders. This helps in maintaining a continuous feedback loop and keeps the process ongoing.
- *Safe Environment:* Create a safe and supportive environment where people feel comfortable sharing their thoughts and ideas. This fosters honest and candid feedback.

4. Act on Feedback:

- *Timely Response:* Act on feedback in a timely manner. Delaying action can lead to missed opportunities for improvement.
- *Visible Changes:* Make visible changes based on feedback. This shows stakeholders that their input is valued and encourages continued participation.

5. Document and Track Feedback:

- *Feedback Log:* Maintain a feedback log to document all input received. This helps in tracking feedback over time and ensures that no valuable insights are lost.
- *Action Tracker:* Use an action tracker to monitor the implementation of changes based on feedback. This helps in keeping the process organized and accountable.

Overcoming Common Challenges

While feedback loops are valuable, they can come with challenges. Here's how to overcome some common obstacles:

1. Feedback Overload:

- *Filter and Prioritize:* Filter and prioritize feedback to focus on the most critical and relevant input. Avoid trying to address all feedback at once.
- *Manage Expectations:* Manage stakeholder expectations by communicating which feedback will be addressed and why.

2. Resistance to Feedback:

- *Build Trust:* Build trust with stakeholders by showing that their feedback is valued and acted upon. This encourages more open and honest input.

- *Address Concerns:* Address any concerns or fears about providing feedback. Reassure stakeholders that their input is welcome and will not have negative consequences.

3. Inconsistent Feedback:

- *Clarify Objectives:* Clarify the objectives and focus of the feedback sessions. This helps in gathering consistent and relevant input.
- *Standardize Process:* Standardize the feedback process to ensure that all stakeholders are providing input on the same aspects.

4. Implementing Feedback:

- *Resource Allocation:* Allocate the necessary resources to implement changes based on feedback. This ensures that the feedback loop leads to tangible improvements.
- *Iterative Approach*: Use an iterative approach to implement feedback gradually. This allows for continuous improvement without overwhelming the team.

Feedback loops are a powerful tool for driving continuous improvement and innovation. By regularly seeking input from peers, mentors, and potential users, you can gather valuable insights that help shape and enhance your ideas. This iterative refinement process ensures that your concepts evolve to meet the needs and expectations of your target audience, ultimately leading to more successful outcomes.

Embrace feedback loops as a regular practice in your creative process. Use them to gather diverse perspectives, uncover blind spots, and validate assumptions. With each iteration, you'll move closer to a final product or solution that performs exceptionally well and meets the needs of your audience. Whether you're developing a new product

The Importance of Collaboration and Diverse Perspectives in the Ideation Process

Collaboration and diversity are essential elements of successful ideation. When people from different backgrounds, experiences, and disciplines come together, they bring a wealth of perspectives that can spark creativity and lead to innovative solutions. This section will delve into how working collaboratively and embracing diverse viewpoints can enhance the ideation process, uncover unique insights, and ultimately drive more effective and inclusive innovation. By fostering an environment where diverse ideas are valued and collaboration is encouraged, we can unlock the full potential of creative problem-solving and innovation.

Cross-Functional Teams:

Cross-functional teams are powerful drivers of innovation. By bringing together members from different departments and backgrounds, you create a melting pot of diverse skill sets and perspectives. This diversity can significantly enhance creativity and lead to more robust, well-rounded solutions. Let's explore how cross-functional teams can be formed, the benefits they bring, and how to maximize their potential for innovation.

Diverse Skillsets

The foundation of a cross-functional team is its diversity in skills and experiences. Each member brings unique expertise, which collectively enriches the team's ability to tackle complex problems.

Why Diverse Skillsets Matter:

- *Comprehensive Problem-Solving:* Different departments often have distinct ways of approaching problems. By combining these methods, the team can consider a wider range of solutions.

- *Broader Knowledge Base:* A diverse team has a broader knowledge base to draw value from. This can be particularly valuable in understanding different aspects of a problem or project.
- *Enhanced Flexibility:* Teams with diverse skill sets can be more flexible and adaptable. They can pivot more easily when faced with unexpected challenges or opportunities.

How to Form Cross-Functional Teams:

Identify Core Objectives:

- *Define Goals:* Clearly define the goals and objectives of the team. Understanding the end goal helps in selecting the right mix of skills and expertise.
- *Key Competencies:* Identify the key competencies needed to achieve these goals. This helps in ensuring that all necessary skills are represented within the team.

Select Team Members:

- *Departmental Representation:* Ensure that each relevant department is represented. For example, if the project involves product development, include members from R&D, marketing, sales, and customer service.
- *Diverse Experiences:* Look for team members with varied experiences and backgrounds. This diversity can bring fresh perspectives and innovative ideas.
- *Complementary Skills:* Aim for a mix of complementary skills. This balance ensures that the team can cover all aspects of the project effectively.

Facilitate Effective Integration:

- *Team Orientation:* Conduct an orientation session to help team members understand each other's roles and expertise. This fosters mutual respect and collaboration from the start.
- *Define Roles and Responsibilities:* Clearly define the roles and responsibilities of each team member. This clarity helps in avoiding overlap and ensures accountability.
- *Communication Channels:* Establish clear communication channels. Regular meetings, collaborative tools, and open forums for discussion can facilitate smooth communication.

Enhancing Creativity

The diversity in cross-functional teams not only broadens the skillset but also significantly enhances creativity. Different perspectives can lead to novel solutions and innovative breakthroughs.

Why Diversity Enhances Creativity:

- *Varied Perspectives:* Different backgrounds and experiences bring varied perspectives to the table. This variety can lead to more creative and out-of-the-box thinking.
- *Challenge Assumptions:* Diverse teams are more likely to challenge assumptions and question the status quo. This critical thinking is essential for innovation.
- *Combining Ideas:* Collaboration among diverse members can lead to the combination of different ideas, resulting in unique and innovative solutions.

Strategies to Enhance Creativity in Cross-Functional Teams:

Foster an Inclusive Environment:

- *Encourage Openness:* Create an environment where all team members feel comfortable sharing their ideas. Encourage openness and active participation.
- *Value Every Contribution:* Ensure that every contribution is valued. Recognize and appreciate the unique perspectives that each member brings.
- *Avoid Groupthink:* Actively work to avoid groupthink by encouraging dissenting opinions and alternative viewpoints. This helps in exploring a wider range of ideas.

Use Creative Techniques:

- *Brainstorming Sessions:* Organize regular brainstorming sessions to generate ideas. Use techniques like mind mapping, reverse thinking, and SCAMPER to stimulate creative thinking.
- *Idea Journals:* Encourage team members to maintain idea journals where they can jot down thoughts and inspirations. Share these ideas regularly to spark further creativity.
- *Design Thinking:* Implement design thinking principles that emphasize empathy, experimentation, and iterative improvement. This user-centered approach can lead to innovative solutions.

Promote Collaboration and Interaction:

- *Cross-Departmental Projects:* Initiate cross-departmental projects that require collaboration among different teams. This helps build relationships and foster a collaborative culture.
- *Team-Building Activities:* Organize team-building activities to

strengthen bonds and improve collaboration. Activities that require problem-solving can also stimulate creativity.

- *Shared Spaces:* Create shared workspaces where team members can interact informally. These interactions can lead to spontaneous idea generation and collaboration.

Practical Applications of Cross-Functional Teams

Cross-functional teams can be applied in various contexts to drive innovation and achieve organizational goals. Here are some practical applications:

Product Development:

- *Holistic Approach:* By including members from R&D, marketing, sales, and customer service, the team can take a holistic approach to product development. This ensures that all aspects, from design to customer feedback, are considered.
- *User-Centered Design*: Involve user experience (UX) designers and customer service representatives to ensure that the product meets user needs and provides a seamless experience.

Process Improvement:

- *Operational Efficiency:* Form cross-functional teams to identify and implement process improvements. Include members from different departments to ensure that all parts of the process are optimized.
- *Continuous Improvement:* Foster a culture of continuous improvement by regularly reviewing and refining processes based on feedback and performance data.

Strategic Initiatives:

- *Business Strategy:* Use cross-functional teams to develop and execute strategic initiatives. This ensures that all perspectives are considered, leading to more comprehensive and effective strategies.

- *Change Management:* Involve representatives from various departments in change management projects. Their insights can help anticipate and address potential challenges.

Customer Experience:

- *360-Degree View:* Create teams that focus on enhancing the customer experience. Include members from customer service, marketing, product development, and sales to get a 360-degree view of the customer journey.
- *Feedback Integration:* Use cross-functional teams to integrate customer feedback into product and service improvements. This helps in aligning offerings with customer expectations.

Tips for Effective Cross-Functional Teams

To maximize the benefits of cross-functional teams, consider the following tips:

1. Clear Goals and Objectives:

- *Define Success:* Clearly define what success looks like for the team. This provides direction and helps in aligning efforts towards common goals.
- *Measurable Objectives*: Set measurable objectives that can be tracked and evaluated. This helps in monitoring progress and ensuring accountability.

2. *Leadership and Facilitation:*

- *Strong Leadership:* Appoint a strong leader or facilitator who can guide the team and ensure that all voices are heard. The leader should foster collaboration and keep the team focused on its goals.
- *Facilitation Skills:* The facilitator should possess strong facilitation skills to manage discussions, resolve conflicts, and drive the team toward consensus.

3. *Effective Communication:*

- *Regular Updates:* Provide regular updates on the team's progress. This helps in maintaining transparency and keeping all stakeholders informed.
- *Open Dialogue:* Encourage open dialogue and active listening. Ensure that all team members have the opportunity to contribute and that their inputs are considered.

4. *Continuous Learning:*

- *Training and Development:* Provide opportunities for training and development. This helps team members enhance their skills and stay updated with the latest trends and techniques.
- *Learning from Experience:* Encourage the team to learn from both successes and failures. Reflect on experiences and use the insights gained to improve future performance.

5. *Recognition and Rewards:*

- *Celebrate Successes:* Celebrate the team's successes and achievements. This boosts morale and motivates the team to continue striving for excellence.
- *Recognize Contributions:* Recognize the contributions of individual

team members. This fosters a sense of belonging and encourages continued engagement.

Overcoming Common Challenges

While cross-functional teams offer numerous benefits, they can also face challenges. Here's how to overcome some common obstacles:

1. Conflicting Priorities:

- *Align Goals:* Ensure that the team's goals are aligned with organizational priorities. This helps in managing conflicting priorities and ensuring that the team's efforts are supported.
- *Negotiation and Compromise:* Encourage negotiation and compromise to resolve conflicts. Foster a collaborative mindset where team members work together to find mutually beneficial solutions.

2. Communication Barriers:

- *Clear Channels:* Establish clear communication channels to facilitate smooth interaction. Use collaborative tools and platforms to support communication.
- *Cultural Sensitivity*: Be aware of cultural differences and communication styles. Foster an inclusive environment where all team members feel comfortable expressing themselves.

3. Resistance to Change:

- *Stakeholder Engagement:* Engage stakeholders early in the process to gain their buy-in and support. Clearly communicate the benefits of cross-functional collaboration.
- *Change Champions:* Identify and empower change champions

within the team who can advocate for the initiative and help drive adoption.

4. Accountability and Responsibility:

- *Define Roles:* Clearly define roles and responsibilities to ensure accountability. This helps in avoiding overlap and ensuring that all tasks are covered.
- *Performance Metrics:* Use performance metrics to track progress and hold team members accountable. Regularly review and adjust responsibilities as needed.

Cross-functional teams are a powerful mechanism for driving innovation and achieving organizational goals. By bringing together diverse skillsets and perspectives, these teams can enhance creativity, solve complex problems, and develop well-rounded solutions. Embrace the concept of cross-functional collaboration to unlock the full potential of your team and drive meaningful change within your organization.

Form cross-functional teams with clear goals, strong leadership, and effective communication. Foster an inclusive environment where diverse ideas are valued, and collaboration is encouraged. By leveraging the unique strengths of each team member and embracing continuous learning, you can create a dynamic and innovative team capable of achieving extraordinary results.

Inclusive Environment:

Creating an inclusive environment is fundamental to fostering innovation and collaboration. An inclusive environment encourages participation from all team members, ensuring that everyone feels comfortable sharing their ideas. It values all inputs, fostering a culture of respect and openness. By embracing inclusivity, you can unlock the full potential of your team, drive creativity, and achieve remarkable results.

Encouraging Participation

Encouraging participation is about creating a space where everyone feels welcome to contribute their thoughts and ideas. It involves actively inviting input, making participation easy, and ensuring that all voices are heard.

Why Encouraging Participation Matters:

- *Diverse Perspectives:* Encouraging participation brings diverse perspectives to the table, enriching the ideation process with a variety of viewpoints.
- *Boosts Engagement*: When team members feel their contributions are valued, they are more engaged and committed to the project's success.
- *Fosters Innovation:* A participatory environment fosters innovation by allowing for the free flow of ideas and encouraging creative thinking.

Strategies to Encourage Participation:

1. Active Listening:

- *Be Present:* Practice active listening by being fully present during discussions. Show interest in what others are saying and avoid interrupting.
- *Acknowledge Contributions:* Acknowledge and appreciate contributions, even if they are not immediately applicable. This reinforces that all input is valued.

2. Open Dialogue:

- *Facilitate Conversations:* Create opportunities for open dialogue. Encourage team members to share their thoughts and ideas freely.
- *Ask Open-Ended Questions:* Use open-ended questions to stimulate

discussion and explore ideas in depth. Questions like "What do you think?" or "How might we approach this?" invite participation.

3. Create Safe Spaces:

- *Psychological Safety:* Foster psychological safety by ensuring that team members feel safe to express their ideas without fear of judgment or ridicule.
- *Supportive Environment:* Create a supportive environment where mistakes are seen as learning opportunities. Encourage risk-taking and experimentation.

4. Leverage Technology:

- *Collaboration Tools:* Use collaboration tools to facilitate participation, especially in remote or hybrid work settings. Tools like Slack, Microsoft Teams, and Zoom can support real-time collaboration.
- *Anonymous Feedback:* Provide options for anonymous feedback to encourage honest input. This can help gather candid insights that might not be shared openly.

5. Inclusive Meetings:

- *Agenda and Structure:* Set clear agendas for meetings and ensure that there is time allocated for everyone to contribute.
- *Round-Robin Technique:* Use techniques like the round-robin to ensure that each team member has the opportunity to speak.

6. Encourage Diverse Contributions:

- *Value Different Perspectives:* Encourage contributions from team members with diverse backgrounds and experiences. Recognize that diversity enhances creativity and problem-solving.

- *Rotating Roles:* Rotate roles within the team to provide different members the opportunity to lead discussions and share their perspectives.

Valuing All Inputs

Valuing all inputs is about fostering a culture where every contribution is respected and considered. It ensures that all team members feel that their ideas matter, which is crucial for maintaining motivation and engagement.

Why Valuing All Inputs Matters:

- *Builds Trust:* When team members see that their inputs are valued, it builds trust and strengthens team cohesion.
- *Encourages Creativity:* A culture that values all inputs encourages creativity by allowing for the exploration of diverse ideas.
- *Enhances Collaboration:* Valuing contributions from all team members enhances collaboration and creates a sense of ownership and shared purpose.

Strategies to Value All Inputs:

1. Create a Culture of Respect:

- *Respectful Communication:* Foster respectful communication by encouraging team members to listen actively and respond thoughtfully to each other's ideas.
- *Positive Reinforcement*: Use positive reinforcement to acknowledge and appreciate contributions. Recognize the effort and thought behind each idea.

2. Provide Constructive Feedback:

- *Balanced Feedback*: Provide balanced feedback that highlights both the strengths and areas for improvement. This helps in refining ideas without discouraging the contributor.

- *Specific and Actionable*: Ensure that feedback is specific and actionable. General comments are less helpful than detailed suggestions for improvement.

3. Encourage Collaboration:

- *Collaborative Brainstorming*: Encourage collaborative brainstorming sessions where ideas are built upon collectively. This reinforces the value of each contribution.

- *Co-Creation:* Involve team members in the co-creation process. This ensures that their inputs are integrated into the final solution, enhancing ownership and commitment.

4. Document and Share Contributions:

- *Idea Logs*: Maintain an idea log to document all contributions. This ensures that no idea is lost and provides a reference for future discussions.

- *Shared Platforms*: Use shared platforms to document and share contributions. Tools like Trello, Asana, or Google Docs can help in organizing and tracking inputs.

5. Recognize and Celebrate Contributions:

- *Public Recognition*: Recognize and celebrate contributions publicly. This can be done during team meetings, through company newsletters, or on collaboration platforms.

- *Incentives and Rewards*: Provide incentives and rewards for valuable contributions. This could be in the form of bonuses, awards, or additional responsibilities.

Practical Applications of an Inclusive Environment

Creating an inclusive environment can be applied in various contexts to drive innovation and enhance team performance. Here are some practical applications:

Project Teams:

- *Inclusive Planning:* Involve all team members in the planning phase of projects. This ensures that diverse perspectives are considered from the outset.
- *Regular Check-Ins:* Conduct regular check-ins to gather feedback and ensure that all team members are aligned and engaged.

Product Development:

- *User-Centered Design:* Incorporate inputs from diverse user groups in the product development process. This ensures that the product meets the needs of a broad audience.
- *Cross-Functional Collaboration:* Foster cross-functional collaboration to integrate diverse skills and expertise into the product development cycle.

Organizational Culture:

- *Diversity and Inclusion Programs:* Implement diversity and inclusion programs to promote an inclusive culture across the organization. This can include training, workshops, and initiatives that celebrate diversity.
- *Inclusive Policies:* Develop and enforce policies that promote inclusivity and prevent discrimination. This creates a safe and supportive work environment for all employees.

Leadership Development:

- *Inclusive Leadership Training:* Provide training for leaders on inclusive leadership practices. This equips them with the skills to foster an inclusive environment within their teams.
- *Mentorship Programs:* Establish mentorship programs that connect employees from diverse backgrounds with experienced mentors. This supports their professional growth and inclusion.

Tips for Creating an Inclusive Environment

To create and maintain an inclusive environment, consider the following tips:

1. Lead by Example:

- *Inclusive Leadership:* Leaders should model inclusive behaviors and set the tone for the rest of the team. This includes actively seeking input, valuing contributions, and fostering a culture of respect.
- *Visible Commitment:* Demonstrate a visible commitment to inclusivity through actions and decisions. This reinforces the importance of inclusivity within the organization.

2. Foster Open Communication:

- *Transparent Communication:* Maintain transparent communication to build trust and ensure that all team members are informed and engaged.
- *Feedback Loops:* Establish feedback loops to continuously gather input and improve processes. This helps address concerns and make necessary adjustments.

3. Invest in Training and Development:

- *Inclusivity Training:* Provide training on inclusivity and unconscious bias to raise awareness and promote inclusive behaviors.
- *Skill Development:* Invest in skill development programs that enhance the capabilities of all team members. This ensures that everyone has the opportunity to contribute effectively.

4. Promote Collaboration:

- *Team-Building Activities:* Organize team-building activities that promote collaboration and strengthen relationships among team members.
- *Cross-Functional Projects:* Encourage cross-functional projects that require collaboration among diverse teams. This fosters an inclusive and collaborative culture.

5. Measure and Improve:

- *Track Progress:* Track progress on inclusivity initiatives through surveys, feedback, and performance metrics. This helps in identifying areas for improvement.
- *Continuous Improvement:* Continuously improve inclusivity practices based on feedback and data. This ensures that the environment remains inclusive and supportive.

Overcoming Common Challenges

Creating an inclusive environment can come with challenges, but they can be effectively managed. Here's how to overcome some common obstacles:

1. Resistance to Change:

- *Engage Stakeholders:* Engage stakeholders early in the process to gain their buy-in and support. Clearly communicate the benefits of an inclusive environment.

- *Change Champions:* Identify and empower change champions who can advocate for inclusivity and drive adoption.

2. Unconscious Bias:

- *Awareness Training:* Provide training on unconscious bias to raise awareness and mitigate its impact. Encourage self-reflection and open dialogue on biases.
- *Bias Mitigation Strategies:* Implement bias mitigation strategies in recruitment, performance evaluations, and decision-making processes.

3. Ensuring Fair Participation:

- *Equal Opportunities:* Ensure that all team members have equal opportunities to participate and contribute. Address any barriers that may prevent fair participation.
- *Inclusive Practices:* Implement inclusive practices such as rotating meeting facilitators, using inclusive language, and actively seeking input from quieter team members.

Creating an inclusive environment is fundamental to fostering innovation, collaboration, and overall team success. By encouraging participation and valuing all inputs, you can unlock the full potential of your team, drive creativity, and achieve remarkable results. Embrace inclusivity as a core value and integrate it into your daily practices, policies, and culture.

Lead by example, foster open communication, and invest in training and development. Promote collaboration, measure progress, and continuously improve your inclusivity practices. Overcome challenges by engaging stakeholders, addressing unconscious bias, and ensuring fair participation.

An inclusive environment not only enhances team performance but also creates a supportive and fulfilling workplace where everyone feels valued and empowered. By cultivating inclusivity, you can drive meaningful change, foster innovation, and achieve extraordinary outcomes.

Collaborative Tools:

In today's digital age, collaborative tools have become indispensable for fostering innovation and enhancing teamwork. Utilizing digital platforms like shared documents, online whiteboards, and project management software can facilitate idea sharing and development. These tools enable real-time collaboration, making it easier for teams to work together regardless of their location. Let's dive into the various collaborative tools available, their benefits, and how to effectively integrate them into your workflow.

Digital Platforms

Digital platforms are essential for modern collaboration. They provide a space where teams can share documents, brainstorm ideas, manage projects, and communicate seamlessly. Here's how different types of digital platforms can be utilized to enhance collaboration:

Shared Documents:

- *Google Docs:* Google Docs allows multiple users to work on a document simultaneously. Team members can add comments, suggest edits, and see changes in real time. This tool is particularly useful for collaborative writing, creating reports, and developing presentations.
- *Microsoft Office 365:* With tools like Word, Excel, and PowerPoint available online, Microsoft Office 365 enables real-time collaboration. Multiple users can work on the same document, making it easy to gather input and refine content collaboratively.

Online Whiteboards:

- *Miro:* Miro is an online whiteboard platform that provides a space for brainstorming, planning, and visual collaboration. Teams can create mind maps, flowcharts, and diagrams together, making it ideal for ideation sessions and strategic planning.
- *Jamboard:* Google's Jamboard is another excellent tool for online whiteboarding. It integrates seamlessly with other Google Workspace tools, allowing teams to brainstorm and collaborate visually in real time.

Project Management Software:

- *Trello:* Trello is a popular project management tool that uses boards, lists, and cards to help teams organize tasks and projects. It's highly visual and intuitive, making it easy to track progress and collaborate on tasks.
- *Asana:* Asana offers a robust platform for project management, allowing teams to assign tasks, set deadlines, and monitor progress. It provides various views, such as lists, boards, and calendars, to accommodate different project management styles.
- *Monday.com:* Monday.com is a flexible work operating system that allows teams to customize workflows, track projects, and collaborate efficiently. It's highly adaptable and integrates with numerous other tools, enhancing its functionality.

Real-Time Collaboration

One of the most significant advantages of digital collaborative tools is the ability to facilitate real-time collaboration. This capability allows teams to work together seamlessly, regardless of their physical location. Real-time collaboration breaks down geographical barriers and enables instant communication and feedback.

Benefits of Real-Time Collaboration:

- *Immediate Feedback:* Real-time collaboration allows for immediate feedback, which accelerates the decision-making process and helps teams quickly address issues and refine ideas.
- *Enhanced Productivity:* Teams can work together simultaneously, reducing delays caused by waiting for input or approvals. This streamlined workflow enhances overall productivity.
- *Increased Engagement:* Real-time collaboration fosters a sense of engagement and inclusivity, as all team members can actively participate in discussions and contribute their ideas.
- *Seamless Communication:* Tools that enable real-time collaboration often include chat and video conferencing features, ensuring that communication remains seamless and efficient.

Implementing Real-Time Collaboration:

1. Communication Platforms:

- *Slack:* Slack is a widely used communication platform that supports real-time messaging, file sharing, and integrations with other tools. Teams can create channels for different projects or topics, making it easy to stay organized and communicate effectively.
- *Microsoft Teams:* Microsoft Teams offers chat, video conferencing, and integration with Microsoft Office 365 tools. It's an excellent platform for real-time collaboration, allowing teams to work together on documents and projects while maintaining clear communication.

2. Video Conferencing:

- *Zoom:* Zoom provides robust video conferencing capabilities, enabling virtual meetings, webinars, and collaborative sessions. Features like screen sharing and breakout rooms facilitate interactive and productive discussions.
- *Google Meet:* Integrated with Google Workspace, Google Meet offers video conferencing with real-time collaboration features. Teams can share screens, collaborate on documents, and communicate effectively during meetings.

3. Collaborative Design Tools:

- *Figma:* Figma is a powerful design tool that allows teams to collaborate on design projects in real time. Designers can work together on interfaces, prototypes, and other visual elements, ensuring a cohesive and efficient design process.
- *Adobe XD:* Adobe XD supports real-time collaboration, enabling designers to create and share prototypes, gather feedback, and make adjustments collaboratively.

4. Development Platforms:

- *GitHub*: GitHub is a platform for version control and collaboration, particularly useful for software development projects. Teams can work on code simultaneously, review changes, and manage projects through issues and pull requests.
- *Bitbucket:* Similar to GitHub, Bitbucket provides tools for version control and collaboration. It integrates with other Atlassian products like Jira, enhancing its project management capabilities.

Integrating Collaborative Tools into Your Workflow

To maximize the benefits of collaborative tools, it's essential to integrate them effectively into your workflow. Here are some strategies to ensure a smooth and productive integration:

1. Assess Your Needs:

- *Identify Requirements:* Determine the specific needs of your team and projects. Consider factors such as the type of work, team size, and communication preferences.
- *Evaluate Tools:* Evaluate different tools based on your requirements. Look for features that align with your workflow and enhance collaboration.

2. Onboard Your Team:

- *Training and Orientation:* Provide training sessions and orientation to familiarize your team with the chosen tools. Ensure that everyone understands how to use the tools effectively.
- *Create Guidelines:* Develop guidelines for using the tools, including best practices for communication, file sharing, and project management. This helps maintain consistency and efficiency.

3. Foster a Collaborative Culture:

- *Encourage Participation:* Encourage all team members to actively participate in using the collaborative tools. Foster an inclusive culture where everyone feels comfortable sharing their ideas and feedback.
- *Promote Transparency:* Use the tools to promote transparency in your projects. Share updates, progress, and decisions openly to keep everyone informed and engaged.

4. Monitor and Adjust:

- *Regular Check-Ins:* Conduct regular check-ins to gather feedback on the use of the tools. Identify any challenges or areas for improvement.
- *Adjust as Needed:* Be flexible and willing to adjust your approach based on feedback. Continuously refine your use of the tools to enhance collaboration and productivity.

Practical Applications of Collaborative Tools

Collaborative tools can be applied in various contexts to drive innovation and enhance teamwork. Here are some practical applications:

Remote Work:

- *Virtual Collaboration:* Use collaborative tools to facilitate virtual collaboration among remote teams. Platforms like Slack, Zoom, and Trello can help maintain clear communication and coordinated efforts.
- *Document Sharing:* Shared documents and online whiteboards enable remote teams to work on projects simultaneously, ensuring that everyone stays aligned and productive.

Project Management:

- *Task Management:* Use project management software to assign tasks, set deadlines, and track progress. Tools like Asana and Monday.com help teams stay organized and focused.
- *Resource Allocation:* Collaborative tools can help manage resources effectively by providing visibility into team members' workloads and availability.

Creative Projects:

- *Design Collaboration:* Utilize collaborative design tools like Figma and Adobe XD to work on creative projects. These tools enable real-time feedback and iteration, ensuring a cohesive final product.
- *Brainstorming Sessions:* Online whiteboards and mind-mapping tools facilitate virtual brainstorming sessions, allowing teams to generate and refine ideas collaboratively.

Sales and Marketing:

- *Campaign Planning:* Use project management and collaboration tools to plan and execute marketing campaigns. Teams can track progress, share assets, and gather feedback in real time.
- *Customer Relationship Management:* Collaborative CRM platforms like Salesforce enable sales teams to manage customer interactions, share insights, and coordinate efforts.

Education and Training:

- *Virtual Classrooms:* Tools like Google Classroom and Microsoft Teams support virtual classrooms, enabling real-time collaboration between teachers and students.
- *Training Programs:* Collaborative platforms can enhance training programs by providing interactive learning experiences, shared resources, and continuous feedback.

Tips for Effective Use of Collaborative Tools

To maximize the benefits of collaborative tools, consider the following tips:

1. Choose the Right Tools:

- *Feature Fit:* Select tools that fit the specific needs of your team and projects. Ensure that the features align with your workflow and enhance collaboration.

- *User-Friendly:* Choose tools that are user-friendly and intuitive. This reduces the learning curve and encourages adoption.

2. Encourage Consistent Use:

- *Standardize Tools:* Standardize the use of collaborative tools across your team or organization. This ensures consistency and makes it easier to manage projects and communication.
- *Regular Use:* Encourage regular use of the tools to maintain engagement and familiarity. Make the tools an integral part of your daily workflow.

3. Provide Training and Support:

- *Ongoing Training:* Offer ongoing training and support to help team members get the most out of the tools. Provide resources like tutorials, guides, and Q&A sessions.
- *Help Desk:* Set up a help desk or support channel to address any questions or issues that arise. This ensures that team members can quickly get assistance when needed.

4. Monitor Usage and Effectiveness:

- *Usage Metrics:* Monitor usage metrics to understand how the tools are being used and identify any gaps or areas for improvement.
- *Feedback Loop:* Establish a feedback loop to gather input from team members on the effectiveness of the tools. Use this feedback to make necessary adjustments and improvements.

5. Foster a Collaborative Mindset:

- *Encourage Collaboration:* Promote a collaborative mindset by encouraging teamwork, open communication, and mutual support.

- *Recognize Contributions:* Recognize and celebrate contributions from team members. This fosters a positive and collaborative culture.

Collaborative tools are essential for modern innovation and teamwork. By utilizing digital platforms like shared documents, online whiteboards, and project management software, teams can enhance their ability to share ideas, develop projects, and work together seamlessly. Real-time collaboration further breaks down geographical barriers, allowing teams to engage and innovate regardless of location.

To integrate collaborative tools effectively, assess your team's needs, onboard your team, foster a collaborative culture, and continuously monitor and adjust your approach. Practical applications of these tools span various contexts, from remote work and project management to creative projects and education.

By choosing the right tools, encouraging consistent use, providing training and support, monitoring usage, and fostering a collaborative mindset, you can maximize the benefits of collaborative tools and drive innovation and success within your team or organization. Embrace the power of collaboration and leverage these tools to unlock the full potential of your collective creativity and expertise.

Peer Review:

Peer review is a powerful tool in the innovation process, providing a structured way for team members to offer constructive criticism and valuable feedback on each other's ideas. By implementing a peer review process, you create a culture of continuous improvement and collaboration, ensuring that ideas are constantly refined and enhanced. Let's explore how to establish an effective peer review process, the benefits it brings, and strategies to maximize its impact.

Constructive Criticism

Constructive criticism is the cornerstone of a successful peer review process. It involves offering specific, actionable feedback that helps improve the idea or project without discouraging the contributor. Constructive criticism should be framed positively, focusing on areas for improvement while recognizing the strengths of the idea.

Why Constructive Criticism Matters:

- *Enhances Ideas:* Constructive criticism helps in identifying areas for improvement and refining ideas, leading to more robust and well-developed solutions.
- *Fosters Growth:* Providing and receiving constructive criticism fosters personal and professional growth. It encourages continuous learning and development.
- *Builds Trust:* A culture of constructive criticism builds trust among team members. When feedback is given respectfully and positively, it strengthens relationships and collaboration.

Strategies for Providing Constructive Criticism:

1. Be Specific:

- *Clear Feedback:* Provide clear and specific feedback that addresses particular aspects of the idea. Avoid vague comments that can be interpreted in multiple ways.
- *Examples:* Use examples to illustrate your points. This helps the recipient understand the feedback and how to apply it.

2. Focus on Improvement:

- *Positive Framing:* Frame your feedback positively by highlighting areas for improvement rather than just pointing out flaws.

- *Actionable Suggestions:* Offer actionable suggestions that the recipient can implement to improve their idea. This makes the feedback more practical and useful.

3. Balance Praise and Critique:

- *Highlight Strengths:* Start by highlighting the strengths of the idea. This creates a positive tone and acknowledges the contributor's efforts.
- *Address Weaknesses:* Follow with constructive criticism that addresses the weaknesses. Ensure that the critique is balanced and fair.

4. Be Respectful and Supportive:

- *Respectful Language:* Use respectful and supportive language when providing feedback. Avoid harsh or critical tones that can discourage the recipient.
- *Encouragement:* Encourage the recipient by expressing confidence in their ability to improve and refine the idea.

5. Foster Open Communication:

- *Two-Way Dialogue:* Foster a two-way dialogue where the recipient can ask questions and seek clarification on the feedback.
- *Active Listening:* Practice active listening when the recipient responds. Show that you value their perspective and are willing to engage in constructive discussions.

Continuous Improvement

The peer review process is not a one-time event but a continuous feedback loop that promotes ongoing improvement. By regularly reviewing and refining ideas, teams can ensure that their concepts evolve and improve over time. Continuous improvement is about embracing an iterative approach, where each round of feedback leads to incremental enhancements.

Why Continuous Improvement Matters:

- *Iterative Refinement:* Continuous improvement ensures that ideas are constantly refined and enhanced. Each iteration brings the idea closer to its optimal form.
- *Adaptability:* A culture of continuous improvement fosters adaptability. Teams can quickly respond to feedback and make necessary adjustments.
- *Sustained Innovation:* Continuous improvement sustains innovation by encouraging ongoing experimentation and learning. It keeps the innovation process dynamic and forward-looking.

Steps to Implement Continuous Improvement:

1. Establish a Feedback Loop:

- *Regular Reviews:* Schedule regular peer review sessions to gather feedback and make improvements. This keeps the process ongoing and consistent.
- *Feedback Channels:* Create clear channels for providing and receiving feedback. Use tools like shared documents, project management software, and communication platforms to facilitate this.

2. Track Progress:

- *Documentation:* Document all feedback and the changes made based on it. This creates a record of the improvement process and ensures that no valuable insights are lost.
- *Metrics:* Use metrics to track progress and measure the impact of the improvements. This helps in evaluating the effectiveness of the peer review process.

3. Implement Changes:

- *Action Plans:* Develop action plans to implement the feedback. Assign responsibilities and set deadlines to ensure that the changes are made promptly.
- *Iterative Updates:* Make iterative updates to the idea based on the feedback. Implement changes incrementally and test their impact.

4. Reflect and Adjust:

- *Reflection Sessions:* Hold reflection sessions to review the feedback and changes made. Discuss what worked well, what didn't, and what can be improved in the next iteration.
- *Adjust Strategy:* Adjust your strategy based on the reflections and insights gained. This iterative approach ensures that the idea continues to evolve and improve over time.

Practical Applications of Peer Review

Peer review can be applied in various contexts to drive innovation and enhance team performance. Here are some practical applications:

Product Development:

- *Prototype Testing:* Use peer review to test and refine product prototypes. Gather input from colleagues to identify areas for improvement and enhance the product's design and functionality.
- *Feature Development:* Continuously gather feedback on product features and updates. Use this input to prioritize feature development and ensure that the product meets user needs.

Service Design:

- *Service Blueprints:* Develop and test service blueprints with input from team members. Use peer review to refine service processes and improve service delivery.

- *Customer Experience:* Use peer review to continuously improve the customer experience. Gather feedback from team members on different aspects of the service and make necessary adjustments.

Marketing and Branding:

- *Campaign Testing:* Test marketing campaigns with input from peers before launching them widely. Gather feedback on the campaign's message, visuals, and effectiveness, and refine the campaign based on this input.
- *Brand Perception:* Continuously gather feedback on brand perception from team members. Use this input to adjust branding strategies and ensure alignment with audience expectations.

Education and Training:

- *Curriculum Development:* Use peer review to develop and refine educational curricula. Gather input from colleagues to ensure that the curriculum is relevant and effective.
- *Training Programs:* Continuously gather feedback on training programs and materials. Use this input to improve the content, delivery methods, and overall effectiveness of the training.

Tips for Effective Peer Review

To maximize the benefits of peer review, consider the following tips:

1. Create a Positive Culture:

- *Encourage Positivity:* Foster a positive culture where feedback is seen as an opportunity for growth and improvement.

- *Celebrate Contributions:* Recognize and celebrate the contributions of team members. This creates a supportive environment where everyone feels valued.

2. *Provide Training:*

- *Feedback Training:* Provide training on how to give and receive constructive feedback. This helps team members develop the skills needed for effective peer review.
- *Continuous Learning:* Encourage continuous learning and development. Provide resources and opportunities for team members to enhance their skills.

3. *Foster Open Communication:*

- *Transparent Communication:* Maintain transparent communication to build trust and ensure that all team members are informed and engaged.
- *Feedback Loops:* Establish feedback loops to continuously gather input and improve processes. This helps address concerns and make necessary adjustments.

4. *Monitor and Adjust:*

- *Track Feedback:* Track feedback and the changes made based on it. This helps in evaluating the effectiveness of the peer review process.
- *Adjust as Needed:* Be flexible and willing to adjust your approach based on feedback. Continuously refine your peer review process to enhance its effectiveness.

5. *Encourage Collaboration:*

- *Collaborative Approach:* Encourage a collaborative approach to peer review. Foster a culture where team members work together to improve ideas and achieve common goals.

- *Shared Responsibility:* Make peer review a shared responsibility. Ensure that all team members are actively involved in providing and receiving feedback.

Overcoming Common Challenges

While peer review offers numerous benefits, it can also face challenges. Here's how to overcome some common obstacles:

1. Resistance to Feedback:

- *Build Trust:* Build trust with team members by showing that their feedback is valued and acted upon. This encourages more open and honest input.
- *Address Concerns:* Address any concerns or fears about providing feedback. Reassure team members that their input is welcome and will not have negative consequences.

2. Inconsistent Feedback:

- *Clarify Objectives:* Clarify the objectives and focus of the peer review sessions. This helps in gathering consistent and relevant input.
- *Standardize Process:* Standardize the peer review process to ensure that all team members are providing input on the same aspects.

3. Implementing Feedback:

- *Resource Allocation:* Allocate the necessary resources to implement changes based on feedback. This ensures that the peer review process leads to tangible improvements.
- *Iterative Approach:* Use an iterative approach to implement feedback gradually. This allows for continuous improvement without overwhelming the team.

Peer review is a powerful mechanism for driving continuous improvement and innovation. By implementing a structured peer review process, teams can provide constructive criticism, gather valuable feedback, and iteratively refine their ideas. This continuous feedback loop ensures that concepts evolve to meet the needs and expectations of the target audience, ultimately leading to more successful outcomes.

To maximize the benefits of peer review, create a positive culture, provide training, foster open communication, and monitor and adjust your approach. Encourage collaboration and make peer review a shared responsibility. By overcoming common challenges and embracing the power of peer review, you can drive innovation, enhance team performance, and achieve extraordinary results.

Workshops and Retreats:

Workshops and retreats are powerful tools for fostering ideation and brainstorming. These focused sessions provide the perfect environment for deep dives into specific problems or opportunities, enabling intensive collaboration and creative thinking. By taking teams out of their usual work environment and immersing them in a dedicated space for innovation, you can unlock new ideas and drive meaningful progress. Let's explore the benefits of workshops and retreats, how to organize them effectively, and strategies to maximize their impact.

Focused Sessions

Workshops and retreats offer a unique opportunity for focused sessions, where team members can concentrate on specific challenges or opportunities without the usual distractions of the workplace. These sessions are designed to foster creativity and collaboration, providing a structured yet flexible environment for idea generation.

Why Focused Sessions Matter:

- *Dedicated Time:* Focused sessions provide dedicated time for brainstorming and problem-solving, allowing team members to fully engage with the task at hand.
- *Eliminate Distractions:* By removing the usual workplace distractions, team members can concentrate more effectively and think more creatively.
- *Structured Approach:* Workshops and retreats offer a structured approach to ideation, with clear goals, agendas, and facilitation, ensuring that the time is used productively.

Strategies for Organizing Focused Sessions:

1. Set Clear Objectives:

- *Define Goals:* Clearly define the goals and objectives of the workshop or retreat. Understanding the desired outcomes helps in planning the session and keeping it focused.
- *Specific Challenges:* Identify specific challenges or opportunities that the session will address. This helps in ensuring that the discussion remains targeted and relevant.

2. Plan the Agenda:

- *Detailed Agenda:* Create a detailed agenda that outlines the structure and flow of the session. Include time for introductions, brainstorming, group discussions, and wrap-up.
- *Flexible Segments:* Plan flexible segments within the agenda to allow for spontaneous discussions and idea exploration. This flexibility can lead to unexpected insights and breakthroughs.

3. Facilitate Participation:

- *Inclusive Environment:* Foster an inclusive environment where all team members feel comfortable sharing their ideas. Encourage active participation and respect diverse viewpoints.
- *Interactive Activities:* Include interactive activities such as group exercises, role-playing, and games to stimulate creativity and engagement.

4. Provide Resources:

- *Materials and Tools:* Provide necessary materials and tools such as whiteboards, sticky notes, markers, and digital devices. These resources facilitate brainstorming and idea visualization.
- *Support Staff:* Consider having support staff to assist with logistics, note-taking, and other administrative tasks. This allows participants to focus entirely on the session.

5. Choose the Right Location:

- *Inspiring Venue*: Select a location that inspires creativity and collaboration. This could be an offsite venue, a retreat center, or even a unique workspace designed for innovation.
- *Comfort and Convenience:* Ensure that the venue is comfortable and convenient, with amenities such as catering, Wi-Fi, and breakout areas.

Deep Dives

Workshops and retreats are ideal for deep dives into specific problems or opportunities. These intensive sessions allow teams to explore issues in depth, understand the root causes, and develop innovative solutions.

Why Deep Dives Matter:

- *Thorough Exploration:* Deep dives allow for a thorough exploration of complex problems or opportunities, ensuring that all aspects are considered.
- *Focused Collaboration*: Intensive collaboration during deep dives brings together diverse perspectives and expertise, leading to well-rounded solutions.
- *Creative Problem-Solving:* Deep dives foster creative problem-solving by encouraging team members to think critically and explore different angles.

Strategies for Conducting Deep Dives:

1. Identify Key Issues:

- *Root Cause Analysis:* Use techniques such as root cause analysis to identify the key issues or opportunities that need to be addressed. This helps in focusing the deep dive on the most critical areas.
- *Stakeholder Input:* Gather input from stakeholders to understand their perspectives and priorities. This ensures that the deep dive is aligned with the needs and expectations of all relevant parties.

2. Use Structured Methods:

- *NEWT Analysis:* Conduct a NEWT analysis as discussed earlier to evaluate the nurturing strengths, eliminating weak areas, winning opportunities, and identifying threats related to the issue. This structured approach helps in organizing thoughts and insights.
- *Design Thinking:* Apply design thinking principles to understand user needs, define problems, ideate solutions, prototype, and test. This user-centered approach ensures that the solutions are practical and effective.

3. Facilitate Group Discussions:

- *Breakout Groups:* Divide participants into breakout groups to explore different aspects of the issue. This encourages detailed discussions and allows for diverse viewpoints to be considered.
- *Roundtable Discussions:* Conduct roundtable discussions where each participant can share their insights and ideas. This collaborative approach fosters a sense of shared ownership and commitment.

4. Visualize Ideas:

- *Mind Mapping:* Use mind mapping to visualize ideas and their connections. This helps in seeing the bigger picture and identifying new angles.
- *Prototyping:* Develop prototypes of proposed solutions to test their feasibility and gather feedback. This iterative process helps refine ideas and make them more practical.

5. Capture and Document Insights:

- *Detailed Notes:* Take detailed notes during the deep dive to capture all insights and ideas. This ensures that no valuable information is lost.
- *Visual Records:* Use visual records such as diagrams, charts, and sketches to document the discussions. These visual aids help in communicating the ideas effectively.

Practical Applications of Workshops and Retreats

Workshops and retreats can be applied in various contexts to drive innovation and enhance team performance. Here are some practical applications:

Strategic Planning:

- *Visioning Workshops:* Use workshops to develop a shared vision and strategic plan for the organization. Engage team members in identifying key goals, strategies, and action plans.
- *Scenario Planning:* Conduct scenario planning sessions to explore different future scenarios and develop strategies to address potential challenges and opportunities.

Product Innovation:

- *Ideation Retreats:* Organize ideation retreats to brainstorm new product ideas and features. Encourage cross-functional collaboration to bring diverse perspectives to the table.
- *Prototyping Workshops:* Use prototyping workshops to develop and test new product concepts. Gather feedback from team members and refine the prototypes based on their input.

Process Improvement:

- *Lean Workshops:* Conduct lean workshops to identify and eliminate waste in processes. Use techniques such as value stream mapping to visualize and optimize workflows.
- *Continuous Improvement Retreats:* Organize retreats focused on continuous improvement. Engage team members in identifying areas for improvement and developing action plans.

Team Building:

- *Collaborative Exercises:* Use workshops and retreats for team-building exercises. Activities such as trust-building exercises, problem-solving challenges, and outdoor adventures strengthen team bonds and enhance collaboration.

- *Conflict Resolution:* Conduct workshops focused on conflict resolution and communication. Provide a safe space for team members to address and resolve conflicts constructively.

Tips for Effective Workshops and Retreats

To maximize the benefits of workshops and retreats, consider the following tips:

1. Prepare Thoroughly:

- *Detailed Planning:* Plan the workshop or retreat in detail, including the agenda, activities, materials, and logistics.
- *Pre-Session Preparation:* Provide participants with pre-session materials and instructions to help them prepare for the session. This ensures that everyone is aligned and ready to contribute.

2. Facilitate Effectively:

- *Experienced Facilitator*: Use an experienced facilitator to guide the session. The facilitator should be skilled in managing discussions, encouraging participation, and keeping the session on track.
- *Engagement Techniques:* Use engagement techniques such as icebreakers, energizers, and interactive activities to keep participants engaged and motivated.

3. Encourage Collaboration:

- *Collaborative Activities:* Include collaborative activities that require participants to work together and share ideas. This fosters a sense of teamwork and collective ownership.
- *Open Dialogue:* Encourage open dialogue and active listening. Ensure that all voices are heard and that diverse perspectives are considered.

4. Capture and Share Outcomes:

- *Document Insights:* Capture all insights, ideas, and decisions made during the session. Use tools such as flip charts, whiteboards, and digital devices to document the discussions.
- *Share Outcomes*: Share the outcomes of the workshop or retreat with all participants and relevant stakeholders. This ensures that everyone is informed and aligned with the next steps.

5. Follow Up:

- *Action Plans:* Develop action plans based on the outcomes of the session. Assign responsibilities and set deadlines to ensure that the ideas are implemented.
- *Continuous Feedback:* Gather feedback from participants on the effectiveness of the workshop or retreat. Use this feedback to improve future sessions.

Overcoming Common Challenges

While workshops and retreats offer numerous benefits, they can also face challenges. Here's how to overcome some common obstacles:

1. Resistance to Participation:

- *Engage Early:* Engage participants early in the planning process to gain their buy-in and support. Clearly communicate the benefits of the session.
- *Incentives:* Provide incentives for participation, such as recognition, rewards, or professional development opportunities.

2. Managing Time:

- *Time Management:* Manage time effectively to ensure that all activities are completed within the allocated time. Use timekeepers and agenda reminders to stay on track.
- *Prioritize Activities:* Prioritize activities based on their importance and relevance. Focus on high-impact activities that drive the session's goals.

3. Ensuring Alignment:

- *Clear Objectives:* Ensure that the objectives of the session are clearly defined and communicated to all participants. This helps in maintaining focus and alignment.
- *Facilitator Role:* The facilitator should actively manage discussions to ensure that they stay aligned with the session's goals. Use techniques such as summarizing and redirecting to keep the discussion on track.

4. Managing Group Dynamics:

- *Inclusive Environment:* Foster an inclusive environment where all participants feel comfortable sharing their ideas. Address any dominant behaviors that may hinder participation.
- *Conflict Resolution:* Address conflicts constructively and ensure that they do not derail the session. Use techniques such as mediation and negotiation to resolve conflicts.

Workshops and retreats are powerful mechanisms for driving innovation and enhancing team performance. By organizing focused sessions and deep dives, you can create a structured yet flexible environment for ideation and problem-solving. These sessions foster intensive collaboration and creative thinking, leading to well-rounded and innovative solutions.

To maximize the benefits of workshops and retreats, prepare thoroughly, facilitate effectively, encourage collaboration, capture and share outcomes, and follow up with action plans. Overcome common challenges by engaging participants early, managing time effectively, ensuring alignment, and managing group dynamics.

By embracing the power of workshops and retreats, you can unlock the full potential of your team, drive meaningful progress, and achieve extraordinary results. Create an environment where creativity and collaboration thrive, and watch as your team generates innovative ideas and solutions that drive success.

External Collaboration:

In the land of innovation, external collaboration stands as a vital strategy for bringing in fresh perspectives and specialized knowledge. Partnering with experts, industry partners, and academia can significantly expand your horizons, providing new insights and uncovering opportunities that might otherwise remain hidden. Let's delve into the benefits of external collaboration, how to establish effective partnerships, and strategies to maximize their impact.

Partnering with Experts

Collaborating with external experts can inject new energy and ideas into your innovation process. Experts bring specialized knowledge and experience that can help you navigate complex challenges and identify novel solutions.

Why Partnering with Experts Matters:

- *Specialized Knowledge:* External experts possess deep knowledge in specific areas, offering insights that may not be available within your organization.

- *Innovative Solutions:* Experts can introduce innovative solutions and approaches that you might not have considered, broadening your problem-solving toolkit.
- *Accelerated Learning:* Collaborating with experts accelerates the learning process, enabling your team to quickly acquire new skills and knowledge.

Strategies for Partnering with Experts:

1. Identify Relevant Experts:

- *Industry Leaders:* Look for leaders in your industry who have a track record of innovation and success. Their experience can provide valuable guidance and inspiration.
- *Academic Researchers:* Collaborate with researchers from universities and research institutions who are at the forefront of scientific and technological advancements.
- *Consultants and Advisors:* Engage consultants and advisors who specialize in areas relevant to your projects. Their expertise can help you overcome specific challenges and optimize your strategies.

2. Establish Clear Objectives:

- *Define Goals:* Clearly define the goals and objectives of the collaboration. Understanding what you aim to achieve helps in aligning efforts and expectations.
- *Scope of Work:* Outline the scope of work and specific deliverables. This ensures that both parties are on the same page and working towards common goals.

3. Foster Open Communication:

- *Regular Updates:* Maintain regular communication with external experts to stay updated on progress and address any issues promptly.

- *Feedback Mechanism:* Establish a feedback mechanism to gather input and suggestions from the experts. This helps in continuously refining your approach.

4. Leverage Their Network:

- *Extended Network:* External experts often have extensive networks of professionals and organizations. Leverage these connections to explore additional collaboration opportunities and resources.
- *Collaborative Platforms*: Use collaborative platforms to facilitate communication and information sharing. Tools like Slack, Microsoft Teams, and project management software can enhance collaboration.

Expanding Horizons

External collaborations can significantly expand your horizons by providing new insights and opportunities for innovation. By engaging with industry partners, academia, and other external entities, you can tap into diverse perspectives and explore new avenues for growth.

Why Expanding Horizons Matters:

- *Diverse Perspectives:* External collaborations bring diverse perspectives to the table, enriching your innovation process with a variety of viewpoints.
- *New Opportunities:* Collaborating with external partners can uncover new opportunities for innovation that you might not have identified on your own.
- *Enhanced Creativity:* Exposure to different ideas and approaches enhances creativity, leading to more innovative and effective solutions.

Strategies for Expanding Horizons:

1. Engage with Industry Partners:

- *Joint Ventures:* Form joint ventures with industry partners to explore new markets, develop new products, or enhance existing offerings. Collaborative efforts can lead to shared success and mutual growth.
- *Industry Consortia:* Participate in industry consortia and alliances. These collaborative groups bring together companies to address common challenges and drive collective innovation.

2. Collaborate with Academia:

- *Research Partnerships:* Establish research partnerships with universities and research institutions. These collaborations can provide access to cutting-edge research, advanced technologies, and top talent.
- *Innovation Hubs:* Engage with innovation hubs and technology transfer offices. These entities facilitate collaboration between academia and industry, fostering the commercialization of research and technological advancements.

3. Leverage Open Innovation Platforms:

- *Crowdsourcing:* Use open innovation platforms to crowdsource ideas and solutions from a global community of innovators. This approach broadens your reach and taps into a diverse pool of creativity.
- *Innovation Challenges:* Host innovation challenges and competitions to attract external contributors. These events can generate a wealth of innovative ideas and identify potential collaborators.

4. Explore Cross-Industry Collaboration:

- *Interdisciplinary Projects:* Explore interdisciplinary projects that bring together expertise from different industries. This cross-pollination of ideas can lead to breakthrough innovations.

- *Knowledge Exchange*: Facilitate knowledge exchange between industries. Attend conferences, workshops, and seminars to learn from other sectors and apply their insights to your own challenges.

Practical Applications of External Collaboration

External collaboration can be applied in various contexts to drive innovation and enhance organizational performance. Here are some practical applications:

Product Development:

- *Collaborative R&D:* Partner with research institutions to conduct collaborative R&D projects. This can accelerate the development of new products and technologies.
- *Supplier Innovation:* Collaborate with suppliers to innovate and improve product components. Suppliers often have unique insights and capabilities that can enhance product quality and performance.

Process Improvement:

- *Lean Manufacturing:* Collaborate with lean manufacturing experts to streamline production processes and reduce waste. External expertise can help identify inefficiencies and implement best practices.
- *Quality Management:* Engage with quality management consultants to enhance your quality control processes. Their specialized knowledge can lead to significant improvements in product quality and customer satisfaction.

Market Expansion:

- *Strategic Alliances:* Form strategic alliances with companies in complementary markets. These alliances can help you expand your reach and tap into new customer segments.

- *Distribution Partnerships:* Partner with distributors and sales channels to expand your market presence. External partners can provide valuable market insights and enhance your distribution capabilities.

Technology Adoption:

- *Digital Transformation:* Collaborate with technology firms to adopt and implement new digital technologies. External expertise can guide you through the digital transformation process and ensure successful integration.
- *Cybersecurity:* Engage with cybersecurity experts to enhance your organization's security posture. Their specialized knowledge can help protect your assets and data from cyber threats.

Tips for Effective External Collaboration

To maximize the benefits of external collaboration, consider the following tips:

1. Choose the Right Partners:

- *Alignment of Goals:* Ensure that your goals and values align with those of your external partners. This alignment is crucial for a successful collaboration.
- *Complementary Skills:* Look for partners with complementary skills and expertise. This diversity enhances the overall capability of the collaboration.

2. Establish Trust:

- *Transparent Communication:* Maintain transparent communication with your partners. Share information openly and honestly to build trust and foster a positive working relationship.

- *Mutual Respect:* Show mutual respect for each other's expertise and contributions. Recognize and appreciate the value that each partner brings to the collaboration.

3. Define Roles and Responsibilities:

- *Clear Roles:* Clearly define the roles and responsibilities of each partner. This ensures that everyone knows what is expected of them and helps prevent misunderstandings.
- *Accountability:* Establish accountability mechanisms to ensure that all partners fulfill their commitments. Regular progress reviews and performance assessments can help maintain accountability.

4. Foster a Collaborative Culture:

- *Inclusive Environment:* Create an inclusive environment where all partners feel comfortable sharing their ideas and insights. Encourage open dialogue and active participation.
- *Collaborative Tools:* Use collaborative tools to facilitate communication and information sharing. Tools like shared documents, project management software, and video conferencing can enhance collaboration.

5. Monitor and Evaluate:

- *Track Progress:* Monitor the progress of the collaboration regularly. Use metrics and KPIs to measure success and identify areas for improvement.
- *Evaluate Outcomes***:** Evaluate the outcomes of the collaboration to assess its impact and effectiveness. Gather feedback from all partners to learn from the experience and make necessary adjustments.

Overcoming Common Challenges

While external collaboration offers numerous benefits, it can also face challenges. Here's how to overcome some common obstacles:

1. Cultural Differences:

- *Cultural Sensitivity:* Be aware of and respect cultural differences between partners. Foster cultural sensitivity and inclusivity within the collaboration.
- *Cross-Cultural Training:* Provide cross-cultural training to team members to enhance their understanding and appreciation of different cultures.

2. Intellectual Property Concerns:

- *IP Agreements:* Establish clear intellectual property (IP) agreements that outline the ownership and use of IP generated during the collaboration. This protects the interests of all partners.
- *Confidentiality:* Implement confidentiality agreements to protect sensitive information. Ensure that all partners understand and adhere to these agreements.

3. Communication Barriers:

- *Effective Communication:* Foster effective communication by using clear and concise language. Avoid jargon and technical terms that may be unfamiliar to some partners.
- *Language Support:* Provide language support if there are language barriers. This could include translation services or bilingual team members.

External collaboration is a powerful strategy for driving innovation and enhancing organizational performance. By partnering with experts, industry partners, and academia, you can bring in fresh perspectives, specialized knowledge, and new opportunities for growth. These collaborations expand your horizons, enrich your innovation process, and lead to more innovative and effective solutions.

To maximize the benefits of external collaboration, choose the right partners, establish trust, define roles and responsibilities, foster a collaborative culture, and monitor and evaluate the collaboration's progress. Overcome common challenges by addressing cultural differences, intellectual property concerns, and communication barriers.

Embrace the power of external collaboration to unlock the full potential of your organization, drive meaningful progress, and achieve extraordinary results. By leveraging the expertise and insights of external partners, you can stay ahead of the competition, explore new opportunities, and create lasting value for your organization and stakeholders.

User Involvement:

Engaging end-users in the ideation process is an essential component of successful innovation. By involving users directly through co-creation sessions, focus groups, and user testing, you can ensure that your ideas are grounded in real-world needs and preferences. This user-centered approach not only increases the chances of success but also builds stronger relationships with your customers. Let's explore the benefits of user involvement, how to implement it effectively, and strategies to maximize its impact.

Co-Creation

Co-creation is a collaborative approach that involves end-users in the development of new products, services, or solutions. By bringing users into the ideation process, you can gather valuable insights and feedback that help shape your innovations.

Why Co-Creation Matters:

- *Real-World Relevance:* Co-creation ensures that your innovations are aligned with the actual needs and preferences of users, making them more relevant and valuable.
- *Enhanced Creativity:* Involving users in the creative process brings diverse perspectives and ideas, leading to more innovative and effective solutions.
- *User Buy-In:* When users are involved in the creation process, they feel a sense of ownership and are more likely to support and adopt the final product or service.

Strategies for Effective Co-Creation:

1. Identify Key Users:

- *Target Audience:* Identify the key users who represent your target audience. These could be current customers, potential customers, or other stakeholders who will be affected by the innovation.
- *Diverse Representation:* Ensure that your co-creation sessions include a diverse representation of users. This diversity enhances the richness of the insights and ideas generated.

2. Facilitate Collaborative Sessions:

- *Workshops:* Organize co-creation workshops where users can collaborate with your team to generate and refine ideas. Use interactive activities such as brainstorming, role-playing, and prototyping to stimulate creativity and engagement.
- *Online Platforms:* Use online platforms to facilitate co-creation with remote users. Tools like virtual whiteboards, collaborative documents, and video conferencing can enable real-time collaboration and idea sharing.

3. Gather and Incorporate Feedback:

- *Continuous Feedback:* Gather feedback from users throughout the co-creation process. Use surveys, interviews, and focus groups to collect their input and insights.
- *Iterative Development:* Incorporate user feedback into the development process iteratively. Regularly update users on the progress and changes made based on their feedback, fostering a sense of collaboration and transparency.

Real-World Insights

Involving users in the ideation process provides real-world insights that are crucial for the success of your innovations. These insights help you understand the actual needs, preferences, and behaviors of users, ensuring that your solutions are practical and effective.

Why Real-World Insights Matter:

- *User-Centric Design:* Real-world insights enable you to design solutions that are user-centric, addressing the specific needs and pain points of your target audience.
- *Market Validation:* Engaging users early in the process provides market validation, reducing the risk of developing products or services that do not resonate with the market.
- *Enhanced User Experience:* Understanding user behaviors and preferences allows you to create a seamless and enjoyable user experience, increasing customer satisfaction and loyalty.

Strategies for Gathering Real-World Insights:

1. Conduct Focus Groups:

- *User Discussions:* Organize focus groups where users can discuss their needs, preferences, and experiences. Facilitate open and honest discussions to gather deep insights.
- *Topic Exploration:* Explore specific topics related to your innovation, such as usability, functionality, and user experience. Use guided questions to steer the discussion and uncover valuable insights.

2. Implement User Testing:

- *Prototype Testing:* Develop prototypes of your ideas and test them with users. Gather feedback on usability, functionality, and overall experience to identify areas for improvement.
- *A/B Testing:* Use A/B testing to compare different versions of your product or service. This helps you understand user preferences and make data-driven decisions.

3. Analyze Behavioral Data:

- *Usage Analytics:* Analyze usage data to understand how users interact with your product or service. Look for patterns and trends that indicate user preferences and pain points.
- *User Journeys:* Map out user journeys to visualize the steps users take when engaging with your product or service. Identify touchpoints and areas for improvement.

Practical Applications of User Involvement

User involvement can be applied in various contexts to drive innovation and enhance user experience. Here are some practical applications:

Product Development:

- *Feature Prioritization:* Use user feedback to prioritize product features and enhancements. This ensures that your product development efforts are aligned with user needs.
- *User-Centered Design:* Involve users in the design process to create products that are intuitive and user-friendly. Gather input on design elements, usability, and overall user experience.

Service Design:

- *Service Blueprinting:* Use co-creation sessions to develop service blueprints that map out the user experience. Gather feedback on each touchpoint to ensure a seamless and enjoyable service journey.
- *Customer Support:* Involve users in the design of customer support processes. Gather insights on common issues and preferences to create a more effective and user-friendly support system.

Marketing and Branding:

- *Campaign Development:* Involve users in the development of marketing campaigns. Gather feedback on messaging, visuals, and overall campaign strategy to ensure that it resonates with your target audience.
- *Brand Positioning:* Use user insights to inform your brand positioning and messaging. Understand how users perceive your brand and what values resonate with them.

Education and Training:

- *Curriculum Development:* Involve learners in the development of educational curricula. Gather feedback on content, delivery methods, and overall learning experience to create more effective and engaging programs.

- *Training Programs:* Use user feedback to design training programs that address specific needs and preferences. Gather input on training content, format, and delivery to ensure maximum impact.

Tips for Effective User Involvement

To maximize the benefits of user involvement, consider the following tips:

1. Engage Users Early:

- *Early Involvement:* Engage users early in the ideation process to gather initial insights and feedback. This helps in shaping the direction of your innovation efforts.
- *Ongoing Engagement:* Maintain ongoing engagement with users throughout the development process. Regularly update them on progress and gather their input at key stages.

2. Create a Safe Space:

- *Open Environment:* Create a safe and open environment where users feel comfortable sharing their thoughts and ideas. Encourage honest and constructive feedback.
- *Respect Privacy:* Respect user privacy and confidentiality. Ensure that their feedback is used responsibly and ethically.

3. Use Diverse Methods:

- *Multiple Channels:* Use multiple channels to gather user feedback, such as surveys, interviews, focus groups, and user testing. This ensures a comprehensive understanding of user needs and preferences.
- *Qualitative and Quantitative:* Combine qualitative and quantitative methods to gather rich and actionable insights. Use qualitative methods to explore user experiences and quantitative methods to validate findings.

4. Act on Feedback:

- *Implement Changes:* Act on user feedback by making necessary changes and improvements. Show users that their input is valued and has a tangible impact.
- *Close the Loop:* Close the feedback loop by informing users about the changes made based on their feedback. This fosters a sense of collaboration and trust.

Overcoming Common Challenges

While user involvement offers numerous benefits, it can also face challenges. Here's how to overcome some common obstacles:

1. User Fatigue:

- *Engagement Strategies:* Use engagement strategies to keep users motivated and interested. Provide incentives, recognize their contributions, and create enjoyable and meaningful experiences.
- *Manage Frequency:* Manage the frequency of user involvement to avoid overburdening users. Balance regular engagement while respecting their time and availability.

2. Diverse Perspectives:

- *Inclusive Approach:* Foster an inclusive approach that values diverse perspectives. Ensure that your user involvement efforts include a wide range of users with different backgrounds and experiences.
- *Facilitate Dialogue:* Facilitate open and respectful dialogue to manage differing opinions and perspectives. Use techniques such as mediation and consensus-building to find common ground.

3. Implementation Challenges:

- *Resource Allocation:* Allocate the necessary resources to implement user feedback effectively. Ensure that you have the time, budget, and personnel to act on user input.
- *Prioritization:* Prioritize user feedback based on its impact and feasibility. Focus on changes that will have the most significant positive effect on the user experience.

User involvement is a powerful strategy for driving innovation and enhancing user experience. By engaging end-users in the ideation process through co-creation sessions, focus groups, and user testing, you can gather valuable real-world insights and create solutions that truly resonate with your audience. This user-centered approach not only increases the chances of success but also builds stronger relationships with your customers.

To maximize the benefits of user involvement, engage users early, create a safe space for feedback, use diverse methods, and act on the feedback gathered. Overcome common challenges by managing user fatigue, fostering an inclusive approach, and ensuring that you have the resources to implement changes effectively.

Embrace the power of user involvement to unlock the full potential of your innovation efforts, drive meaningful progress, and achieve extraordinary results. By placing users at the center of your innovation process, you can create solutions that meet their needs, exceed their expectations, and deliver lasting value.

Frameworks and Tools for Creating Innovative Solutions

Using structured frameworks and tools can significantly enhance the process of developing innovative solutions. Over the years, I've found that having a clear methodology not only streamlines ideation and concept development but also ensures that no valuable insights are overlooked. This section will dive into various methodologies that have proven effective in my experience and can help you navigate the complexities of innovation. Whether you're just starting with a new idea or looking to refine an existing concept, these tools will provide the structure and guidance needed to bring your vision to life and achieve impactful results.

Design Thinking

Design thinking is a powerful framework for developing user-centric solutions. It's an iterative process that emphasizes empathy, creativity, and rationality, aiming to understand and address the real needs of users. The design thinking process consists of five key stages: Empathize, Define, Ideate, Prototype, and Test. Each stage is crucial in creating solutions that are both innovative and effective.

Empathize

The first stage, Empathize, involves immersing yourself in the user's world to gain a deep understanding of their needs, challenges, and desires. This stage is about putting yourself in the user's shoes and seeing the world through their eyes.

Methods to Empathize:

- *Interviews:* Conduct in-depth interviews with users to uncover their experiences, motivations, and pain points. Open-ended questions can reveal valuable insights that structured surveys might miss.

- *Observation:* Spend time observing users in their natural environment. Watch how they interact with products and services, and note any frustrations or workarounds they employ.
- *Immersion:* Engage in the same activities as your users. If you're designing a tool for chefs, for example, spend time cooking in a professional kitchen to experience their daily challenges firsthand.

A great example of empathizing in action is IDEO's work with Gyrus ACMI, a medical device company. To redesign surgical instruments, IDEO designers observed surgeries and interviewed surgeons and nurses to understand their needs. This empathy work revealed insights that led to significant design improvements.

Define

Once you have gathered sufficient data through empathy, the next step is to Define the problem. This stage is about synthesizing the insights gathered and clearly articulating the core problem to be addressed.

Crafting a Problem Statement:

- *Insight Synthesis:* Analyze the data collected during the empathy stage to identify patterns and key insights. Look for recurring themes and underlying issues that users face.
- *Problem Statement:* Formulate a clear and concise problem statement that captures the essence of the user's need. A well-defined problem statement guides the ideation process and keeps the focus on solving the right problem.

For instance, after observing and interviewing surgeons, IDEO defined the problem as the need for more ergonomic and intuitive surgical instruments. This clear problem statement provided a focused direction for the subsequent design efforts.

Ideate

With a well-defined problem, the next stage is to Ideate, where you generate a wide range of ideas and potential solutions. This stage encourages creativity and divergent thinking.

Generating Ideas:

- *Brainstorming Sessions:* Hold brainstorming sessions where participants are encouraged to share as many ideas as possible without judgment. The goal is to generate a diverse array of concepts.
- *Mind Mapping:* Use mind mapping to visually organize and connect different ideas. This technique helps in exploring various angles and relationships between concepts.
- *Sketching:* Encourage participants to sketch their ideas. Visual representations can make abstract ideas more tangible and easier to discuss.

IDEO's approach to ideation often involves diverse teams, including designers, engineers, and users, collaborating to generate a broad spectrum of ideas. This collaborative effort ensures that multiple perspectives are considered.

Prototype

The Prototype stage involves creating tangible representations of your ideas. Prototypes can range from simple sketches and mock-ups to more detailed models and interactive simulations. The goal is to bring ideas to life and test them in a real-world context.

Building Prototypes:

- *Low-Fidelity Prototypes:* Start with low-fidelity prototypes such as sketches, paper models, or digital wireframes. These are quick and inexpensive to create, allowing you to explore multiple ideas without significant investment.

- *High-Fidelity Prototypes:* As ideas are refined, develop high-fidelity prototypes that more closely resemble the final product. These can be functional models or interactive simulations that provide a realistic user experience.

IDEO's work with the global design company, Steelcase, is a great example of effective prototyping. To redesign the office chair, IDEO created multiple prototypes, ranging from simple cardboard models to fully functional chairs. Each prototype was tested and refined based on user feedback.

Test

The final stage, Test, involves evaluating your prototypes with real users. This stage provides valuable feedback and insights that help refine and improve the solution.

Testing Prototypes:

- *User Testing:* Conduct user testing sessions where users interact with the prototype and provide feedback. Observe their behavior, note any difficulties they encounter, and gather their impressions.
- *Iterative Refinement:* Use the feedback from testing to make iterative improvements to the prototype. This cycle of testing and refining continues until the solution meets the users' needs effectively.

For example, after developing prototypes for the office chair, IDEO tested them with office workers in various settings. The feedback gathered during these tests informed further refinements, resulting in a final design that was both innovative and user-friendly.

Applying Design Thinking: A Live Example

A live example of applying design thinking can be seen in the work of Airbnb. In its early days, Airbnb faced significant challenges with user trust and engagement. The founders decided to use design thinking to address these issues.

Empathize: The founders traveled to New York City to meet with hosts and guests. They stayed in the listings, talked to users, and observed their experiences. This immersion provided deep insights into the users' needs and pain points.

Define: Based on their empathy work, the founders defined the core problem: users needed better visuals and descriptions to trust the listings. They identified that low-quality photos and insufficient information were significant barriers to booking.

Ideate: The Airbnb team brainstormed various solutions to improve the listings. Ideas included professional photography, detailed descriptions, and user-generated reviews. They also considered ways to enhance the user interface to make it more intuitive and trustworthy.

Prototype: Airbnb decided to implement professional photography as a key solution. They hired photographers to take high-quality photos of the listings. Additionally, they redesigned the listing page to include more detailed descriptions and user reviews. These prototypes were tested with a small group of users.

Test: The prototypes were tested in real-world scenarios. Hosts and guests provided feedback, which was used to refine the features. The professional photos significantly increased bookings, and the detailed descriptions and reviews improved user trust.

The iterative process of testing and refining led to a significant increase in user engagement and trust, contributing to Airbnb's rapid growth and success.

The Importance of User Focus

One of the core principles of design thinking is its user-centric focus. Throughout the entire process, from empathizing to testing, the user remains at the center. This iterative approach ensures that the solutions developed are not only innovative but also highly relevant and effective.

User-Centric Benefits:

- *Enhanced Relevance:* By focusing on real user needs and preferences, design thinking ensures that the solutions developed are highly relevant to the target audience.
- *Improved Adoption:* Solutions that are designed with the user in mind are more likely to be adopted and embraced. Users feel that their needs and feedback are valued, leading to greater satisfaction.
- *Continuous Improvement:* The iterative nature of design thinking allows for continuous improvement. Regular user feedback ensures that solutions evolve to meet changing needs and expectations.

Design thinking is a powerful framework for developing user-centric solutions that are both innovative and effective. By following the stages of Empathize, Define, Ideate, Prototype, and Test, you can create solutions that address real user needs and preferences. The iterative nature of design thinking ensures continuous improvement and relevance.

I have used design thinking extensively in my projects and have witnessed firsthand its impactful power. By focusing on empathy, collaboration, and iteration, design thinking can help you create solutions that truly resonate with your audience and drive meaningful progress.

Lean Startup Method

The Lean Startup Method is a powerful approach to innovation that emphasizes rapid development, real-world feedback, and iterative improvement. This methodology helps entrepreneurs and innovators to build products that meet market needs while minimizing waste and maximizing efficiency. The core principles of the Lean Startup Method are encapsulated in the Build-Measure-Learn cycle, which provides a structured yet flexible framework for turning ideas into successful products.

Build-Measure-Learn Cycle

At the heart of the Lean Startup Method is the Build-Measure-Learn cycle. This iterative process involves creating a Minimum Viable Product (MVP), measuring its performance in the market, and learning from the results to refine and improve the product. This cycle repeats until the product meets the needs of the target audience effectively.

Build: The first step in the Lean Startup Method is to build an MVP. The MVP is a simplified version of the product that includes only the most essential features necessary to test the core assumptions about the product. The goal is to develop the MVP quickly and with minimal resources, allowing you to gather initial feedback without investing too much time or money.

For example, Dropbox began with a simple MVP—a video demonstrating how the service would work. This allowed the founders to gauge interest and gather feedback without building a full-scale product. The overwhelmingly positive response to the video validated their assumptions and justified further development.

Measure: Once the MVP is built, the next step is to measure its performance in the market. This involves collecting data on how users interact with the product, what features they use, and any issues they encounter. This data is crucial for understanding whether the product is meeting user needs and identifying areas for improvement.

To measure effectively, it's important to define clear metrics that align with your goals. These could include user engagement, conversion rates, customer satisfaction, and other relevant indicators. Tools like Google Analytics, customer surveys, and user testing sessions can provide valuable insights into how the MVP is performing.

Learn: The final step in the cycle is to learn from the data collected during the measurement phase. This involves analyzing the data to identify patterns, understand user behavior, and draw conclusions about the product's effectiveness. Based on these insights, you can make informed decisions about what changes to make in the next iteration of the product.

For instance, if users are consistently struggling with a particular feature, it may indicate a need for redesign or additional functionality. Alternatively, if a feature is highly popular, you might prioritize enhancing it in future updates.

Minimizing Waste

One of the key principles of the Lean Startup Method is minimizing waste. This approach focuses on avoiding unnecessary work and resources by iterating quickly and learning from real-world feedback. By concentrating on building only what is necessary to test assumptions, you can avoid investing time and money into features or products that may not succeed in the market.

Developing an MVP: The concept of the MVP is central to minimizing waste. By starting with a basic version of the product, you can test your assumptions without committing significant resources. This allows you to validate your ideas early on and make adjustments before investing heavily in development.

Iterative Improvement: The iterative nature of the Build-Measure-Learn cycle ensures continuous improvement and reduces the risk of developing a product that doesn't meet market needs. Each iteration provides valuable feedback that guides the next steps, enabling you to refine the product based on real-world data rather than assumptions.

Live Example: Zappos

A compelling example of the Lean Startup Method in action is the story of Zappos, an online shoe and clothing retailer. In its early days, Zappos founder Nick Swinmurn wanted to test whether people would buy shoes online. Instead of building a full-fledged e-commerce platform, he started with a simple MVP.

Build: Swinmurn took photos of shoes from local stores and posted them online. When a customer placed an order, he would purchase the shoes from the store and ship them directly to the customer. This approach allowed him to test the core assumption—that people would be willing to buy shoes online—without investing in inventory or a sophisticated website.

Measure: By tracking sales and customer feedback, Swinmurn gathered valuable data on user behavior and preferences. He measured key metrics such as the types of shoes that were popular, the average order size, and customer satisfaction levels. This data provided insights into the viability of the business model and areas for improvement.

Learn: The feedback from early customers validated the idea that there was a market for buying shoes online. Based on these learnings, Swinmurn was able to secure funding and gradually expand the business. He invested in building a dedicated e-commerce platform, developing a robust supply chain, and enhancing customer service.

By starting small and iterating based on real-world feedback, Zappos was able to grow into a successful and innovative company. This approach minimized waste by focusing on essential features and continuously improving based on user data.

Applying the Lean Startup Method

Implementing the Lean Startup Method in your organization involves adopting a mindset of experimentation and continuous improvement. Here are some strategies to effectively apply this methodology:

1. **Start with Hypotheses:** Begin with clear hypotheses about your product and market. These hypotheses form the basis for your MVP and guide your testing and measurement efforts. For example, you might hypothesize that users will prefer a certain feature or that a specific pricing model will be effective.

2. **Prioritize Learning:** Prioritize learning over perfection. The goal of the MVP is to gather feedback, not to create a flawless product. Be open to making mistakes and learning from them, as this is a crucial part of the iterative process.

3. **Focus on Key Metrics:** Identify key metrics that align with your business goals and focus on measuring them. These metrics will help you understand user behavior and make data-driven decisions. Common metrics include customer acquisition cost, lifetime value, churn rate, and user engagement.

4. **Iterate Quickly:** Move quickly through the Build-Measure-Learn cycle. Rapid iterations allow you to test assumptions and make adjustments before committing significant resources. This agility helps you stay responsive to market changes and user feedback.

5. **Engage with Users:** Actively engage with users throughout the process. Their feedback is invaluable for refining your product and ensuring it meets

their needs. Use surveys, interviews, and user testing sessions to gather insights and validate your assumptions.

Benefits of the Lean Startup Method

The Lean Startup Method offers several benefits for innovators and entrepreneurs:

Reduced Risk: By testing assumptions early and iterating based on feedback, you reduce the risk of developing a product that doesn't meet market needs.

Cost Efficiency: Focusing on an MVP and iterating in time helps you avoid unnecessary expenses and allocate resources more efficiently.

Faster Time to Market: Rapid iterations enable you to bring products to market faster, gaining a competitive advantage and capturing market share.

Customer-Centric Approach: Engaging with users and incorporating their feedback ensures that your product is aligned with their needs and preferences.

Continuous Improvement: The iterative nature of the Lean Startup Method fosters a culture of continuous improvement, driving long-term success and innovation.

The Lean Startup Method is a powerful framework for developing innovative solutions efficiently and effectively. By following the Build-Measure-Learn cycle, you can rapidly test assumptions, gather real-world feedback, and iterate on your product to ensure it meets user needs. This approach minimizes waste and maximizes the chances of success by focusing on what truly matters.

I have seen firsthand the impact of the Lean Startup Method in various projects and ventures. By prioritizing learning, engaging with users, and iterating quickly, you can navigate the complexities of innovation and bring successful products to market. Whether you're an entrepreneur starting a new venture or an established company looking to innovate, the Lean Startup Method provides a structured yet flexible approach to achieving your goals.

•

TRIZ (Theory of Inventive Problem Solving)

TRIZ is all about systematic innovation. Unlike other creative problem-solving techniques that rely on brainstorming and intuition, TRIZ uses a structured approach to identify and solve problems. This methodology is particularly effective in addressing complex issues where traditional methods may fall short.

The foundation of TRIZ is its focus on contradictions. Altshuller discovered that most inventive problems arise from contradictions—situations where improving one aspect of a system leads to the deterioration of another. TRIZ provides tools and principles to resolve these contradictions, enabling innovators to find solutions that balance competing demands.

Innovation Patterns

One of the key strengths of TRIZ is its use of innovation patterns. Altshuller's analysis of patents revealed that many inventions followed similar patterns or principles. By categorizing these patterns, TRIZ offers a toolbox of strategies that can be applied to various problems. These patterns, known as the "40 Inventive Principles," provide a starting point for generating innovative solutions.

Applying TRIZ: A Live Example

To illustrate the power of TRIZ, let's look at the example of Samsung. Samsung has successfully applied TRIZ to enhance its product development processes, particularly in its home appliance division.

Identifying the Problem

Samsung engineers faced a challenge with their washing machines. Customers wanted machines that were both energy-efficient and capable of handling large loads. However, increasing the drum size to accommodate larger loads often led to increased energy consumption and decreased washing efficiency—classic contradictions.

Using TRIZ to Solve the Problem

The engineers applied TRIZ to address this issue. They started by identifying the specific contradictions: increasing drum size improved load capacity but negatively impacted energy efficiency and washing performance.

Applying Inventive Principles

Using the TRIZ framework, the engineers explored various inventive principles. One of the principles they considered was "Segmentation," which involves dividing an object into independent parts. By applying this principle, they came up with the idea of segmenting the washing drum into multiple smaller drums that could operate independently.

Prototyping and Testing

The next step was to prototype this segmented drum design. The engineers created a model with multiple smaller drums, each capable of operating at different speeds and handling different load sizes. This design allowed for greater flexibility and efficiency.

They then tested the prototype to see how it performed in real-world conditions. The segmented drums proved to be highly efficient, handling large loads while consuming less energy. This innovative approach resolved the contradictions that had previously hindered their designs.

Steps to Apply TRIZ

Applying TRIZ involves several key steps, each designed to systematically address and solve inventive problems.

1. **Define the Problem:** Begin by clearly defining the problem and identifying any contradictions. What are the competing demands or conflicting requirements? For example, in Samsung's case, the problem was to increase load capacity without sacrificing energy efficiency.

2. **Analyze the Problem:** Break down the problem into its fundamental components. What are the key factors and variables involved? This analysis helps to understand the underlying structure of the problem.

3. **Identify Contradictions:** Identify the contradictions within the problem. What improvements lead to negative side effects? These contradictions are central to the TRIZ approach.

4. **Apply Inventive Principles:** Refer to the 40 Inventive Principles of TRIZ. These principles offer a range of strategies for overcoming contradictions. Select and apply the principles that are most relevant to your problem.

5. **Develop Solutions:** Generate potential solutions based on the selected principles. This step involves creative thinking within the structured framework of TRIZ.

6. **Prototype and Test:** Create prototypes of the proposed solutions and test them in real-world conditions. This iterative process allows you to refine and improve the solutions.

7. **Evaluate and Implement:** Evaluate the test results and select the best solution for implementation. Ensure that the chosen solution effectively resolves the contradictions and meets the desired objectives.

Benefits of TRIZ

The TRIZ methodology offers several benefits for innovators and organizations:

Systematic Approach: TRIZ provides a structured and systematic approach to problem-solving, making it easier to tackle complex issues.

Predictable Outcomes: By leveraging proven patterns of innovation, TRIZ increases the likelihood of finding effective solutions.

Time Efficiency: TRIZ can accelerate the problem-solving process by providing clear guidelines and principles to follow.

Versatility: TRIZ is applicable across various industries and domains, from engineering and technology to business and management.

Innovation Culture: Adopting TRIZ fosters a culture of innovation within organizations, encouraging employees to systematically approach problems and think creatively.

TRIZ, the Theory of Inventive Problem Solving, is a powerful methodology for systematic innovation. By focusing on contradictions and leveraging patterns of invention, TRIZ provides a structured approach to problem-solving that can lead to breakthrough solutions. The example of Samsung demonstrates how TRIZ can be effectively applied to resolve complex issues and drive innovation.

In my experience, TRIZ has been an invaluable tool for addressing challenging problems and developing innovative solutions. Its structured approach ensures that no stone is left unturned, and its focus on contradictions leads to solutions that balance competing demands. Whether you're facing a technical challenge or a business problem, TRIZ can provide the framework and principles needed to find effective solutions and achieve extraordinary results.

Business Model Canvas

The Business Model Canvas is an essential tool for visualizing and planning the key components of your business model. Developed by Alexander Osterwalder, it provides a structured framework for understanding, analyzing, and innovating your business. This canvas offers a holistic view of your business, helping to identify areas for innovation and improvement, enabling you to align all aspects of your operations with your strategic goals.

Understanding the Business Model Canvas

The Business Model Canvas is divided into nine building blocks that cover the core elements of any business. These building blocks are: Customer Segments, Value Propositions, Channels, Customer Relationships, Revenue Streams, Key Resources, Key Activities, Key Partnerships, and Cost Structure. Each of these blocks plays a critical role in defining how your business creates, delivers, and captures value.

Customer Segments

Customer Segments define the different groups of people or organizations your business aims to reach and serve. Identifying and understanding your target customer segments is crucial for tailoring your value propositions and marketing strategies to meet their specific needs.

For example, when Nike expanded its focus to include female athletes, it identified women as a distinct customer segment. This led to the creation of targeted marketing campaigns and products designed specifically for women, which significantly increased their market share in this segment.

Value Propositions

Value Propositions describe the unique benefits and solutions your business offers to each customer segment. This block focuses on what makes your product or service attractive and differentiates it from competitors. It's about solving customer problems and fulfilling their needs.

A compelling example is Dollar Shave Club, which disrupted the razor industry by offering high-quality razors through a convenient subscription model at a low cost. Their value proposition addressed the high cost and inconvenience of traditional razor purchases, attracting a loyal customer base.

Channels

Channels outline the various ways your business delivers its value propositions to customers. This includes all the touchpoints through which customers interact with your brand, from marketing and sales to distribution and after-sales support.

Zara uses both physical retail stores and a robust online presence to reach its customers. This multi-channel approach allows Zara to offer a seamless shopping experience, whether customers prefer to shop in-store or online.

Customer Relationships

Customer Relationships define the type of relationship your business establishes with each customer segment. This can range from personal assistance and dedicated support to self-service and automated interactions. Building strong customer relationships is essential for customer retention and loyalty.

Zappos excels in this area by offering exceptional customer service, including free returns and 24/7 customer support. This commitment to customer satisfaction has built a strong, loyal customer base and set Zappos apart from other online retailers.

Revenue Streams

Revenue Streams represent the ways in which your business generates income from each customer segment. This includes all the different pricing mechanisms, such as sales, subscriptions, leasing, licensing, and more.

Adobe transitioned from selling software licenses to a subscription-based model with its Creative Cloud. This shift to recurring revenue streams allowed Adobe to stabilize its income and foster deeper customer relationships through continuous updates and support.

Key Resources

Key Resources describe the critical assets required to deliver your value propositions, reach your customer segments, and sustain your business operations. These resources can be physical, intellectual, human, or financial.

For Netflix, key resources include its extensive content library, proprietary recommendation algorithms, and a growing base of subscribers. These resources enable Netflix to deliver a compelling entertainment experience and maintain its competitive edge in the streaming industry.

Key Activities

Key Activities encompass the essential actions your business must perform to operate successfully and deliver its value propositions. This includes activities related to production, marketing, sales, and customer service.

For example, Dyson's key activities include continuous research and development to innovate in the field of home appliances. This focus on R&D has led to groundbreaking products like the bagless vacuum cleaner and the bladeless fan.

Key Partnerships

Key Partnerships outline the network of suppliers, partners, and alliances that help your business operate and grow. These partnerships can provide access to resources, expertise, and distribution channels that are critical for success.

For example, Spotify has partnered with various record labels, artists, and tech companies to provide a vast music library and seamless streaming experience. These partnerships are crucial for maintaining and expanding its service offerings.

Cost Structure

Cost Structure details the major costs involved in operating your business. This includes costs associated with key activities, key resources, and key partnerships. Understanding your cost structure is vital for managing profitability and financial sustainability.

For Uber, significant costs include driver incentives, marketing, technology development, and regulatory compliance. By carefully managing these costs, Uber aims to achieve operational efficiency and long-term profitability.

Applying the Business Model Canvas: A Live Example

A practical example of applying the Business Model Canvas is LEGO. In the early 2000s, LEGO faced significant financial difficulties and needed to rethink its business model. By using the Business Model Canvas, LEGO was able to map out and refine its business strategy, leading to a remarkable turnaround.

Customer Segments

LEGO identified several key customer segments: children, parents, adult fans of LEGO (AFOL), and educators. This broad segmentation allowed LEGO to tailor its products and marketing efforts to meet the unique needs of each group.

Value Propositions

For children, LEGO's value proposition centers on imaginative play and creativity. For parents, it offers educational benefits and high-quality, durable products. For AFOLs, LEGO provides complex and challenging sets that cater to their hobby and passion. For educators, LEGO offers educational kits that support STEM learning.

Channels

LEGO uses a mix of direct and indirect channels to reach its customers. This includes physical retail stores, an extensive online store, and a network of third-party retailers. LEGO also engages customers through branded stores and LEGO-themed amusement parks, enhancing the overall brand experience.

Customer Relationships

LEGO maintains strong customer relationships through various initiatives. For children and parents, it offers membership in the LEGO Club, which provides exclusive content and activities. For AFOLs, LEGO supports fan conventions and online communities. For educators, LEGO offers training and resources to integrate its products into educational curricula.

Revenue Streams

LEGO's revenue streams include direct sales from its stores and online platform, sales through third-party retailers, and licensing agreements for LEGO-themed merchandise and media content. The diversification of revenue streams has helped LEGO stabilize its income and expand its market presence.

Key Resources

LEGO's key resources include its brand, extensive product portfolio, proprietary brick design, and intellectual property related to its themes and characters. These resources enable LEGO to continuously innovate and deliver high-quality products that resonate with its diverse customer base.

Key Activities

LEGO's key activities involve continuous product development, marketing, and maintaining strong retail and online sales channels. LEGO also invests heavily in research and development to create new products and themes that capture the interest of its customers.

Key Partnerships

LEGO has established key partnerships with various stakeholders. This includes collaborations with media companies to produce LEGO-themed movies and TV shows, partnerships with educational institutions to develop learning kits, and alliances with other brands for co-branded products.

Cost Structure

LEGO's cost structure includes expenses related to manufacturing, marketing, distribution, and research and development. By managing these costs effectively, LEGO has been able to maintain profitability while investing in growth and innovation.

Benefits of the Business Model Canvas

The Business Model Canvas offers several benefits for businesses of all sizes and stages:

Holistic View: The canvas provides a comprehensive view of your business model, allowing you to see how different components interact and affect each other.

Clarity and Focus: By breaking down your business model into key components, the canvas helps clarify your value proposition and strategic priorities.

Identifying Opportunities: The canvas highlights areas for innovation and improvement, helping you identify new opportunities for growth and differentiation.

Alignment and Communication: The visual nature of the canvas makes it an excellent tool for aligning your team and communicating your business model to stakeholders.

Iterative Improvement: The canvas is flexible and can be updated as your business evolves. This iterative approach ensures that your business model remains relevant and effective.

The Business Model Canvas is a powerful tool for visualizing, planning, and innovating your business model. By breaking down your business into nine key components, the canvas provides a structured framework for understanding how your business creates, delivers, and captures value.

I have personally used the Business Model Canvas in various projects and have found it invaluable for gaining clarity, identifying opportunities, and aligning team efforts. Whether you are a startup looking to define your business model or an established company seeking to innovate, the Business Model Canvas can provide the insights and structure needed to achieve your goals. By leveraging this tool, you can create a more resilient, adaptable, and successful business.

Value Proposition Canvas

The Value Proposition Canvas is a powerful tool for aligning your product or service with the needs and desires of your customers. Created by Alexander Osterwalder, this tool focuses on understanding and addressing customer needs to ensure that your innovation delivers real value. By dissecting both the customer profile and the value map, the Value Proposition Canvas helps you create a compelling value proposition that resonates with your target audience.

Understanding the Value Proposition Canvas

The Value Proposition Canvas consists of two main sections: the Customer Profile and the Value Map. Each section is further divided into specific components that help you analyze and align your product or service with customer expectations.

Customer Profile

The Customer Profile helps you understand your target audience in detail. It includes three key components: Customer Jobs, Pains, and Gains.

Customer Jobs: Customer jobs describe what your customers are trying to achieve in their personal and professional lives. This includes functional, social, and emotional tasks. Understanding these jobs is crucial for creating a product or service that fits seamlessly into their lives.

For example, when Slack was developed, its creators focused on the customer's job of improving team communication and collaboration. By addressing the need for efficient and centralized communication, Slack became an essential tool for many businesses.

Pains: Pains refer to the challenges, frustrations, and obstacles that customers face while trying to accomplish their jobs. Identifying these pains helps you understand what customers are trying to avoid and where they experience difficulties.

When Netflix expanded its streaming services, it identified a major pain point: the inconvenience of DVD rentals, including late fees and limited selection. By eliminating these pains, Netflix significantly enhanced the user experience.

Gains: Gains are the benefits and positive outcomes that customers seek. These can include functional utility, social gains, positive emotions, and cost savings. Understanding the desired gains allows you to tailor your product or service to exceed customer expectations.

For instance, Spotify recognized that users wanted easy access to a vast library of music without the hassle of downloads or ads. By providing this gain through their premium subscription, Spotify created a compelling value proposition.

Value Map

The Value Map details how your product or service creates value for customers. It includes three components: Products and Services, Pain Relievers, and Gain Creators.

Products and Services: This section lists the specific products and services you offer that help customers achieve their jobs. It's important to ensure that these offerings directly address the identified customer jobs.

For example, Peloton offers a range of products and services, including high-quality exercise bikes, live-streamed fitness classes, and on-demand workout sessions. These offerings align perfectly with the customer's job of maintaining a fitness routine from home.

Pain Relievers: Pain relievers describe how your product or service alleviates customer pains. This involves directly addressing the challenges and frustrations identified in the Customer Profile.

When Tesla introduced its electric vehicles, one of the pain relievers was reducing the environmental impact and operational costs associated with traditional gasoline cars. This directly addressed the growing concern for sustainability among consumers.

Gain Creators: Gain creators explain how your product or service provides benefits that customers seek. This involves delivering the desired gains identified in the Customer Profile.

For example, Airbnb provides gain creators by offering unique, personalized travel experiences that traditional hotels cannot match. This caters to the customer's desire for authentic and diverse lodging options.

Applying the Value Proposition Canvas: A Live Example

A practical example of applying the Value Proposition Canvas is the story of Fitbit. Fitbit revolutionized the fitness industry by creating a product that seamlessly aligned with customer needs and desires.

Customer Profile

Customer Jobs: Fitbit's primary customers were individuals looking to improve their health and fitness. The customer job was to track physical activity, monitor health metrics, and achieve fitness goals.

Pains: Fitbit identified several pains: the complexity of tracking fitness manually, the lack of motivation, and the inability to monitor health metrics accurately. These pain points were common among fitness enthusiasts and individuals looking to improve their health.

Gains: The desired gains for Fitbit's customers included easy and accurate tracking of fitness metrics, motivation through goal setting and community support, and actionable health insights. Customers wanted a simple yet effective way to stay on top of their fitness routines.

Value Map

Products and Services: Fitbit developed a range of wearable devices that track physical activity, heart rate, sleep patterns, and other health metrics. These products provided the tools needed to achieve fitness goals.

Pain Relievers: Fitbit's devices simplified the process of tracking fitness metrics. The intuitive interface and easy-to-use app made it simple for users to monitor their progress and stay motivated. Additionally, the community features provided social support and encouragement, addressing the pain point of lack of motivation.

Gain Creators: Fitbit's gain creators included detailed health insights, personalized recommendations, and progress tracking. The ability to set and achieve goals, earn badges, and participate in challenges created a sense of accomplishment and motivation.

Benefits of the Value Proposition Canvas

The Value Proposition Canvas offers several benefits for businesses looking to innovate and align their offerings with customer needs:

Customer-Centric Focus: The canvas emphasizes understanding and addressing customer needs, ensuring that your product or service delivers real value.

Clarity and Alignment: By mapping out the customer profile and value map, the canvas provides clarity on how your offerings align with customer expectations.

Identifying Gaps: The canvas helps identify gaps between what customers want and what your product or service delivers, highlighting areas for improvement.

Enhanced Communication: The visual nature of the canvas makes it an excellent tool for communicating your value proposition to stakeholders and aligning your team.

Iterative Improvement: The canvas is flexible and can be updated as customer needs and market conditions change, allowing for continuous refinement of your value proposition.

The Value Proposition Canvas is a powerful tool for ensuring that your innovation efforts are aligned with customer needs and desires. By thoroughly understanding the customer profile and mapping out how your product or service delivers value, you can create a compelling value proposition that resonates with your target audience.

I have found the Value Proposition Canvas to be an invaluable tool in various projects. It provides a structured approach to understanding customer needs and aligning your offerings to meet those needs effectively. Whether you are developing a new product or refining an existing service, the Value Proposition Canvas can help you create solutions that deliver real value and drive customer satisfaction.

By leveraging this tool, you can ensure that your innovations are not only creative but also meaningful and impactful. It's about putting the customer at the center of your innovation process and continuously striving to exceed their expectations.

Blue Ocean Strategy

The Blue Ocean Strategy is a groundbreaking approach to business strategy that emphasizes creating new market space, making the competition irrelevant, and driving value innovation. Developed by W. Chan Kim and Renée Mauborgne, this strategy helps businesses break away from the saturated "red oceans" of intense competition and venture into "blue oceans" of uncontested market space. By focusing on value innovation, companies can differentiate their offerings and create new demand, leading to significant growth and profitability.

Understanding Blue Ocean Strategy

The core idea behind Blue Ocean Strategy is to redefine market boundaries and create a unique space where competition is minimal or non-existent. This involves shifting focus from competing within existing market conditions to creating new opportunities that attract non-customers and generate new demand.

Creating Uncontested Market Space

One of the primary goals of Blue Ocean Strategy is to create uncontested market space. This is achieved by identifying and pursuing opportunities that have not yet been tapped by competitors. This approach allows companies to bypass intense competition and focus on areas where they can establish themselves as pioneers.

To illustrate the power of creating uncontested market space, let's look at the example of Cirque du Soleil. When Cirque du Soleil was founded in 1984, the circus industry was struggling with declining audiences and rising costs. Traditional circuses faced intense competition and had little differentiation. Instead of competing within this crowded space, Cirque du Soleil redefined the circus experience.

Cirque du Soleil combined elements of theater, dance, and music with traditional circus acts, creating a unique form of entertainment that appealed to a broader audience, including adults who typically did not attend traditional circuses. By creating this new market space, Cirque du Soleil made the competition irrelevant and attracted a completely new segment of customers.

Value Innovation

Value innovation is at the heart of Blue Ocean Strategy. It involves delivering exceptional value to customers while simultaneously reducing costs. This dual focus on value and cost sets Blue Ocean Strategy apart from traditional competitive strategies, which often involve trade-offs between differentiation and low cost.

Delivering Exceptional Value: Value innovation requires a deep understanding of customer needs and desires. Companies must identify the key factors that drive customer value and focus on enhancing those aspects.

This often involves rethinking traditional industry practices and finding innovative ways to deliver more value.

Reducing Costs: At the same time, companies must look for ways to reduce costs. This can involve streamlining operations, eliminating unnecessary features, or leveraging new technologies. The goal is to deliver a superior product or service at a lower cost, making it difficult for competitors to replicate.

Consider the example of Nintendo with its Wii gaming console. In the early 2000s, the video game industry was dominated by Sony and Microsoft, with their PlayStation and Xbox consoles focusing on high-performance graphics and processing power. Instead of competing directly, Nintendo created a new market space by focusing on motion-sensing gameplay and family-friendly entertainment.

The Wii's innovative motion-sensing technology offered a unique gaming experience that appealed to a broader audience, including non-gamers and older adults. At the same time, Nintendo kept production costs low by using less advanced hardware as compared to its competitors. This combination of value innovation allowed Nintendo to capture a new segment of the market and achieve significant success with the Wii.

Implementing Blue Ocean Strategy

Implementing Blue Ocean Strategy involves several key steps, each designed to help businesses identify and pursue new opportunities. These steps provide a structured approach to creating uncontested market space and driving value innovation.

1. Reconstruct Market Boundaries

The first step in Blue Ocean Strategy is to rethink and redefine market boundaries. This involves looking beyond traditional industry limits and exploring new possibilities. Companies can use the six paths framework to systematically search for opportunities:

- Look across alternative industries
- Look across strategic groups within industries
- Look across the chain of buyers
- Look across complementary product and service offerings
- Look across functional or emotional appeal to buyers
- Look across time

By applying these perspectives, companies can uncover new market spaces that competitors have overlooked.

2. Focus on the Big Picture

Instead of getting bogged down in detailed data and analysis, Blue Ocean Strategy emphasizes the importance of focusing on the big picture. This involves understanding the broader trends and shifts in the market and identifying how they can be leveraged to create new opportunities.

3. Reach Beyond Existing Demand

To create new market space, companies must reach beyond their existing customer base and attract non-customers. This involves understanding the needs and preferences of potential customers who are currently not served by the industry. By addressing the pain points and desires of these non-customers, companies can unlock new sources of demand.

4. Get the Strategic Sequence Right

Blue Ocean Strategy involves following a specific sequence of steps to ensure successful implementation. This includes creating a compelling value proposition, setting a strategic price, and aligning the entire business model to deliver on the value proposition. By carefully sequencing these steps, companies can maximize their chances of success.

A Live Example: Yellow Tail Wine

A compelling example of Blue Ocean Strategy in action is Yellow Tail wine, produced by the Australian company Casella Wines. When Yellow Tail entered the US wine market in the early 2000s, the industry was highly competitive, with numerous brands vying for market share. Traditional wine producers focused on complexity and connoisseurship, often alienating casual drinkers.

Instead of competing directly with established brands, Yellow Tail redefined the wine experience. They simplified their product offerings, focusing on easy-to-drink wines with a fun and approachable brand image. By targeting casual drinkers and making wine more accessible, Yellow Tail created a new market space within the wine industry.

Yellow Tail's value innovation included:

- *Simplified Product Line:* Yellow Tail offered a limited range of wines with straightforward, recognizable labels, making it easy for consumers to choose.
- *Affordable Pricing:* They priced their wines competitively, making them accessible to a broader audience.
- *Approachable Branding:* Yellow Tail's branding emphasized fun and enjoyment rather than sophistication and expertise, appealing to casual drinkers.

This approach allowed Yellow Tail to capture a significant share of the US wine market, becoming one of the top-selling wine brands in the country.

By creating uncontested market space and focusing on value innovation, Yellow Tail made the competition irrelevant and achieved remarkable success.

The Blue Ocean Strategy is a powerful framework for creating uncontested market space and driving value innovation. By focusing on delivering exceptional value to customers while simultaneously reducing costs, companies can differentiate their offerings and create new demand. The examples of Cirque du Soleil, Nintendo, and Yellow Tail demonstrate how this strategy can lead to significant growth and profitability.

I have seen firsthand how the principles of Blue Ocean Strategy can be applied to various industries and businesses. By rethinking market boundaries, focusing on the big picture, reaching beyond existing demand, and getting the strategic sequence right, you can create innovative solutions that resonate with customers and stand out in the market. Whether you're an entrepreneur launching a new venture or an established company seeking to innovate, Blue Ocean Strategy provides the tools and insights needed to achieve extraordinary results.

Innovation is not a distant goal, reserved for the few with extraordinary genius. It is a process, a mindset, and a commitment to continually push the boundaries of what is possible. The spark of an idea can come from anywhere—a casual conversation, a moment of curiosity, or a deep-seated desire to make a difference. What sets successful innovators apart is their willingness to nurture that spark, explore it from every angle, and bring it to life with passion and determination.

Your journey will not be without challenges. There will be moments of doubt, obstacles to overcome, and times when the path forward seems unclear. But it is in these moments that your resilience and creativity will shine the brightest. Embrace each challenge as an opportunity to learn and grow. Trust in your ability to navigate uncertainty and find innovative solutions that others might overlook.

"The future is yours to shape—dare to imagine, create, and innovate"

– Bob Philips –

Chapter 5

I - Implement: Turning Ideas Into Reality

- **The EXECUTE Principle.**
- **The OVERCOME Principle.**
- **Success Stories.**

Bringing ideas to life has always been one of the most exhilarating and challenging parts of my innovation journey. This chapter is close to my heart because it dives into the implementation phase—the moment where dreams change into reality, where meticulous plans start to take shape, and where you finally see tangible results from your hard work. Implementation is not just about executing a plan; it's about overcoming obstacles, adapting to new challenges, and celebrating every success along the way.

I'm going to share with you the strategies and insights that have guided me through the highs and lows of bringing ideas to life. There are two principles that I will share here and my goal is to provide you with the confidence you need to turn your innovative ideas into impactful realities.

Executing an idea is a meticulous process that requires planning, commitment, and adaptability. Here, I'd like to introduce you to a principle I follow called the EXECUTE Principles. These steps will guide you through turning your innovative ideas into actionable projects.

The EXECUTE Principles

E - Establish a Clear Vision

One of the most crucial steps in turning your innovative ideas into reality is establishing a clear vision. This vision acts as the foundation for every action you take moving forward. It's your North Star, guiding you through each phase of the implementation process and helping you stay focused and aligned.

Start by writing down your goals. Use SMART goals. When your goals are clearly defined, you can easily track your progress and make necessary adjustments along the way. This clarity also helps in communicating your vision to your team and stakeholders, ensuring that everyone is on the same page.

Now, let's take this a step further. Close your eyes and visualize your end goal. Picture it vividly in your mind. Imagine you've reached the pinnacle of success with your idea. How do you feel at that moment? What emotions are you experiencing? See your product or service fully realized, operating just as you envisioned. What does it look like? What features and benefits stand out? How are people interacting with it?

Next, visualize your customers. How are they responding to your product? Are they excited, satisfied, and eager to share their positive experiences? What feedback are they giving you? Imagine the impact your product is having on their lives. How has it made things better, easier, or more enjoyable for them?

Now, open your eyes and write down everything you just envisioned. Describe your feelings, the appearance and functionality of your product, and the reactions of your customers. Be as detailed and specific as possible. This exercise not only helps solidify your vision but also serves as a powerful motivator. It reminds you why you embarked on this journey in the first place and what you're working towards.

Having a clear vision is more than just knowing what you want to achieve; it's about feeling connected to your goal on an emotional level. This connection fuels your passion and determination, keeping you driven even when challenges arise. It also helps you make decisions that are aligned with your ultimate objective, ensuring that every step you take brings you closer to your vision.

When I first started my journey, I vividly remember envisioning the impact I wanted my innovations to have. I saw my products changing lives, solving problems, and creating value. This vision kept me motivated, guiding me through the complexities and uncertainties of the implementation process. It's what pushed me to refine my ideas, overcome obstacles, and celebrate the milestones along the way.

Establishing a clear vision is not a one-time task. It's an ongoing process of refining and reaffirming your goals. As you progress, revisit your vision regularly. Adjust it as necessary, and use it to stay aligned with your purpose. Your vision is your compass—keep it clear, keep it strong, and let it guide you to success.

X - eXpand with a Strategic Plan

Once you have a clear vision, the next crucial step is to expand it into a strategic plan. Think of your strategic plan as the roadmap to success, guiding you from where you are now to where you want to be. It breaks down your grand vision into smaller, manageable tasks and sets milestones to track progress along the way. This structured approach ensures that every step is purposeful and directed towards achieving your ultimate goal.

Start by identifying the major components of your vision. What are the key areas you need to focus on to bring your idea to life? These might include product development, market research, customer acquisition, or any other critical elements specific to your project. Break these components down into smaller tasks that are easier to manage and complete. This decomposition helps in making the seemingly overwhelming vision more attainable.

Setting milestones is an essential part of your strategic plan. Milestones are significant points in your project timeline that signify progress and achievement. They serve as checkpoints to ensure you are on track. Think of them as mini-goals that keep you motivated and provide a sense of accomplishment as you move forward. Make sure each milestone is clear, achievable, and directly aligned with your overall vision.

Timelines are another crucial aspect of your strategic plan. Assign deadlines to each task and milestone. This not only helps in maintaining momentum but also creates a sense of urgency and discipline. Be realistic with your timelines, considering the complexity of tasks and available resources. Remember, the goal is to make steady progress, not to rush and compromise on quality.

Resource allocation is a critical element of strategic planning. Identify the resources you will need for each task—whether it's financial, human, or technological resources. Ensure that you have everything you need to proceed efficiently. If certain resources are lacking, plan how to acquire them before they become bottlenecks. Effective resource management ensures that each part of your project is adequately supported and can move forward without unnecessary delays.

Assigning responsibilities is also key to a successful strategic plan. Clearly define who is responsible for each task and milestone. This clarity prevents confusion and ensures accountability. Each team member should understand their role and how it contributes to the overall vision. Encourage open communication and collaboration among team members to foster a supportive and cohesive working environment.

A well-structured strategic plan provides clarity and direction, ensuring everyone involved knows their roles and responsibilities. It translates your vision into actionable steps, making it easier to track progress and make adjustments as needed. It also helps in identifying potential risks and challenges early on, allowing you to develop contingency plans and stay prepared.

Reflecting on my own experiences, I can attest to the power of a strategic plan. When I first embarked on my journey, having a detailed roadmap was invaluable. It kept me focused, organized, and motivated. Each milestone reached was a reminder of progress, and each completed task brought me closer to my vision. The strategic plan acted as a guide, helping me navigate through complexities and uncertainties with confidence.

Remember, your strategic plan is a living document. As you progress, revisit and revise it regularly. Stay flexible and adapt to new insights or changes in circumstances. By expanding your vision with a strategic plan, you set yourself up for success, ensuring that every step you take is deliberate, informed, and aligned with your ultimate goals.

E - Engage the Right Team

Having the right team is absolutely crucial when it comes to turning innovative ideas into reality. Your vision, no matter how brilliant, needs the support and collaboration of a team with diverse skills and expertise. Engaging the right team can make the difference between success and stagnation.

First, it's essential to choose individuals who bring a variety of skills and perspectives to the table. Diversity in your team is not just about different professional backgrounds; it also includes diverse ways of thinking, problem-solving approaches, and personal experiences. This diversity fosters creativity and innovation, allowing for a richer pool of ideas and solutions. When assembling your team, look for people who excel in areas where you might need support, whether it's technical expertise, marketing savvy, or strategic thinking.

Passion is another key ingredient. Choose team members who are genuinely enthusiastic about the project. Passion drives commitment, and committed individuals are more likely to go the extra mile, especially when challenges arise. When people are passionate about what they do, their energy is contagious, creating a motivated and dynamic team environment.

Once you have your team, it's vital that each member understands the vision and their specific role in achieving it. Clearly communicate your vision, goals, and the importance of each role. This not only helps in aligning everyone's efforts but also fosters a sense of ownership and responsibility. When people understand how their work contributes to the bigger picture, they are more engaged and invested in the project's success.

Fostering a collaborative environment is essential for a productive team. Encourage open communication where everyone feels comfortable sharing their ideas, feedback, and concerns. Create an atmosphere of mutual respect, where each team member's contributions are valued. Collaboration thrives in an environment where people trust and respect one another, and where there is a shared commitment to the project's success.

Open communication is the backbone of effective teamwork. Regular team meetings, updates, and check-ins help keep everyone on the same page. Use collaborative tools and platforms that facilitate easy information sharing and real-time communication. Encourage team members to voice their opinions and suggestions, and listen actively. This not only helps in refining ideas but also builds a strong team dynamic where everyone feels heard and valued.

Mutual respect is another cornerstone of a strong team. Celebrate the unique strengths and contributions of each team member. Acknowledge and appreciate their efforts, and create opportunities for them to grow and shine. When people feel respected and appreciated, they are more likely to be motivated and engaged.

Reflecting on my own experiences, I've seen firsthand the impact of having the right team. In one of my early projects, the diversity of skills and perspectives within the team was a game-changer. Each member brought something unique to the table, and together, we were able to navigate challenges and come up with innovative solutions that I couldn't have achieved alone. The passion and commitment of the team kept us going, even during the toughest times.

Remember, building the right team is an ongoing process. As your project evolves, so might your team's needs. Stay attuned to the dynamics within your team, and be prepared to make adjustments as necessary. Investing time and effort in engaging the right team pays off immensely in the long run.

By engaging the right team, you create a solid foundation for your project's success. Your team's diverse skills, passion, and collaborative spirit will drive the implementation process, turning your innovative ideas into reality. Embrace the journey with your team, and together, you'll achieve extraordinary results.

C - Consolidate Resources

Once you have your vision set, a strategic plan in place, and the right team engaged, the next crucial step is to consolidate your resources. This is about gathering and securing everything you need to turn your innovative idea into reality. Resources come in many forms, including financial backing, technology, tools, and materials. Being strategic in how you allocate these resources is essential to ensuring every aspect of your project is adequately supported.

Start by identifying the key resources you will need. Financial resources are often at the top of the list. This could include securing funding through investors, loans, grants, or internal budgeting. Understanding your financial requirements and planning your budget meticulously can prevent many problems down the line. Ensure you have a clear picture of your financial landscape, including potential costs, revenue streams, and contingencies for unexpected expenses.

Technology and tools are another critical area. Depending on your project, this might involve specific software, hardware, or specialized equipment. Make a comprehensive list of the technological resources you need and ensure they are readily available when required. Investing in the right technology can significantly enhance efficiency and effectiveness, so choose tools that align well with your project's needs.

In addition to technology, consider the materials and supplies necessary for your project. This could range from raw materials for manufacturing to office supplies for day-to-day operations. Having a clear inventory of required materials and a reliable supply chain is crucial to avoid any disruptions during the implementation phase.

Be strategic in how you allocate your resources. Not every part of your project will require the same level of support, so prioritize accordingly. Focus on areas that are critical to your project's success and allocate resources to ensure these areas are robustly supported. For example, if product development is key to your innovation, channel more resources into R&D and prototyping. On the other hand, if market penetration is your main challenge, allocate more resources to marketing and sales efforts.

Resource allocation is not a one-time task. It requires continuous monitoring and adjustment. As your project progresses, you may find certain areas need more support while others require less. Stay flexible and be prepared to reallocate resources as needed to address emerging challenges and opportunities.

One effective strategy is to create a resource management plan. This plan outlines how resources will be allocated, monitored, and adjusted throughout the project lifecycle. It serves as a reference point to ensure that you are on track and helps make informed decisions when adjustments are necessary.

In my experience, consolidating resources effectively can make or break a project. I remember a time when we underestimated the technological resources needed for a particular innovation. This oversight caused significant delays and setbacks. However, by quickly recognizing the gap and reallocating resources, we were able to get back on track. This experience underscored the importance of thorough resource planning and the ability to adapt quickly.

Lastly, don't hesitate to seek external support if needed. This could involve partnerships, collaborations, or outsourcing certain tasks. Leveraging external resources can provide additional expertise and capacity, ensuring your project is well-supported.

By consolidating resources effectively, you lay a strong foundation for the successful implementation of your innovative ideas. Ensure every aspect of your project is adequately supported, and remain agile in your approach to resource management. With the right resources in place, you can confidently move forward, knowing you have the necessary tools and support to bring your vision to life.

U - Utilize Prototyping

Prototyping is one of the most vital steps in turning your innovative ideas into reality. It's where your concept begins to take a tangible form, allowing you to test its feasibility and functionality. Creating a preliminary model or version of your product or service can reveal insights that are not apparent during the planning stages. This hands-on approach is essential for identifying potential issues early and making necessary adjustments before you move to full-scale implementation.

Start by developing a basic prototype that captures the core elements of your idea. This doesn't have to be a fully developed product; it can be a simple model or a mock-up that demonstrates the key features and functionality. The goal is to bring your idea to life in a way that allows you and others to interact with it, providing a concrete basis for feedback and improvement.

Once you have your prototype, put it to the test. Gather a diverse group of testers who can provide different perspectives and insights. These could be potential customers, team members, or industry experts. Encourage them to use the prototype as they would in a real-world setting and observe their interactions closely. Take note of any issues they encounter, questions they have, or suggestions they offer. This feedback is invaluable for refining your prototype.

Prototyping is not just about identifying flaws; it's also an opportunity to explore new possibilities. Sometimes, the act of creating and testing a prototype can spark fresh ideas and inspire further innovation. Don't be afraid to experiment with different approaches and configurations. The iterative nature of prototyping means that each version of your prototype should be better than the last, gradually evolving into a more polished and effective product.

Incorporate the feedback you receive into the next iteration of your prototype. Address any issues that were identified and make improvements based on the suggestions and observations. This process of continuous refinement ensures that your final product is well-tested and optimized for success. Remember, the earlier you catch and fix problems, the less costly and time-consuming it will be to address them later.

Prototyping also helps build confidence among your stakeholders. When investors, partners, or customers can see and interact with a tangible representation of your idea, it becomes easier for them to understand its value and potential. A well-developed prototype can serve as a powerful tool for securing support and buy-in, demonstrating your commitment and progress in a concrete way.

Reflecting on my own journey, I recall a project where prototyping was a game-changer. We had a concept that looked perfect on paper, but when we created the first prototype, several practical issues emerged. Through multiple iterations and extensive testing, we were able to refine the product, resulting in a final version that was far superior to our initial concept. This experience underscored the importance of prototyping and the value of an iterative, hands-on approach.

Utilize prototyping not just as a step in your process, but as an integral part of your innovation journey. Embrace the opportunity to learn, adapt, and improve. With each iteration, your idea will become more robust and ready for full-scale implementation. Prototyping bridges the gap between concept and reality, ensuring that when you finally launch your product or service, it is well-tested, refined, and poised for success.

T - Test with Phased Implementation

Implementing your project in phases is a strategic approach to managing risk and ensuring quality. This methodical process allows you to test your concept on a smaller scale before committing to full-scale implementation, providing invaluable insights and minimizing potential setbacks.

Start with a pilot phase. This is your opportunity to test the waters with your innovative idea. By launching a limited version of your product or service, you can gather critical data and observe how it performs in a real-world setting. The pilot phase is not just a trial run; it's a learning experience. It allows you to identify any issues or challenges early on, giving you the chance to make necessary adjustments before a broader rollout.

During the pilot phase, focus on gathering as much data as possible. Track key performance indicators (KPIs) that are relevant to your project's success. This could include user engagement, customer satisfaction, operational efficiency, or any other metrics that provide insight into how well your idea is functioning. Collect feedback from users and stakeholders to understand their experiences and gather suggestions for improvement. This feedback is a goldmine of information that can guide your next steps.

Use the insights gained from the pilot phase to refine your approach. Analyze the data and feedback to identify patterns and pinpoint areas that need improvement. This might involve tweaking certain features, addressing unforeseen issues, or enhancing aspects that received positive responses. The goal is to optimize your product or service based on real-world performance, ensuring it meets the needs and expectations of your target audience.

As you make adjustments, prepare for the next phase of implementation. Gradually scale up your project, expanding its reach and impact. This could mean increasing the number of users, entering new markets, or enhancing the product's functionality. Each phase of expansion should be informed by the lessons learned from the previous one, ensuring that you build on a solid foundation.

Phased implementation also allows you to manage resources more effectively. By starting small, you can allocate resources judiciously and avoid the risk of overextending yourself too soon. As confidence in your project grows with each successful phase, you can invest more heavily, knowing that your approach is validated and refined.

This approach is not just about mitigating risks; it's about enhancing quality. By iterating through phases, you continually improve and fine-tune your product or service. This iterative process helps you deliver a final offering that is well-tested, polished, and ready to meet the demands of a larger audience.

Reflecting on my own experiences, I've seen the power of phased implementation firsthand. In one particular project, we launched a pilot phase to test a new training module. The initial feedback revealed several areas for improvement that we hadn't anticipated. By addressing these issues early, we were able to enhance the module significantly before rolling it out to a wider audience. This phased approach not only improved the quality of the final product but also boosted our confidence in its success.

Testing with phased implementation is a disciplined approach that balances ambition with practicality. It allows you to manage risks, ensure quality, and gather valuable insights at every step. By starting with a pilot phase and gradually scaling up, you create a pathway to success that is informed, strategic, and adaptable. Embrace this method to turn your innovative ideas into impactful realities, one phase at a time.

E - Evaluate and Adjust

Continuous evaluation and adjustment are fundamental to the successful implementation of any innovative idea. It's not enough to simply set a plan in motion; you must consistently monitor progress, gather feedback, and be prepared to make necessary changes. This ongoing process ensures that your project stays on track and can adapt to any challenges or changes that arise.

Start by tracking your progress against the milestones you've established. These milestones act as checkpoints, allowing you to assess whether you are on the right path and making the desired progress. Regularly reviewing these benchmarks helps identify any deviations from the plan early, giving you the chance to address issues before they become major obstacles.

Gathering feedback is an integral part of the evaluation process. Feedback can come from various sources: your team, stakeholders, customers, or any other parties involved in the project. Encourage open and honest communication to gain valuable insights into what's working well and what needs improvement. This feedback provides a reality check, helping you see the project from different perspectives and uncovering areas you might have overlooked.

Flexibility and adaptability are crucial qualities during implementation.

Even with the best-laid plans, unforeseen challenges and changes in circumstances are inevitable. Whether it's a shift in market dynamics, technological advancements, or unexpected internal issues, being rigid in your approach can lead to setbacks. Instead, embrace a flexible mindset and be ready to pivot when necessary. This might involve reassigning resources, modifying timelines, or even altering the project's direction to better align with new realities.

Consider this flexibility as a strength rather than a weakness. Being adaptable allows you to respond proactively to changes, turning potential disruptions into opportunities for improvement. It ensures that your project remains relevant and resilient, capable of navigating the unpredictable landscape of innovation.

Reflecting on my journey, there were numerous instances where evaluation and adjustment were pivotal to success. One project, in particular, required multiple iterations and feedback loops. Initially, we faced significant hurdles that threatened to derail our progress. However, by continuously monitoring our performance and seeking feedback, we were able to identify critical issues and make timely adjustments. This iterative process ultimately led to a much stronger and more successful outcome than if we had stuck rigidly to our original plan.

Regular evaluation also involves celebrating progress. Acknowledge the milestones you've achieved and the improvements you've made along the way. Celebrating small wins boosts morale and keeps the team motivated. It also reinforces the importance of the continuous improvement process, highlighting that every step forward, no matter how small, is valuable.

Documenting your evaluation and adjustment process is equally important. Keeping detailed records of the feedback received, changes made, and the reasons behind these adjustments provides a valuable reference for future projects. It builds a repository of knowledge and lessons learned, which can guide you in refining your approaches and avoiding past mistakes.

In conclusion, the principle of Evaluate and Adjust is about embracing a dynamic and responsive approach to implementation. Continuous monitoring, gathering feedback, and being prepared to adapt are essential practices that ensure your innovative ideas not only survive but thrive. By remaining flexible and open to change, you can navigate challenges effectively and steer your project toward success. Remember, innovation is a journey, and the ability to evaluate and adjust is what keeps you moving forward, no matter what obstacles you encounter along the way.

The EXECUTE principles serve as your trusted guide in bringing innovative ideas to life. These steps are not just processes but a mindset—a commitment to excellence and adaptability. As you begin your implementation journey, let these principles inspire confidence and drive. Follow each step with passion and determination, knowing that you have the tools to turn your innovative dreams into achievements.

The OVERCOME Principles

Now, let's move to the next principle. Overcoming challenges in innovation demands resilience, strategic thinking, and adaptability. Here, I'd like to introduce you to a principle I follow called the OVERCOME Principles. These strategies will help you navigate obstacles and ensure the successful implementation of your innovative ideas.

O - Open Communication

Resistance to change is a common obstacle that can hinder the implementation of innovative ideas. People naturally resist altering their routines and stepping out of their comfort zones. To overcome this resistance, open communication is key. It's crucial to communicate the benefits of the change clearly and involve stakeholders in the process from the beginning. This approach helps in building trust, understanding, and commitment, which are essential for a smooth transition.

Start by clearly articulating the reasons behind the change and the benefits it will bring. People need to understand why the change is necessary and how it will positively impact them and the organization. Highlight the advantages, such as improved efficiency, better performance, enhanced job satisfaction, or long-term growth. Use specific examples and data to support your message, making it more relatable and convincing. The goal is to create a shared vision that everyone can buy into and support.

Involving stakeholders in the change process is another critical aspect of open communication. When people feel included, and their opinions are valued, they are more likely to support the change. Engage stakeholders early on by seeking their input and feedback. This can be done through meetings, surveys, or informal conversations. Listen to their concerns and address them thoughtfully. By involving stakeholders, you also gain valuable insights and ideas that can improve the implementation process.

Providing training and support is essential to help people adapt to the new way of doing things. Change often requires new skills or knowledge, and without proper training, employees may feel overwhelmed and resistant. Develop a comprehensive training program that addresses the specific needs of your team. This could include workshops, online courses, or one-on-one coaching sessions. Ensure that the training is accessible and practical, enabling employees to apply what they learn effectively.

Support goes beyond training. Be available to answer questions and provide guidance as needed. Create a support system where employees can seek help without hesitation. This could be in the form of a help desk, peer support groups, or regular check-ins with managers. Recognize and reward efforts and progress, no matter how small, to encourage a positive attitude towards the change.

Open communication also involves being transparent about the challenges and setbacks that may arise. Honesty fosters trust and shows that you are committed to navigating the change together. Share updates regularly and keep the lines of communication open. Encourage a culture where feedback is welcomed and acted upon. This continuous loop of communication helps in maintaining momentum and addressing issues promptly.

I have seen the power of open communication in overcoming resistance to change. In one project, we faced significant pushback from stakeholders who were skeptical about a new technology we were introducing. By taking the time to explain the benefits, involving them in the process, and providing thorough data, training and support, we were able to turn resistance into enthusiasm. The open communication fostered a sense of ownership and commitment, ultimately leading to a successful implementation.

Open communication is the foundation for overcoming resistance to change. By clearly communicating the benefits, involving stakeholders, providing training and support, and maintaining transparency, you can build a supportive environment where change is embraced rather than resisted. Embrace open communication as a powerful tool to navigate the challenges of innovation and ensure the successful implementation of your ideas.

V - Value Resources

Resource constraints are a common challenge when implementing innovative ideas. Whether it's a lack of funds, time, or manpower, these limitations can present significant barriers to progress. To navigate these obstacles, it's essential to value and optimize your resources. This involves prioritizing your needs, seeking creative solutions, and making the most of what you have.

First, take a comprehensive inventory of your available resources. Identify what you have in terms of financial capital, human resources, and time. Understanding your baseline is crucial for effective planning and prioritization. Once you have a clear picture of your resources, prioritize your needs based on your project's goals and critical milestones. Focus on the most impactful areas that will drive your project forward. This strategic prioritization ensures that you allocate resources where they are needed most.

Reallocating existing resources can also help address constraints. Sometimes, shifting resources from less critical areas to more pressing needs can make a significant difference. Evaluate your current allocations and identify areas where resources can be redirected without compromising overall operations. This might involve reassigning team members to higher-priority tasks or adjusting budget allocations to support essential activities.

Seeking external funding is another way to overcome resource limitations. This could include applying for grants, securing investments, or exploring crowdfunding options. Each of these avenues has its own set of requirements and potential benefits. Grants often come with specific criteria and reporting requirements but can provide substantial financial support. Investment from venture capitalists or angel investors can bring not only funds but also valuable expertise and networking opportunities. Crowdfunding allows you to engage directly with your potential customers, generating both financial support and market validation.

Leveraging partnerships can also be a powerful strategy. Collaborating with other organizations, institutions, or even individuals can provide access to additional resources and capabilities. For instance, partnering with a tech company might give you access to cutting-edge technology and expertise that you otherwise couldn't afford. Academic partnerships can provide research support and fresh perspectives, while collaborations with non-profits can open doors to grants and additional funding sources.

Innovation often requires thinking outside the box, especially when resources are limited. Explore creative solutions that maximize the impact of your available resources. This might involve adopting lean methodologies to streamline processes and reduce waste, or using open-source tools and technologies to minimize costs. Embrace the mindset of doing more with less and look for ways to innovate within your constraints.

I've faced numerous instances where resource constraints seemed insurmountable. One particular project comes to mind where we were operating on a tight budget with limited manpower. By prioritizing our needs, reallocating existing resources, and seeking external funding, we were able to move forward. Additionally, forming strategic partnerships provided us with access to expertise and technology that were pivotal to our success. These experiences taught me the value of resourcefulness and creativity in overcoming limitations.

Ultimately, valuing resources is about being strategic, innovative, and adaptable. It requires a keen understanding of what you have, a clear prioritization of needs, and a willingness to explore unconventional solutions. By effectively managing and optimizing your resources, you can navigate the challenges of implementation and bring your innovative ideas to life. Embrace the mindset of resourcefulness, and you'll find that even with limited resources, you can achieve remarkable results.

E - Establish Clarity

A lack of clarity in objectives can easily lead to confusion and misalignment within your team. When goals and expectations are not clearly defined, it becomes difficult for everyone to work cohesively towards the same vision. Establishing clarity is crucial to ensure that all team members are aligned, motivated, and focused on achieving the common goal.

Start by clearly defining your objectives. What are you aiming to achieve? Break down your overarching vision into specific, actionable goals. Each goal should be precise and well-articulated, leaving no room for ambiguity. When everyone understands what the targets are, it becomes easier to develop strategies and tasks that directly contribute to achieving these goals.

Once your objectives are defined, communicate them effectively to your team. Use various communication channels—meetings, emails, and project management tools—to ensure that everyone is on the same page. During these communications, encourage questions and discussions to clarify any doubts. This open dialogue helps in ensuring that everyone fully understands the objectives and their roles in achieving them.

It's not enough to communicate your objectives just once. Regularly revisit and reaffirm these goals to maintain focus and direction. In the fast-paced world of innovation, priorities can shift, and new challenges can arise. By consistently reviewing your objectives, you can adjust your strategies and keep your team aligned with the overall vision. Regular check-ins and progress meetings are effective ways to reaffirm goals and address any emerging issues.

Visual aids can also play a significant role in establishing clarity. Use charts, diagrams, and timelines to map out your objectives and the steps needed to achieve them. These visual tools can provide a clear and concise representation of the project's direction, making it easier for everyone to grasp the plan and stay focused on their tasks.

Clarity in roles and responsibilities is equally important. Each team member should know exactly what is expected of them and how their work contributes to the larger goal. Define roles clearly and ensure that there is no overlap or confusion about who is responsible for what. This clarity not only improves efficiency but also fosters a sense of ownership and accountability.

Another aspect of establishing clarity is setting clear expectations for performance and outcomes. Define what success looks like for each objective and how progress will be measured. This helps in keeping everyone focused on the desired results and provides a benchmark for evaluating performance. Regular feedback and performance reviews can help in ensuring that everyone stays on track and meets the set expectations.

Reflecting on my own experiences, I've learned that clarity is a cornerstone of successful implementation. There have been times when projects faced delays and setbacks simply because the objectives were not clearly communicated. However, once we took the time to define and communicate our goals effectively, the team became more aligned, motivated, and productive. This clarity helped us navigate challenges and stay focused on our vision.

Establishing clarity is not just a one-time task; it's an ongoing process. As your project evolves, new objectives may emerge, and existing ones may need to be adjusted. Stay proactive in communicating these changes and ensuring that everyone remains aligned. By maintaining a clear and consistent focus on your goals, you can drive your team toward success and turn your innovative ideas into impactful realities.

Establishing clarity in your objectives and expectations is vital for effective implementation. It ensures that everyone understands the goals, knows their roles, and stays focused on the desired outcomes. Embrace clarity as a fundamental principle, and you will create a cohesive, motivated, and productive team capable of achieving great things.

R - Rigorous Planning

Inadequate planning can easily derail even the most promising implementation efforts. A solid, comprehensive plan is the backbone of successful execution. Rigorous planning ensures that all aspects of the project are addressed, potential risks are anticipated, and clear milestones are established. This meticulous approach provides a roadmap that keeps everyone on track and focused on the end goal.

Start by developing a detailed project plan. This plan should cover every facet of your project, from initial stages to final implementation. Break down the project into manageable phases and outline the tasks required for each phase. This helps in understanding the scope of the project and allocating resources effectively. Ensure that each task is clearly defined, with specific objectives and expected outcomes.

Establishing a timeline is crucial. Create a schedule that includes all the major milestones and deadlines. These milestones serve as checkpoints to measure progress and ensure that the project is moving in the right direction. Be realistic with your timelines, considering the complexity of tasks and the availability of resources. A well-structured timeline helps in maintaining momentum and provides a clear path to follow.

Contingency planning is an essential part of rigorous planning. No matter how well you plan, unexpected challenges and risks can arise. Identify potential risks and develop contingency plans to address them. This might involve having backup resources, alternative strategies, or flexibility in timelines. Being prepared for unforeseen events ensures that you can navigate challenges without derailing the entire project.

Regularly review and update your plan. The implementation phase is dynamic, and circumstances can change. Regular check-ins and progress reviews allow you to assess where you stand, identify any deviations from the plan, and make necessary adjustments. This continuous evaluation keeps the project aligned with its goals and allows for timely interventions to address any issues.

Communication is key to effective planning. Ensure that all team members are aware of the plan, their roles, and the timelines. Use project management tools to share the plan and track progress. Regular meetings and updates help maintain transparency and keep everyone on the same page. Encourage team members to provide feedback and raise any concerns they might have. This open communication fosters collaboration and ensures that everyone is working towards the same objectives.

Reflecting on my own experiences, rigorous planning has always been a cornerstone of successful projects. I recall a particularly complex project where meticulous planning made all the difference. By breaking down the project into detailed phases, establishing clear milestones, and preparing for potential risks, we were able to navigate challenges and stay on track. The regular reviews and updates ensured that we adapted to changes effectively, ultimately leading to a successful outcome.

Moreover, rigorous planning instills confidence among stakeholders. When you present a well-thought-out plan, it demonstrates that you have thoroughly considered all aspects of the project and are prepared for potential challenges. This builds trust and support, which are crucial for successful implementation.

Rigorous planning is essential for the successful implementation of innovative ideas. It provides a clear roadmap, anticipates risks, and establishes milestones to measure progress. By continuously reviewing and updating the plan, you ensure that the project stays on track and adapts to changing circumstances. Make rigorous planning as a fundamental principle, and you'll create a solid foundation for turning your innovative visions into reality.

C - Clear Communication

Clear communication is the lifeblood of successful implementation. Poor communication can lead to misunderstandings, delays, and frustration, all of which can derail your project. Fostering a culture of open communication where feedback is encouraged and valued is essential for maintaining alignment and momentum. Using the right tools and platforms can facilitate effective information sharing and collaboration, ensuring that everyone is on the same page.

Start by setting the tone for open communication. Encourage your team to share their thoughts, ideas, and concerns freely. When team members feel heard and valued, they are more likely to engage actively and contribute to the project's success. Create an environment where feedback is not only accepted but sought after. This open dialogue helps identify potential issues early and find collaborative solutions.

Establish regular communication channels. Weekly meetings, daily check-ins, and progress reports can help maintain transparency and keep everyone updated on the project's status. Use these opportunities to address any questions or concerns, celebrate milestones, and realign on goals. Regular communication ensures that everyone remains focused and motivated, reducing the chances of misunderstandings and misalignment.

Choosing the right tools and platforms is crucial for facilitating effective communication. Project management tools like Asana, Trello, or Jira can help track progress, assign tasks, and share updates. Communication platforms like Slack or Microsoft Teams allow for real-time messaging and collaboration. These tools provide a centralized place for information, making it easier for team members to access the data they need and stay informed.

Visual aids can also enhance communication. Use charts, graphs, and dashboards to present complex information in a clear and concise manner. Visual representations can help team members understand project status, identify bottlenecks, and track progress at a glance. This clarity reduces confusion and helps everyone stay aligned with the project's goals.

Encourage transparency in all communications. Be open about challenges and setbacks, and discuss how the team can address them together. This honesty builds trust and fosters a collaborative spirit. When team members feel that they are part of the solution, they are more likely to take ownership and contribute proactively.

Another important aspect of clear communication is active listening. Encourage your team to listen to each other's ideas and feedback without judgment. Active listening promotes understanding and empathy, creating a supportive and cohesive team dynamic. It ensures that all voices are heard and that the best ideas can emerge from collective input.

I have seen the impactful power of clear communication. In one project, a breakdown in communication led to significant delays and frustration. By implementing regular check-ins, using effective communication tools, and fostering an open environment, we were able to turn the situation around. The team became more cohesive, aligned, and motivated, ultimately leading to a successful project outcome.

Regularly revisit and refine your communication strategies. As the project evolves, so might the communication needs. Stay flexible and adapt your methods to ensure that they remain effective. Continuously seek feedback on how communication can be improved and make adjustments as needed.

Clear communication is essential for the successful implementation of innovative ideas. By fostering a culture of open communication, using the right tools, and encouraging active listening, you can prevent misunderstandings and keep the project on track. Make clear communication a core principle, and you'll create a collaborative and motivated team capable of achieving remarkable results.

O - Ownership and Accountability

Ownership and accountability are critical for the successful implementation of any project. Without clear roles and responsibilities, tasks can fall through the cracks, progress can stall, and the overall project can suffer. By fostering a culture of accountability, you ensure that everyone is committed to their contributions and aligned with the project's goals.

Start by clearly defining roles and responsibilities. Each team member should know exactly what is expected of them and how their work contributes to the overall success of the project. This clarity helps prevent overlap and confusion, allowing everyone to focus on their specific tasks. When people understand their roles, they can take ownership of their work, which increases motivation and engagement.

Assigning roles is just the beginning. It's essential to communicate these responsibilities clearly to the entire team. Use project management tools to document and share this information, making it accessible to everyone involved. When team members can see how their work fits into the bigger picture, it fosters a sense of accountability and ownership.

Regular check-ins and progress reviews are vital for maintaining accountability. These meetings provide an opportunity to assess how well tasks are being executed, address any challenges, and realign efforts if necessary. Use these sessions to review progress against milestones and deadlines, ensuring that everyone is on track. Celebrate achievements and recognize those who are meeting or exceeding their commitments, as this positive reinforcement encourages continued accountability.

Holding team members accountable doesn't mean micromanaging them.

Instead, it's about creating a supportive environment where individuals feel responsible for their contributions and understand the importance of their role. Encourage team members to set personal goals and track their own progress. This self-monitoring approach fosters a sense of ownership and helps individuals stay committed to their tasks.

Encourage open communication about challenges and obstacles. When team members encounter difficulties, they should feel comfortable discussing these issues without fear of blame. This transparency allows for collaborative problem-solving and ensures that the team can address issues promptly. By tackling challenges together, you reinforce a culture of accountability and support.

In one project, we implemented a system where each team member was responsible for specific deliverables, with clear deadlines and regular check-ins. This approach not only kept everyone on track but also empowered individuals to take pride in their work. The sense of ownership led to higher-quality outputs and a more cohesive team effort.

It's also important to provide the necessary resources and support for team members to fulfill their responsibilities. Ensure that everyone has the tools, training, and information they need to succeed. When people feel equipped and supported, they are more likely to take ownership of their tasks and deliver their best work.

Accountability should be a two-way street. As a leader, demonstrate accountability by following through on your commitments and being transparent about your own progress. This sets a positive example and reinforces the importance of accountability within the team.

Fostering a culture of ownership and accountability is essential for effective project implementation. Clearly define roles and responsibilities, maintain regular check-ins and progress reviews, and encourage open communication about challenges. By doing so, you create an environment where everyone feels responsible for their contributions and motivated to achieve the project's goals. Prioritize ownership and accountability, and you'll build a committed and high-performing team capable of delivering outstanding results.

M - Manage Technology

Technology can be both an enabler and a barrier in the implementation of innovative ideas. It has the power to streamline processes, enhance communication, and improve productivity. However, if not managed properly, it can also create hurdles and slow down progress. To ensure that technology serves as a helpful tool rather than a hindrance, it's crucial to choose the right technology, provide adequate training, and be prepared to address any technical issues that may arise.

Start by ensuring that the technology you choose aligns with your project's needs and your team's capabilities. Conduct thorough research to identify tools and systems that match your requirements. Consider factors such as ease of use, scalability, and compatibility with existing systems. The goal is to select technology that simplifies tasks and enhances efficiency rather than adding unnecessary complexity. Involve your team in the selection process to gather their input and ensure that the chosen technology meets their needs as well.

Once the appropriate technology is selected, provide comprehensive training to your team members. Even the most advanced tools are only as effective as the people using them. Develop a training program that covers all aspects of the new technology, from basic functions to advanced features. Ensure that the training is practical and hands-on, allowing team members to familiarize themselves with the technology in a real-world context. Offer ongoing support and resources, such as user manuals, tutorials, and help desks, to assist team members as they adapt to the new tools.

Regularly scheduled training sessions can also be beneficial, especially if the technology evolves or new features are added. Keeping your team updated on the latest developments ensures they can make the most of the technology and remain efficient in their work. Encourage team members to share their experiences and tips, fostering a collaborative learning environment where everyone can benefit from each other's insights.

Be prepared to troubleshoot and address any technical issues that arise. Technical glitches are inevitable, but how you handle them can make a significant difference. Establish a clear protocol for reporting and resolving technical problems. Ensure that you have access to technical support, whether it's through an in-house IT team or external service providers. Quick and effective resolution of technical issues minimizes downtime and keeps the project moving forward.

In addition to troubleshooting, regularly review and evaluate the technology's performance. Assess whether it continues to meet your needs and identify any areas for improvement. This continuous evaluation helps you stay ahead of potential issues and ensures that the technology remains a valuable asset to your project.

An example from my own experience involved a project where we implemented a new project management software. Initially, the team faced difficulties adapting to the new system, leading to delays and frustration. However, by providing comprehensive training and setting up a robust support system, we were able to overcome these challenges. The technology eventually became an integral part of our workflow, significantly improving our efficiency and collaboration.

Effective technology management also involves being adaptable. Be open to upgrading or changing technology if it no longer serves your needs. The digital landscape is constantly evolving, and staying current with the latest advancements can provide a competitive edge. However, ensure that any transitions are smooth and well-planned to avoid disruption.

Managing technology effectively is crucial for the successful implementation of innovative projects. By choosing the right technology, providing adequate training, and being prepared to troubleshoot issues, you can ensure that technology acts as an enabler rather than a barrier. Foster a culture of continuous learning and adaptability, and you'll harness the full potential of technology to drive your projects to success.

E - Embrace Flexibility

Market conditions can change rapidly, presenting challenges to the implementation of your innovative ideas. Staying informed about market trends and being ready to adapt your strategy is essential for navigating these uncertainties. Embracing flexibility and agility ensures that your project remains relevant and resilient in the face of changing circumstances.

Start by cultivating a mindset of flexibility within your team. Encourage an environment where change is viewed as an opportunity rather than a threat. This mindset allows your team to remain open to new ideas and approaches, making it easier to pivot when necessary. Emphasize the importance of staying informed about market trends and developments. Regularly review industry reports, attend relevant conferences, and engage with experts to keep your finger on the pulse of the market.

Having a flexible strategy means being prepared to adjust your plans based on new information. Develop a strategic framework that allows for iterative planning and continuous improvement. This approach involves setting short-term goals and regularly evaluating progress, making adjustments as needed. By breaking down your long-term vision into manageable phases, you can remain agile and responsive to market changes.

Scenario planning is a valuable tool for embracing flexibility. Consider different potential market scenarios and develop contingency plans for each. This proactive approach helps you anticipate potential challenges and prepare for various outcomes. By thinking ahead and exploring different possibilities, you can make informed decisions and reduce the impact of unforeseen changes.

Communication plays a crucial role in maintaining flexibility. Keep an open line of communication with your team, stakeholders, and customers. Regular updates and feedback sessions ensure that everyone is aware of any changes and understands the reasons behind them. Transparent communication builds trust and fosters a collaborative spirit, making it easier to implement adjustments smoothly.

Reflecting on my experiences, there was a project where market conditions shifted significantly midway through implementation. By maintaining a flexible approach and encouraging open communication, we were able to adapt our strategy effectively. We held regular team meetings to discuss the latest market trends and brainstorm potential adjustments. This collective effort allowed us to stay ahead of the curve and successfully navigate the changing landscape.

Flexibility also involves being willing to experiment and take calculated risks. Encourage your team to test new ideas and approaches, even if they deviate from the original plan. This experimental mindset fosters innovation and can lead to unexpected breakthroughs. Celebrate the learning that comes from both successes and failures, as each provides valuable insights that can inform future strategies.

Being agile doesn't mean abandoning your core vision; it means being adaptable in your approach to achieving it. Keep your long-term goals in mind, but be open to changing the path to reach them. This balance between steadfastness and adaptability is key to sustaining progress in a dynamic market.

In conclusion, embracing flexibility is essential for successfully implementing innovative ideas in a rapidly changing market. By staying informed about market trends, fostering a mindset of adaptability, and maintaining open communication, you can navigate uncertainties and keep your project on track. Embrace flexibility as a core principle, and you'll be better equipped to turn challenges into opportunities and drive your project to success.

The OVERCOME principles are your blueprint for navigating the inevitable challenges that arise during the implementation of innovative ideas. By focusing on this principle, you can build a resilient and adaptable framework for success. These strategies are not just about overcoming obstacles but about turning them into opportunities for growth and improvement. As you move forward, let these principles guide and inspire you, knowing that with the right mindset and approach, you can overcome any challenge and turn your innovative visions into reality.

Success Stories of Effective Execution

To inspire you and illustrate the power of effective execution, I'd like to share some success stories that highlight how innovative ideas were successfully implemented, leading to remarkable impact and growth. These examples showcase real-world applications of the principles we've discussed, demonstrating how overcoming challenges and executing solutions effectively can turn visionary ideas into game-changing realities.

Zoom: Revolutionizing Communication

The story of Zoom Video Communications is a powerful example of how innovative execution can lead to significant success. Founded by Eric Yuan in 2011, Zoom entered the highly competitive market of video conferencing, which already had established players like Skype and WebEx. However, Yuan's vision and dedication to addressing common pain points in video communication set Zoom apart and ultimately changed the way we connect virtually.

Yuan, a former lead engineer at WebEx, was acutely aware of the limitations and frustrations users experienced with existing video conferencing tools. Frequent call drops, poor video quality, and complicated interfaces made remote communication cumbersome. Yuan's goal with Zoom was simple yet ambitious: to create a video conferencing solution that was reliable, easy to use, and provided high-quality video and audio.

From the outset, Yuan prioritized understanding user needs. He and his team engaged in extensive user research, gathering feedback from individuals and businesses to identify the most critical pain points. This user-centric approach informed Zoom's design and functionality, ensuring that the platform addressed the real-world challenges faced by its users.

One of Zoom's standout features was its user-friendly interface. Unlike many of its competitors, Zoom was designed to be intuitive and easy to navigate, even for those who were not tech-savvy. This simplicity, combined with robust performance, made Zoom an attractive option for a wide range of users, from small businesses to large enterprises.

Zoom also invested heavily in developing innovative features that enhanced the user experience. High-definition video, noise suppression, and virtual backgrounds were just a few of the features that set Zoom apart from other video conferencing tools. Additionally, Zoom's ability to support large-scale meetings and webinars made it a versatile solution for various use cases, from one-on-one meetings to large corporate events.

Despite entering a crowded market, Zoom's commitment to continuous improvement and user satisfaction drove its rapid adoption. Yuan's team regularly updated the platform based on user feedback, addressing issues and adding new features that kept Zoom ahead of the competition. This iterative approach ensured that Zoom remained relevant and valuable to its users.

Zoom's moment of explosive growth came during the COVID-19 pandemic. As the world shifted to remote work and virtual communication, the demand for reliable video conferencing solutions skyrocketed. Zoom was uniquely positioned to meet this demand due to its ease of use, high-quality performance, and scalability. The platform quickly became a household name, with millions of people using Zoom for work meetings, virtual classrooms, social gatherings, and more.

The success of Zoom during this period underscored the importance of understanding user needs and continuously refining the product based on feedback. Yuan's dedication to solving real problems and his willingness to adapt and innovate were key factors in Zoom's rise to prominence. By staying true to its core mission of making video communication seamless and accessible, Zoom was able to capture a significant share of the market and become a critical tool for global communication.

Zoom's journey from a startup to a leader in video conferencing highlights the power of effective execution. Eric Yuan's vision, combined with a relentless focus on user needs and continuous improvement, turned Zoom into a platform that revolutionized the way we communicate. Zoom's story serves as an inspiring example of how innovative ideas, when executed with precision and dedication, can lead to remarkable success and widespread impact.

Peloton: Innovating Home Fitness

Peloton's journey is a compelling example of how innovative execution can redefine an industry. Co-founded by John Foley in 2012, Peloton entered the fitness market with a bold vision: to bring the energy and motivation of group fitness classes into people's homes. Despite initial skepticism and significant financial challenges, Peloton's commitment to creating an engaging, community-driven fitness experience has paid off, making it a leader in the home fitness market.

John Foley's inspiration for Peloton came from his own busy lifestyle. As a fitness enthusiast, he loved attending group workout classes but found it increasingly difficult to fit them into his schedule. He envisioned a solution that combined high-quality exercise equipment with live and on-demand fitness classes, allowing users to enjoy the benefits of group fitness without leaving home. This vision was ambitious, aiming to blend technology, fitness, and community in a seamless way.

Peloton's journey was not without hurdles. The concept faced initial skepticism from both investors and consumers. Many doubted whether people would be willing to invest in expensive fitness equipment and subscribe to online classes. Additionally, the company faced significant financial challenges, with Foley even having to mortgage his home to keep the business afloat. However, Foley and his team remained steadfast in their belief in the product and its potential.

A key factor in Peloton's success was its focus on customer engagement. Peloton didn't just sell exercise bikes; it sold a fitness experience. The company invested heavily in creating high-quality content, with live and on-demand classes led by charismatic and motivational instructors. This content was designed to be engaging and inspiring, fostering a sense of community among users. Peloton's instructors became integral to the brand, building personal connections with members and encouraging them to push their limits.

Technology played a crucial role in Peloton's innovation. The company developed a sleek, high-tech exercise bike equipped with a large touchscreen display for streaming classes. The bike was designed to provide a smooth, immersive experience, replicating the feel of a high-end fitness studio. Peloton also leveraged data and analytics to deliver personalized fitness content, tailoring workouts to individual users' preferences and progress. This personalized approach kept users motivated and coming back for more.

Peloton's community-driven model further set it apart. The platform enabled users to participate in live classes, compete on leaderboards, and connect with other members through social features. This sense of community and accountability was a powerful motivator, helping users stay committed to their fitness goals. Peloton's ability to create a supportive, connected community was a key differentiator in the market.

The COVID-19 pandemic accelerated Peloton's growth, as lockdowns and gym closures led to a surge in demand for home fitness solutions. Peloton was uniquely positioned to meet this demand, offering a high-quality, engaging alternative to traditional gyms. The company's subscriber base grew rapidly, and its stock price soared, solidifying its status as a leader in the connected fitness industry.

Peloton's story underscores the importance of understanding customer needs and leveraging technology to deliver a unique and engaging experience. By combining high-quality equipment, immersive content, and a strong sense of community, Peloton created a new market for connected fitness and revolutionized how people approach home workouts.

Peloton's journey from a bold idea to a leader in home fitness highlights the power of innovative execution. John Foley's vision, combined with a relentless focus on customer engagement and technology, redefined the home fitness industry. Peloton's success story serves as an inspiring example of how commitment to a clear vision and the ability to overcome challenges can lead to remarkable impact and growth.

Warby Parker: Disrupting the Eyewear Industry

Warby Parker's story is a brilliant example of how innovation and a keen understanding of customer needs can disrupt an established industry. Founded by Neil Blumenthal, Andrew Hunt, David Gilboa, and Jeffrey Raider in 2010, Warby Parker set out to revolutionize the eyewear market by offering high-quality, affordable glasses directly to consumers online. The company's innovative approach to distribution and commitment to social responsibility quickly resonated with consumers, making it a standout success in the retail space.

The founders of Warby Parker recognized a significant pain point in the eyewear industry: the high cost of designer glasses. Traditional eyewear companies dominated the market, leading to inflated prices that frustrated consumers. The idea for Warby Parker was born out of a simple yet powerful question: Why should people have to overpay for stylish, well-made glasses?

To address this issue, Warby Parker adopted a direct-to-consumer model. By cutting out the middlemen and selling directly to customers online, they were able to offer high-quality eyewear at a fraction of the traditional retail price. This approach not only reduced costs but also allowed Warby Parker to control the entire customer experience, from browsing and purchasing to delivery and returns.

One of the most innovative aspects of Warby Parker's business model was their home try-on program. Understanding that buying glasses online without trying them on could be a deterrent, the company introduced a program that allowed customers to select five frames to try at home for free.

Customers could then choose the frame that suited them best and return the rest, making the online shopping experience more personal and convenient. This program eliminated a major barrier to online eyewear shopping and provided a seamless, risk-free way for customers to find their perfect pair of glasses.

Warby Parker's commitment to social responsibility also set them apart. For every pair of glasses sold, the company donates a pair to someone in need. This "buy a pair, give a pair" model not only addressed a critical global issue—access to vision care—but also resonated deeply with consumers who wanted their purchases to have a positive social impact. This commitment to giving back helped build a loyal customer base and strengthened Warby Parker's brand identity.

The company's innovative marketing strategies further fueled its success. Warby Parker used a combination of digital marketing, social media, and word-of-mouth referrals to reach and engage customers. Their creative, relatable content and strong brand narrative helped build a community of enthusiastic supporters who spread the word about the brand.

Warby Parker's retail strategy also evolved over time. While they started as an online-only retailer, the company later opened brick-and-mortar stores to complement their online presence. These physical locations provided customers with an opportunity to experience the brand in person, try on glasses, and receive personalized service. This omnichannel approach allowed Warby Parker to reach a wider audience and offer a more holistic shopping experience.

Their success underscores the importance of addressing customer pain points and delivering value in new and creative ways. By combining innovative distribution methods, a customer-centric shopping experience, and a commitment to social responsibility, Warby Parker disrupted the traditional eyewear industry and created a new standard for how glasses are sold.

Warby Parker's journey from a bold idea to a leader in the eyewear industry highlights the power of innovation and customer focus. The founders' vision, combined with their willingness to challenge the status quo and address real consumer frustrations, reshaped the market. Warby Parker's story serves as an inspiring example of how understanding and addressing customer needs, leveraging innovative approaches, and committing to social impact can lead to significant success and industry disruption.

Bumble: Empowering Connections

Bumble's success story is a compelling example of how innovative business models and a strong commitment to user experience can disrupt an industry and foster meaningful change. Founded by Whitney Wolfe Herd in 2014, Bumble revolutionized the online dating scene by empowering women to make the first move. In a space traditionally dominated by men and often plagued by issues of harassment and safety, Bumble's unique approach attracted millions of users and set a new standard for online interactions.

Whitney Wolfe Herd, a co-founder of Tinder, recognized the challenges and frustrations women faced in the online dating world. Determined to create a safer and more respectful environment, she launched Bumble with a clear mission: to empower women and give them more control over their dating experiences. Bumble's defining feature, which requires women to initiate the conversation, flipped the traditional dating script and put women in the driver's seat.

This innovative approach not only differentiated Bumble from its competitors but also resonated deeply with users. Women appreciated the increased sense of safety and control, while men found the experience refreshing and respectful. Bumble's emphasis on fostering genuine connections and reducing harassment led to a more positive and enjoyable user experience, contributing to its rapid growth and popularity.

Bumble's commitment to user experience extended beyond its core dating function. Recognizing the potential to expand its empowering ethos, Bumble introduced Bumble BFF and Bumble Bizz, extending its platform to facilitate friendships and professional networking. This strategic expansion elevated Bumble from a dating app into a multi-faceted social networking platform, appealing to a broader audience and meeting a wider range of social needs.

The introduction of Bumble BFF allowed users to find friends in their area, addressing the often-overlooked need for adult friendships. Whether moving to a new city or simply looking to expand their social circle, users could leverage Bumble's familiar swipe-based interface to connect with potential friends. This feature not only broadened Bumble's user base but also reinforced its mission of creating meaningful connections in various aspects of life.

Bumble Bizz took the platform's empowerment philosophy into the professional realm, enabling users to network, find mentors, and explore job opportunities. By applying the same women-first approach, Bumble Bizz created a space where professional interactions were safe, respectful, and productive. This move showcased Bumble's versatility and commitment to fostering positive connections, whether personal or professional.

Bumble's success is a testament to the impact of innovative business models and a strong focus on user experience. By addressing the specific needs and concerns of women in the online dating space, Whitney Wolfe Herd built a platform that not only challenged industry norms but also resonated with a large and growing user base. Bumble's expansion into friendships and professional networking further demonstrated the scalability and adaptability of its core principles.

In addition to its innovative approach, Bumble has been a vocal advocate for social change. The company has taken strong stances on issues such as online harassment, consent, and equality, further solidifying its reputation as a socially responsible brand. Bumble's proactive efforts to create a safer and more inclusive online environment have garnered widespread support and loyalty from its users.

Bumble's journey from a disruptive dating app to a comprehensive social networking platform highlights the power of innovation and user-centric design. Whitney Wolfe Herd's vision and dedication to empowering women have reshaped the online dating landscape and beyond. Bumble's success story serves as an inspiring example of how addressing user needs, challenging industry norms, and expanding with purpose can lead to significant impact and sustained growth.

Swiggy: Revolutionizing Food Delivery

Swiggy's journey is an inspiring tale of how innovative thinking and a deep understanding of customer needs can disrupt an industry and redefine convenience. Founded by Sriharsha Majety, Nandan Reddy, and Rahul Jaimini in 2014, Swiggy redefined the food delivery landscape in India, offering a seamless and reliable service that quickly became a household name. Swiggy's success story underscores the importance of leveraging technology, focusing on user experience, and continuously innovating to meet evolving customer expectations.

The idea for Swiggy was born out of a clear gap in the market. The founders recognized the inefficiencies and inconsistencies in the existing food delivery services in India. Customers often faced long wait times, limited restaurant options, and poor delivery experiences. Determined to address these issues, Majety, Reddy, and Jaimini set out to create a platform that would streamline the food delivery process and provide a superior customer experience.

Swiggy's approach was centered around building a robust logistics network. Unlike many competitors that relied on third-party delivery services, Swiggy developed its own fleet of delivery personnel. This allowed for greater control over the delivery process, ensuring timely and efficient service. The use of technology played a crucial role in optimizing delivery routes, reducing wait times, and providing real-time tracking for customers. This focus on logistics set Swiggy apart and laid the foundation for its success.

From the outset, Swiggy prioritized user experience. The platform was designed to be user-friendly and intuitive, making it easy for customers to browse restaurant menus, place orders, and track deliveries. Swiggy's app and website offer a wide range of restaurant options, catering to diverse tastes and preferences. By continuously expanding its network of partner restaurants, Swiggy ensured that customers had access to a variety of cuisines, from local favorites to international delicacies.

Swiggy's commitment to innovation didn't stop at logistics and user experience. The company introduced several features that further enhanced convenience and customer satisfaction. Swiggy POP, for instance, offered single-serve meals at affordable prices, catering to solo diners and busy professionals. Swiggy Stores expanded the platform's reach beyond food delivery, allowing customers to order groceries and other essentials from local stores. These initiatives demonstrated Swiggy's ability to adapt and evolve in response to customer needs.

One of Swiggy's significant milestones was the introduction of Swiggy Genie, a hyperlocal delivery service that allowed users to send packages, pick up items, or have anything delivered within their city. This service leveraged Swiggy's existing logistics infrastructure, further showcasing the company's innovative spirit and commitment to making everyday life more convenient for its customers.

Swiggy's success is also a testament to its focus on customer engagement and loyalty. The company launched Swiggy Super, a membership program offering benefits such as free deliveries and exclusive discounts. This program not only incentivized repeat orders but also strengthened Swiggy's relationship with its customers.

The COVID-19 pandemic posed significant challenges to the food delivery industry, but Swiggy's adaptability and resilience helped it navigate this crisis. The company implemented stringent safety protocols to ensure the well-being of its customers and delivery personnel. Swiggy also introduced contactless delivery options, addressing health concerns and providing peace of mind to users.

Swiggy's journey from a startup to a leader in the food delivery industry highlights the power of innovation, user-centric design, and strategic adaptation. The founders' vision, combined with their relentless focus on logistics, user experience, and continuous improvement, revolutionized food delivery in India. Swiggy's story serves as an inspiring example of how addressing customer pain points, leveraging technology, and staying agile can lead to remarkable success and lasting impact.

Implementing innovative ideas is a journey filled with challenges and opportunities. By following structured steps, overcoming obstacles, and learning from successful examples, you can turn your vision into reality. Remember, the key to successful implementation lies in meticulous planning, effective communication, and unwavering commitment. As you begin this journey, stay resilient, adaptable, and focused on your goals. Your innovative ideas have the potential to make a significant impact—believe in your vision and take action to bring it to life.

"Great ideas become reality through action, resilience, and unwavering belief."

– Bob Philips –

Chapter 6

C - Change: Leading And Sustaining Innovation

- **Leadership In Driving And Sustaining Innovation.**
- **EmbeddingInnovationIntoOrganizational Culture.**
- **Measuring Success And Learning From Outcomes.**

Bringing innovative ideas to life is a journey that extends beyond the initial spark of creativity. It's about nurturing those ideas, guiding them through challenges, and embedding them into the very culture of your organization. I want to take you through what I've learned about the critical role of leadership in driving and sustaining innovation.

Leadership isn't just about having a title; it's about exemplifying the vision and values that inspire others to follow. It's about being the first to step into the unknown and encouraging your team to come along.

Leadership in Driving Innovation

Innovation starts at the top. As a leader, your vision, commitment, and actions set the tone for the entire organization. Your enthusiasm and dedication to innovative thinking can inspire your team to embrace new ideas and approaches. When you prioritize and model a culture of innovation, it signals to everyone that creativity and continuous improvement are valued. Your commitment to exploring new possibilities, coupled with a willingness to take calculated risks, encourages others to follow suit. Ultimately, your leadership is the catalyst that drives a culture where innovation thrives and impactful ideas are brought to life.

Vision and Inspiration

Leadership begins with a clear, compelling vision that inspires others to innovate. Sharing your passion for innovation and making it a core part of your organization's mission is essential. When I first stepped into a leadership role, I made it a priority to communicate my vision clearly and passionately. This not only motivated my team but also aligned everyone toward a common goal.

A compelling vision is like a lighthouse that guides your team through the uncertainties of the innovation journey. It's not just about having a goal; it's about painting a vivid picture of what success looks like and why it matters. This vision needs to resonate with everyone in the organization, from top executives to frontline employees, creating a sense of shared purpose and direction.

I remember reading about Sara Blakely, the founder of Spanx, and how her vision and passion reinvented an industry. Blakely's vision was to create a comfortable, slimming undergarment that didn't exist in the market at the time. She was driven by her own frustration with traditional pantyhose and shapewear, and she envisioned a product that would empower women by making them feel confident and comfortable.

Blakely's journey wasn't easy. She faced numerous rejections and challenges, but her unwavering belief in her vision kept her moving forward. She didn't just communicate her vision; she lived it. Blakely personally demonstrated her prototypes, explained her vision to potential investors, and relentlessly pitched her idea to department stores. Her passion was contagious, and it eventually convinced others to believe in her product as well.

Her vision didn't stop at the product itself. Blakely also envisioned a company that empowered women in the workplace. She created a corporate culture at Spanx that emphasized female leadership, innovation, and work-life balance. This vision attracted top talent and fostered a loyal, motivated workforce dedicated to the company's mission.

In my own experience, I found that clearly articulating my vision and demonstrating my commitment to it was crucial in rallying my team. I held regular meetings where I shared not just the goals but the bigger picture—the "why" behind our efforts. I encouraged open dialogue, allowing team members to ask questions and share their thoughts on how we could collectively achieve our vision. This inclusive approach helped create a sense of ownership and commitment among the team.

Moreover, I made sure to align our vision with the values and aspirations of my team members. By understanding what motivated them personally, I could connect their individual goals with our collective mission. This alignment made the vision more relatable and inspiring, driving higher levels of engagement and creativity.

To sustain this inspiration, it's important to celebrate milestones and acknowledge contributions along the way. When you recognize and reward the efforts that bring you closer to your vision, it reinforces the message that innovation is valued and that everyone's contributions matter. In my leadership journey, I made it a point to publicly celebrate even small victories, as they built momentum and kept the team motivated.

Sara Blakely's story and my own experiences underscore the power of a clear, passionate vision in driving innovation. It's not just about setting a direction but about inspiring and mobilizing your team to embark on the journey with you. A compelling vision, communicated effectively and lived authentically, can change an organization's approach to innovation and lead to extraordinary outcomes.

Leading by Example

Leaders must model the behavior they wish to see. Demonstrating a willingness to take risks, embrace new ideas, and learn from failures is crucial. In my journey, I've found that my actions speak louder than words. By being open to experimentation and showing resilience in the face of setbacks, I encouraged my team to adopt a similar mindset.

Leading by example means embodying the principles you advocate. It's about being the first to step into the unknown, showing that it's okay to make mistakes, and emphasizing the importance of learning and growing from those experiences. This approach fosters a culture of innovation and resilience within the organization, as team members feel empowered to explore new ideas without fear of failure.

One leader who exemplifies this approach is Indra Nooyi, the former CEO of PepsiCo. Nooyi is renowned for her bold leadership style and her willingness to take significant risks in the pursuit of innovation. Her journey with PepsiCo is a testament to the power of leading by example.

When Nooyi took the helm at PepsiCo, she envisioned a future where the company would not only be profitable but also contribute positively to societal health and environmental sustainability. This vision required significant changes, including the development of healthier product lines and a focus on sustainability. These changes were risky, especially considering PepsiCo's traditional portfolio of sugary drinks and snacks.

Nooyi didn't just make strategic decisions from behind a desk. She was deeply involved in the process, advocating for the necessary changes and leading the charge. She was willing to pivot and adapt, showing her team that flexibility and resilience were crucial in the face of uncertainty. Her leadership during this transition demonstrated a commitment to innovation, even when it meant disrupting their existing business model.

This shift wasn't without its challenges. PepsiCo faced technical hurdles, competition from established players, and skepticism from both investors and consumers. However, Nooyi remained steadfast. She encouraged a culture of experimentation, where failures were seen as opportunities to learn and improve. This mindset allowed PepsiCo to refine its new product lines and sustainability initiatives, ultimately leading to its success in these areas.

I've found that being visible and actively participating in the innovation process makes a significant difference. When I took on a project to develop a new marketing campaign, I didn't just delegate tasks; I got involved in the research, development, and testing phases. By showing my team that I was willing to take risks and learn alongside them, I fostered a collaborative and innovative environment.

I also made it a point to openly discuss my failures and what I learned from them. This transparency helped break down the fear of failure within the team. When team members saw that setbacks were not the end but rather a step towards improvement, they felt more confident in sharing their ideas and taking calculated risks.

These stories highlight the importance of leading by example. When leaders actively demonstrate the behaviors they wish to see, it creates a ripple effect throughout the organization. Team members feel inspired and empowered to innovate, knowing they have the support and encouragement of their leaders. This culture of innovation and resilience is essential for driving sustained success and achieving remarkable outcomes.

Empowering Your Team

Trust and empower your team to explore and implement innovative ideas. Providing them with the resources, autonomy, and support they need to succeed is crucial for fostering a culture of innovation. One of the most effective ways I've fostered innovation is by creating an environment where my team feels confident to take ownership of their projects and think creatively.

Empowerment begins with trust. As a leader, it's essential to trust your team members and their abilities. This trust creates a foundation where individuals feel valued and confident in their roles. I've found that when I trust my team to make decisions and take initiative, they rise to the occasion and often exceed expectations.

Autonomy is another critical aspect of empowerment. Allow your team members the freedom to explore their ideas and experiment with new approaches. This autonomy encourages creativity and innovation. In my experience, giving my team the space to innovate has led to some of our most successful projects. It's important to set clear goals and expectations, but within those parameters, let your team navigate their path.

Supporting your team is about more than just providing resources. It's about being there to guide them, offer feedback, and remove obstacles that might hinder their progress. I've always made it a priority to be accessible to my team, providing the support they need while encouraging them to take the lead on their projects.

A great example of a leader who embodies these principles is Satya Nadella, the CEO of Microsoft. When Nadella took over as CEO, he focused on evolving Microsoft's culture to one that values innovation and collaboration. He empowered his team by promoting a growth mindset, encouraging continuous learning, and fostering an environment where experimentation and risk-taking were encouraged.

Nadella's approach included breaking down silos within the company and promoting cross-functional collaboration. He trusted his teams to take ownership of their projects and supported them in exploring new ideas. This shift in culture led to the development of innovative products and services, revitalizing Microsoft's position in the tech industry.

In my leadership journey, I've also emphasized the importance of providing the necessary resources for innovation. This includes not only financial resources but also access to training, tools, and technology. By investing in my team's development and ensuring they have what they need to succeed, I've seen a significant increase in their ability to generate and implement innovative ideas.

Creating a culture of recognition and celebration is also vital. Acknowledge and reward your team's efforts and successes. Celebrating milestones and achievements not only boosts morale but also reinforces the importance of innovation within the organization. In my experience, regular recognition of my team's contributions has fostered a sense of pride and motivation to continue pushing the boundaries of what's possible.

Encouraging open communication is another key element of empowerment. Create channels where team members can share their ideas, provide feedback, and collaborate freely. I've always made it a point to listen to my team's suggestions and incorporate their input into our projects. This open dialogue fosters a sense of ownership and engagement, driving innovation forward.

Empowering your team is about creating an environment where they feel trusted, supported, and inspired to innovate. By providing autonomy, resources, and recognition, you can unlock your team's potential and drive significant advancements within your organization. Remember, a team that feels empowered and valued is more likely to embrace innovation and contribute to your organization's success.

Building a Supportive Environment

Fostering a culture of psychological safety where team members feel safe to express their ideas without fear of criticism is crucial for innovation. Encouraging open communication, collaboration, and continuous learning creates an environment where creativity can thrive. Early in my career, I realized the importance of creating a supportive environment. I encouraged my team to voice their ideas and provided constructive feedback, which significantly boosted our innovation efforts.

Psychological safety is the foundation of a supportive environment. When team members know they can share their thoughts and ideas without fear of ridicule or retribution, they are more likely to take risks and think outside the box. This sense of safety is essential for fostering innovation. In my leadership journey, I've made it a priority to establish and maintain an atmosphere where everyone feels respected and valued, regardless of their position or the nature of their ideas.

Open communication is another critical element. Encouraging team members to share their thoughts freely and listen actively to one another fosters a collaborative environment. I've always emphasized the importance of open dialogue, where ideas can be discussed and debated constructively. This approach not only leads to better solutions but also strengthens the team's cohesion and trust.

Collaboration is key to driving innovation. Bringing together individuals with diverse backgrounds and perspectives can lead to breakthrough ideas. I've found that by promoting cross-functional teamwork and encouraging collaboration, we've been able to tackle complex challenges more effectively. It's important to create opportunities for team members to work together, share knowledge, and build on each other's strengths.

Continuous learning is vital for sustaining innovation. In a supportive environment, team members should feel encouraged to expand their skills and knowledge. I've always supported my team's professional development by providing access to training, workshops, and other learning resources. This commitment to continuous improvement not only enhances individual capabilities but also drives the overall growth of the organization.

A leader who exemplifies the importance of building a supportive environment is Mary Barra, CEO of General Motors. Barra is known for her inclusive leadership style and her focus on creating a culture of trust and collaboration at GM. She has fostered an environment where employees feel empowered to share their ideas and take initiative, leading to significant advancements in electric and autonomous vehicle technology.

Barra's approach includes regular town hall meetings where employees at all levels can voice their concerns and suggestions. She actively listens to feedback and encourages open dialogue, reinforcing the importance of psychological safety. This open communication has been instrumental in driving innovation and revitalizing GM into a more agile and forward-thinking company.

In my own experience, I've seen the benefits of creating a supportive environment firsthand. When team members feel safe and valued, they are more likely to contribute their best ideas and work collaboratively towards common goals. I've always encouraged a culture of feedback, where constructive criticism is given and received with the intention of fostering growth and improvement.

Providing regular recognition and celebrating successes are also important aspects of a supportive environment. Acknowledging the hard work and achievements of your team not only boosts morale but also reinforces the value of their contributions. In my leadership practice, I make it a point to celebrate milestones and highlight the innovative efforts of my team, creating a positive and motivating atmosphere.

Embedding Innovation into Organizational Culture

For innovation to thrive, it must become a core part of your organization's culture. It's not enough to pursue innovation as a one-time initiative; it must be a continuous process that influences every level of the organization. Fostering an innovative culture involves encouraging collaboration across teams and establishing a mindset of continuous improvement. By integrating innovation into your daily operations and core values, you can create an environment where new ideas are consistently generated, nurtured, and implemented, driving sustained success and growth.

Creating an Innovative Culture

Developing an innovative culture starts with establishing core values that emphasize innovation, creativity, and continuous improvement. These values should guide your organization's actions and decisions, creating a foundation for sustained growth and success. Emphasizing the importance of an innovative culture by integrating these values into everyday practices and recognizing those who embody them is crucial.

First, make innovation a central theme in core values. This means explicitly stating that creativity and continuous improvement are critical to the organization's mission. Communicate these values regularly and integrate them into policies, procedures, and strategic goals. When innovation is a clear priority, it becomes a natural part of how the team operates.

To foster a culture of creativity, create an environment that encourages curiosity and experimentation. Encourage team members to ask questions, explore new ideas, and take calculated risks. Providing opportunities for brainstorming sessions, workshops, and creative thinking exercises can help stimulate innovative thinking. Organizing monthly "innovation days," where team members can work on passion projects or explore new ideas without the usual constraints of their roles, can be very effective.

Celebrating successes is crucial in reinforcing the value of innovation. Publicly recognize and reward team members who contribute innovative ideas and solutions. This not only boosts morale but also motivates others to think creatively and take initiative. Even small gestures, like highlighting innovative contributions in team meetings or internal newsletters, can make a significant impact.

Learning from failures is equally important. In an innovative culture, failure should be seen as a valuable learning opportunity rather than a setback. Encourage a mindset where mistakes are analyzed and understood, not punished. By fostering an environment where team members feel safe to fail, a space is created where they can experiment and innovate without fear. Sharing failures and what was learned from them sets an example that it's okay to take risks and learn from the outcomes.

Embedding continuous improvement into the culture requires a commitment to ongoing development. Provide regular training and development opportunities to keep the team's skills sharp and up to date. Encourage team members to seek out new knowledge, whether through formal education, attending industry conferences, or simply staying curious and informed about the latest trends and technologies.

Transparency and open communication are also vital. Ensure that everyone in the organization is aware of the goals and progress of innovation initiatives. This creates a sense of shared purpose and accountability. Regularly updating the team on successes, challenges, and next steps fosters a sense of collective ownership and commitment to innovation.

Creating an innovative culture involves developing core values that prioritize innovation, fostering a safe environment for creativity and risk-taking, celebrating successes, and learning from failures. By integrating these values into everyday practices and recognizing those who embody them, a culture that continuously generates and nurtures new ideas can be built, driving sustained success and growth. This approach ensures that innovation remains at the heart of everything the organization does.

Encouraging Collaboration and Cross-Pollination

Promoting collaboration across different teams and departments is essential for fostering innovation. Diverse perspectives can lead to breakthrough ideas and solutions that might not emerge within isolated groups. Encouraging collaboration and cross-pollination of ideas ensures that the organization leverages its collective intelligence and creativity to drive innovation.

One effective way to promote collaboration is by initiating cross-departmental projects. Bringing together individuals from different areas of expertise can result in unique combinations of skills and insights. For instance, a project team comprising members from marketing, product development, and customer service can address a challenge from multiple angles, leading to more comprehensive and innovative solutions.

Creating opportunities for regular brainstorming sessions is another powerful strategy. These sessions should be designed to encourage open dialogue and free-thinking, allowing team members to share their ideas without fear of criticism. Structured brainstorming techniques, such as mind mapping or the "six thinking hats" method, can help facilitate these discussions and ensure that all voices are heard.

Establishing innovation labs or hubs within the organization can also foster collaboration. These dedicated spaces can serve as incubators for new ideas, where team members from various departments can come together to work on experimental projects. Innovation labs provide a safe environment for experimentation, allowing teams to test and refine their ideas before implementing them on a larger scale.

Another approach to encouraging collaboration is through job rotation and shadowing programs. Allowing employees to experience different roles within the organization can provide them with a broader understanding of the business and spark new ideas. Job rotation helps break down silos and encourages employees to think beyond their immediate responsibilities, fostering a more holistic and innovative mindset.

Leaders play a crucial role in promoting collaboration. By setting the example and actively participating in cross-departmental initiatives, leaders can demonstrate the importance of collaboration and encourage their teams to do the same. Recognizing and rewarding collaborative efforts also reinforces the value of teamwork and motivates employees to work together towards common goals.

Leveraging technology can further enhance collaboration. Digital collaboration tools, such as project management software, shared document platforms, and communication apps, enable real-time collaboration regardless of geographical location. These tools make it easier for teams to share information, track progress, and coordinate their efforts, ultimately leading to more efficient and effective collaboration.

Encouraging a culture of knowledge sharing is also vital. Create platforms and opportunities for employees to share their expertise and insights. This could include internal webinars, lunch-and-learn sessions, or an online knowledge repository. When employees feel that their knowledge is valued and that they can learn from their peers, it fosters a culture of continuous learning and innovation.

Finally, fostering external collaborations can bring fresh perspectives and new ideas into the organization. Partnering with other companies, academic institutions, or industry experts can provide access to specialized knowledge and resources. These collaborations can lead to joint ventures, research projects, or the co-development of new products and services, further driving innovation.

Encouraging collaboration and cross-pollination of ideas is essential for fostering innovation. By promoting cross-departmental projects, creating opportunities for brainstorming, establishing innovation labs, and leveraging technology, organizations can harness the power of diverse perspectives. Leaders play a crucial role in setting the example and recognizing collaborative efforts, while knowledge sharing and external partnerships further enhance the innovation ecosystem. This collaborative approach ensures that the organization remains agile, creative, and poised for continuous growth and success.

Implementing Continuous Learning Programs

Investing in continuous learning and development programs is essential for keeping your team updated on the latest trends, technologies, and methodologies. Continuous learning not only enhances the skills of your team but also fosters a culture of innovation and adaptability.

One of the first steps in implementing a successful continuous learning program is to identify the specific needs and interests of your team. Conducting surveys or assessments can help you understand the skills gaps and areas where further development is needed. This information can guide you in designing targeted training programs that address these needs effectively.

Offering a variety of learning opportunities is crucial. This could include workshops, seminars, online courses, and certifications. By providing diverse learning formats, you cater to different learning styles and preferences, making it easier for team members to engage with the material. For instance, some might prefer interactive workshops, while others may benefit more from self-paced online courses.

Regularly updating the learning content is also important. The fast-paced nature of today's business environment means that trends and technologies are constantly evolving. Ensure that your training programs are current and relevant by collaborating with industry experts and continuously monitoring developments in your field. This not only keeps your team's skills sharp but also demonstrates a commitment to their professional growth.

Encouraging team members to pursue continuous learning outside of formal programs is another effective strategy. Create a culture where curiosity and self-improvement are valued. Encourage employees to attend industry conferences, read relevant books and articles, and participate in professional networks. Providing resources such as subscriptions to industry publications or memberships to professional organizations can support these efforts.

Leaders play a pivotal role in promoting continuous learning. By actively participating in training programs and demonstrating a commitment to personal development, leaders can set a powerful example for their teams. Sharing your own learning experiences and insights can inspire others to pursue their own development journeys.

Creating opportunities for team members to share their knowledge with each other is also beneficial. Internal knowledge-sharing sessions, such as lunch-and-learn events or peer-led workshops, can help disseminate new information and insights throughout the organization. This not only reinforces the learning but also fosters a sense of community and collaboration.

Recognition and rewards can further motivate employees to engage in continuous learning. Implementing a system that acknowledges and celebrates learning achievements, such as completing a certification or attending a workshop, can boost morale and encourage others to follow suit. Offering incentives, such as career advancement opportunities or bonuses for acquiring new skills, can also drive participation.

One successful approach I've observed is creating personalized learning plans for each team member. Tailoring development programs to individual career goals and aspirations ensures that learning is relevant and aligned with both personal and organizational objectives. Regular check-ins and progress reviews can help keep these plans on track and provide opportunities for feedback and adjustment.

An example of a company that excels in continuous learning is Google. They offer extensive internal training programs, known as "Google University," where employees can take courses on a wide range of topics. This commitment to learning has helped Google maintain its innovative edge and attract top talent.

Implementing continuous learning programs involves identifying the specific needs of your team, offering diverse and up-to-date learning opportunities, and fostering a culture of curiosity and self-improvement. Leaders play a crucial role in promoting and participating in these initiatives, while recognition and personalized learning plans can further enhance engagement. By investing in continuous learning, you equip your team with the skills and knowledge needed to drive innovation and adapt to the ever-changing business landscape.

Scaling Innovations

Developing strategies to scale successful innovations across the organization is crucial for sustaining growth and maintaining a competitive edge. Creating a framework for piloting, refining, and implementing ideas on a larger scale ensures that innovations are effectively integrated into the organization's operations.

One of the key strategies for scaling innovations is to start with small-scale pilots. Piloting innovative ideas on a smaller scale allows you to test their feasibility and gather valuable feedback without committing significant resources. This approach helps identify any potential issues or challenges early on, making it easier to address them before a full-scale implementation. By starting small, you can experiment with new ideas and refine them based on real-world insights.

Once the pilot phase is complete, it's essential to gather and analyze feedback from all stakeholders involved. This includes team members, customers, and any other relevant parties. Collecting detailed feedback helps you understand what worked well and what needs improvement. It's important to create an open feedback loop where people feel comfortable sharing their honest opinions and suggestions.

Refining the innovation based on feedback is a critical step in the scaling process. Use the insights gathered during the pilot phase to make necessary adjustments and improvements. This iterative process ensures that the innovation is optimized and ready for broader implementation. It's important to remain flexible and open to changes, as continuous refinement is key to successful scaling.

Creating a clear and structured framework for scaling innovations is essential. This framework should outline the steps for moving from the pilot phase to full-scale implementation. It should include timelines, resource allocation, and responsibilities for each stage of the process. A well-defined framework provides clarity and direction, ensuring that everyone involved understands their roles and the overall plan.

Leadership support is crucial for scaling innovations. Leaders need to champion the innovation and provide the necessary resources and support to ensure its success. This includes securing funding, allocating personnel, and removing any barriers that may hinder the scaling process. Leaders should also communicate the importance of the innovation and how it aligns with the organization's strategic goals.

Communication plays a vital role in scaling innovations. Ensure that all team members are informed about the innovation and its progress. Regular updates and transparent communication help maintain momentum and keep everyone aligned. Sharing success stories and highlighting the benefits of the innovation can also build excitement and buy-in across the organization.

Another important aspect of scaling innovations is training and support. Provide comprehensive training programs to ensure that all employees understand the new innovation and how to implement it effectively. Ongoing support, such as help desks or dedicated teams, can help address any issues that arise during the scaling process and ensure a smooth transition.

Measuring the success of the scaled innovation is essential to understand its impact and make any necessary adjustments. Develop key performance indicators (KPIs) to track the progress and effectiveness of the innovation. Regularly review these metrics to assess whether the innovation is achieving its intended goals and delivering value to the organization.

A company that successfully scaled innovation is Zara, the fashion retailer. Zara's approach to scaling involves a highly responsive supply chain and close alignment between design, manufacturing, and retail operations. They pilot new designs in select stores, gather customer feedback, and quickly scale successful products across their global network. This strategy allows Zara to stay ahead of fashion trends and meet customer demand efficiently.

Scaling innovations involves starting with small-scale pilots, gathering and analyzing feedback, refining the innovation, and creating a clear framework for full-scale implementation. Leadership support, effective communication, comprehensive training, and ongoing measurement are crucial for successful scaling. By following these strategies, you can ensure that your innovative ideas are effectively integrated into the organization, driving sustained growth and success.

Measuring Success and Learning from Outcomes

Measuring the impact of innovation is crucial for sustaining it. Let us explore methods to evaluate the success of your innovative efforts and how to learn from the outcomes. By tracking key metrics and analyzing results, you can understand what works, identify areas for improvement, and make informed decisions for future innovation initiatives. Learning from both successes and failures helps refine your approach and ensures continuous growth and improvement.

Defining Success Metrics

Understanding the impact of innovation is crucial for sustaining it. To measure this impact effectively, it is essential to establish clear metrics that focus on three main pillars of any business: productivity, quality, and inventory carrying cost. Let us explore the importance of measurement, the impact of not measuring, why we should use metrics, different types of metrics, and how to apply these concepts to productivity, quality, and inventory carrying cost.

What is the Impact of Not Measuring?

Without proper measurement, you can face numerous challenges and uncertainties that hinder progress and growth. Here are some key impacts:

- *Lack of Clear Expectations*: Without measurement, it's challenging to know what is expected of you and your team. Clear expectations are crucial for guiding efforts and aligning actions with strategic goals.
- *Unawareness of Performance*: You won't have a clear understanding of how you are performing on various parameters. This lack of awareness can lead to inefficiencies and missed opportunities for improvement.

- *Inability to Assess Results:* Without metrics, you can't accurately gauge the results of your initiatives. This makes it difficult to determine whether you're moving in the right direction or need to adjust your approach.
- *No Basis for Comparison:* Measurement allows you to compare performance between individuals, teams, or periods. Without it, making informed decisions and identifying best practices becomes challenging.
- *Lack of Recognition:* Metrics help identify and reward efforts and achievements. Without them, recognizing and incentivizing high performers can be subjective and biased.
- *Perception of Bias:* When performance is not measured objectively, it can lead to perceptions of bias and unfairness within the team. This can erode trust and morale.
- *Inability to Justify Actions:* Without data, justifying your actions and decisions to stakeholders becomes challenging. Metrics provide the evidence needed to support your strategies and initiatives.

Why Should We Use Metrics?

Metrics serve multiple vital purposes in managing and improving business performance:

- *Quantifying State*: Metrics allow you to quantify the state of tangibles and intangibles that affect your work. This provides a clear picture of current performance levels.
- *Effective Communication:* They provide a standardized way to communicate the state of tangibles and intangibles, ensuring everyone is on the same page.

- *Tracking Changes*: Metrics help track how much tangibles or intangibles have changed over time, which is essential for monitoring progress and making informed adjustments.
- *Establishing Standards and Goals*: Using metrics helps in setting benchmarks and goals. They provide a reference point to measure progress against.
- *Controlling and Achieving Goals*: Understanding what to control to achieve your goals is crucial. Metrics highlight areas that need attention and improvement.
- *Influencing Behavior:* Metrics can guide the behavior of individuals and teams. They serve as a basis for performance management, ensuring that actions align with organizational objectives.

Types of Metrics

Understanding different types of metrics is essential for effective measurement. Here are some common types:

- *Absolute Metrics*: These are direct measurements using commonly known units, such as revenue, units sold, or time taken. They provide straightforward insights into performance levels.
- *Ratios:* Ratios are derived by dividing one metric by another, such as profit margin (net income divided by revenue). They help in understanding relationships between different aspects of performance.
- *Proxy Metrics:* These represent non-quantifiable metrics through measurable indicators. For example, employee engagement might be measured through proxy metrics like absenteeism rates or survey scores.

- *Surveys:* Surveys gather perceptions and opinions from individuals on various issues. They provide qualitative insights that can complement quantitative data.
- *Composites:* Composite metrics combine multiple individual metrics in specific ratios to create a comprehensive score. An example could be a customer satisfaction index that combines various aspects of service quality.
- *Grading and Calibration:* These metrics are created relative to a static element, such as performance grades (A, B, C) or calibrated scores based on set criteria.

Applying Metrics to Productivity, Quality, and Inventory

Productivity Metrics

Productivity measures how efficiently resources are used to generate output. Common productivity metrics include:

- *Output per Hour:* Measures the amount of product or service produced per hour of work. It's a direct indicator of efficiency.
- *Labor Productivity:* Calculated by dividing total output by the number of labor hours. This metric helps in assessing the effectiveness of workforce utilization.
- *Cost per Unit:* This measures the cost incurred to produce one unit of product. It's useful for identifying cost-saving opportunities.
- *Utilization Rate:* The ratio of actual output to potential output if resources were used to their full capacity. It highlights underutilization or inefficiencies.

Quality Metrics

Quality assesses how well products or services meet or exceed customer expectations. Key quality metrics include:

- *Defect Rate:* The percentage of defective products in a batch. Lower defect rates indicate higher quality.
- *Customer Satisfaction Score (CSAT):* Often derived from surveys, it reflects how satisfied customers are with your products or services.
- *Net Promoter Score (NPS):* Measures customer loyalty by asking how likely customers are to recommend your product or service to others.
- *First-Pass Yield:* The percentage of products that meet quality standards without rework. Higher first-pass yields indicate efficient processes.

Inventory Carrying Cost Metrics

Inventory carrying cost evaluates the costs associated with holding and managing inventory. Important metrics include:

- *Inventory Turnover Ratio:* The number of times inventory is sold and replaced over a period. Higher turnover indicates efficient inventory management.
- *Days Inventory Outstanding (DIO):* The average number of days inventory is held before being sold. Lower DIO indicates faster inventory movement.
- *Carrying Cost Percentage:* The cost of holding inventory as a percentage of the total inventory value. It includes storage, insurance, and obsolescence costs.
- *Stockout Rate:* The frequency at which inventory runs out. Lower stockout rates indicate better inventory planning.

Learning from Metrics

Measuring success is not just about collecting data; it's about learning from the results to drive continuous improvement. Here's how to make the most out of your metrics:

1. *Analyze Trends:* Look for patterns and trends in your data. This can help identify areas for improvement and predict future performance.
2. *Benchmarking:* Compare your metrics against industry standards or competitors. This provides a context for your performance and highlights areas where you can gain a competitive edge.
3. *Actionable Insights:* Use your findings to make informed decisions. Metrics should guide your strategy and operational improvements.
4. *Feedback Loops:* Establish regular feedback loops where you review metrics with your team. Discuss what's working, what's not, and brainstorm solutions for improvement.
5. *Adjust and Adapt:* Be prepared to pivot based on what the data tells you. Flexibility and adaptability are crucial for continuous improvement.
6. *Celebrate Successes:* Recognize and celebrate achievements. This boosts morale and reinforces the behaviors that lead to success.

By focusing on these three main pillars—productivity, quality, and inventory carrying cost—you can gain a comprehensive understanding of your performance. Use the insights gained from these metrics to drive strategic decisions and foster a culture of continuous improvement. Remember, the ultimate goal of measurement is not just to collect data but to learn and improve continuously.

Feedback and Continuous Improvement

In any innovation journey, feedback is the lifeblood that keeps the process dynamic and relevant. Regularly gathering feedback from stakeholders and using it to refine strategies is crucial. Implementing a feedback loop ensures continuous learning and improvement, helping you stay aligned with the needs and expectations of your customers, employees, and other stakeholders.

Feedback provides real-time insights into how your innovations are being received. It helps you understand the strengths and weaknesses of your initiatives and offers a roadmap for future improvements. Feedback should be seen as a valuable asset, guiding your efforts and ensuring that your innovations remain relevant and effective.

To gather meaningful feedback, you need a structured approach. Surveys and questionnaires are excellent tools for collecting quantitative and qualitative data from a large audience. Tailor your questions to gather specific insights about your products, services, and overall customer experience. Engage small groups of stakeholders in detailed discussions through focus groups. This method allows for in-depth understanding and the collection of nuanced feedback. Personal interviews with key stakeholders can provide deep insights and uncover issues that might not emerge in group settings. Utilize online platforms and social media to gather feedback and encourage customers to share their thoughts and experiences openly. Additionally, regularly seek feedback from your employees to understand internal challenges and opportunities for improvement.

Implementing a feedback loop is a systematic process of gathering, analyzing, and acting on feedback. Make feedback collection an ongoing process using surveys, interviews, and other methods to gather continuous input from stakeholders. Once you have collected feedback, analyze the data to identify trends, patterns, and areas for improvement. Look for both positive and negative feedback to get a balanced view. Communicate the feedback findings with your team. Transparency is key to fostering a culture of continuous improvement. Based on the feedback, create action plans to address identified issues and leverage opportunities for enhancement. Assign responsibilities and set timelines for implementation. Execute the action plans and make the necessary adjustments to your strategies, products, or processes. Ensure that changes are communicated clearly to all relevant stakeholders. After implementing changes, follow up with stakeholders to gather their feedback on the adjustments made. This closes the loop and begins the cycle anew.

The feedback loop is not a one-time process but a continuous cycle of learning and adapting. Be willing to adapt your strategies based on the feedback you receive. Flexibility is crucial for continuous improvement. Foster an environment where feedback is valued and encouraged. Recognize and reward those who provide constructive feedback. Regularly review the impact of the changes you have implemented. Use metrics to measure improvements and identify any further adjustments needed. Take time to reflect on the outcomes of your initiatives. Consider what worked well and what didn't, and use these reflections to guide future innovation efforts. Acknowledge and celebrate the successes that come from acting on feedback. This boosts morale and reinforces the importance of continuous improvement.

By prioritizing feedback and integrating it into a continuous improvement process, you can ensure that your innovations remain effective and aligned with the evolving needs of your stakeholders. This approach not only enhances the quality and impact of your innovations but also fosters a culture of learning and growth within your organization.

Celebrating Success and Learning from Failures

In the journey of innovation, both successes and failures play crucial roles. Celebrating successes and analyzing failures are essential practices that provide valuable lessons and guide future efforts. Embracing both outcomes helps create a balanced and resilient culture, fostering continuous growth and improvement.

Successes should be celebrated to recognize the hard work, dedication, and creativity that contributed to achieving goals. Celebrations boost morale, build team spirit, and motivate everyone to strive for further accomplishments. Whether it's a major breakthrough or a small milestone, acknowledging achievements reinforces positive behaviors and encourages a culture of excellence. Success celebrations can take various forms, from formal awards ceremonies to informal team gatherings. Public recognition of individual and team efforts helps build a sense of pride and ownership. It's also an opportunity to reflect on what worked well and why, capturing the strategies and practices that led to success. Sharing these insights across the organization ensures that effective approaches are replicated and built upon in future projects.

On the other hand, failures are inevitable in the innovation process. Instead of viewing failures as setbacks, they should be seen as opportunities for learning and growth. Analyzing failures provides critical insights into what went wrong and why. This process helps identify potential pitfalls, refine strategies, and avoid repeating mistakes. When discussing failures, create an open and non-judgmental environment where team members feel safe to share their experiences. This openness fosters trust and encourages candid conversations about challenges and lessons learned.

Conduct post-mortem analyses to dissect failed projects or initiatives. Examine each aspect, from planning and execution to outcomes, to understand the root causes of failure. Identify specific factors that contributed to the setback, whether they were related to strategy, execution, resources, or external influences. Encourage team members to share their perspectives and insights, promoting a collaborative approach to problem-solving. Document the lessons learned from failures and integrate them into future planning and decision-making processes. By doing so, you turn failures into valuable learning experiences that drive continuous improvement.

Balancing the celebration of successes with the analysis of failures helps create a resilient and adaptive organization. It's essential to foster a culture that values both achievements and learning from mistakes. This balanced approach encourages a mindset of continuous improvement and innovation. One effective way to integrate this balance is to incorporate regular reflection sessions into your organizational routine. Schedule periodic reviews where successes are celebrated and failures are analyzed. Use these sessions to identify key takeaways, share insights, and set new goals. These reflections provide a holistic view of progress and help maintain momentum in your innovation efforts.

Additionally, promoting a growth mindset within the organization is crucial. A growth mindset encourages individuals to view challenges and setbacks as opportunities to learn and grow. Leaders play a pivotal role in modeling this mindset by demonstrating resilience and a willingness to learn from both successes and failures. Encourage team members to take calculated risks and experiment with new ideas. Emphasize that failures are part of the innovation process and that learning from them is more important than avoiding them. Recognize and reward efforts that demonstrate creativity, initiative, and a commitment to continuous improvement, regardless of the outcome.

By celebrating successes and learning from failures, you create a dynamic and resilient culture that thrives on continuous improvement. This balanced approach not only drives innovation but also builds a motivated and engaged workforce. Embracing both outcomes as valuable learning experiences ensures that your organization remains adaptable, forward-thinking, and ready to tackle future challenges with confidence.

Leading and sustaining innovation is a dynamic and ongoing process. It requires strong leadership, a supportive culture, and a commitment to continuous improvement. By embedding innovation into the core of your organization and measuring its impact, you can drive meaningful change and achieve lasting success.

"Anything under the sun can be measured, except maybe the number of times I've lost my keys. But seriously, if you don't measure it, how will you know how far you've come?"

– Bob Philips –

Chapter 7

Navigating The Innovation Journey: Challenges And Solutions

- **Understanding And Overcoming The Challenges.**
- **Building A Resilient Innovation Ecosystem.**

Innovation is a journey filled with peaks and valleys, triumphs and setbacks. Having navigated this path myself, I understand that the challenges can be daunting, but the rewards are equally fulfilling. There have been moments when the road seemed impassable, yet the thrill of a breakthrough and the joy of seeing an idea come to life kept me moving forward. I've faced skepticism, financial hurdles, and the occasional self-doubt, but each obstacle taught me invaluable lessons and strengthened my resolve. We will explore common obstacles encountered during the innovation journey and explore actionable strategies to overcome them. Whether you're just starting out or are deep into your innovation process, my goal is to equip you with the insights needed to persevere and thrive. By sharing my experiences and the lessons learned along the way, I hope to inspire you to navigate your own innovation journey with confidence and resilience. Remember, every setback is an opportunity for growth, and every challenge can be the catalyst for your next big breakthrough. Let's embark on this journey together and turn your innovative ideas into impactful realities.

Understanding and overcoming the challenges

Societal Skepticism

Innovative ideas often face skepticism from society, including family, friends, and professional colleagues. People are naturally resistant to change, especially when it challenges established norms. This societal skepticism is a common obstacle that many innovators encounter, including myself. I vividly remember the initial reactions from my family and friends when I introduced a groundbreaking concept. The raised eyebrows, the doubtful questions, and the hesitation were palpable. It was disheartening, but I quickly learned that this skepticism was not necessarily a rejection of my idea. Instead, it was a manifestation of a natural human response: fear of the unknown.

Fear of the unknown is a powerful force. When people are confronted with something new and different, their instinctive reaction is often to question and resist. This resistance is not rooted in malice or negativity; it is a defense mechanism designed to protect against potential risks and uncertainties. As an innovator, understanding this psychological barrier is crucial. It allows you to approach societal skepticism with empathy and strategic planning.

One of the most effective ways to combat societal skepticism is through education. Early in the process, take the time to educate your stakeholders about your innovative idea. Provide them with a clear, comprehensive understanding of what you are proposing and why it is beneficial. Use data, case studies, and real-world examples to illustrate the value and impact of your innovation. The more informed your stakeholders are, the less fearful they will be. They will begin to see the possibilities and potential rather than just the risks.

Engaging stakeholders early is another critical strategy. When people feel included in the process, they are more likely to support it. Involve your team, clients, and other key stakeholders from the beginning. Seek their input, listen to their concerns, and address their questions. This collaborative approach not only builds trust but also fosters a sense of ownership and commitment. When people feel that they have a stake in the innovation, they are more likely to advocate for it.

I recall a specific instance where engaging stakeholders early made a significant difference. I was working on a project that aimed to revolutionize our company's approach to customer service. The idea was met with considerable skepticism, particularly from the frontline employees who would be directly affected by the change. Rather than pushing the idea through without their buy-in, I decided to involve them in the process. We held workshops, brainstorming sessions, and feedback meetings where their voices were heard and valued. This inclusive approach not only alleviated their fears but also led to valuable insights that improved the final implementation. What started as a skeptical group of employees eventually became the most enthusiastic champions of the new system.

Demonstrating the value and benefits of your innovation is also crucial in overcoming societal skepticism. People need to see tangible proof that your idea works and that it offers significant advantages over the current state. Pilot projects, prototypes, and case studies are excellent tools for this purpose. By showcasing real-world applications and positive outcomes, you can build credibility and trust. When stakeholders witness the success of your innovation firsthand, their skepticism diminishes, and their support grows.

For instance, during one of my projects, we developed a prototype to demonstrate the effectiveness of our new technology. We invited key stakeholders to observe the prototype in action and provided them with detailed reports on its performance. The initial skepticism gradually gave way to excitement as they saw the tangible benefits and potential impact. This shift in perception was instrumental in securing the support and resources needed for full-scale implementation.

Addressing the emotional aspect of skepticism is equally important. Change can be unsettling, and people often need reassurance that their fears and concerns are valid. Acknowledge the challenges and uncertainties that come with innovation and communicate openly about how you plan to address them. Show empathy and understanding towards those who are hesitant. By validating their feelings and providing clear, honest communication, you can build a foundation of trust and openness.

Another strategy that has proven effective, in my experience, is storytelling. Stories have a unique power to connect with people on an emotional level. Share stories of past innovations that faced similar skepticism but ultimately succeeded. Highlight the journey, the obstacles, and the eventual triumphs. These narratives can inspire and motivate stakeholders to embrace the new idea. They serve as powerful reminders that every great innovation initially faced resistance but succeeded because of perseverance and belief.

In addition to these strategies, it is essential to remain patient and persistent. Changing perceptions and overcoming skepticism takes time. There will be moments of doubt and frustration, but it is important to stay committed to your vision. Celebrate small victories along the way and use them as building blocks to gain further support. Persistence, coupled with a strategic approach, can gradually turn skeptics into supporters.

Navigating societal skepticism requires a combination of education, engagement, demonstration, empathy, and persistence. By understanding the root causes of skepticism and addressing them proactively, you can build a supportive environment for your innovation. Remember, every great idea initially faced resistance. It is through your efforts to educate, engage, and inspire that you can turn that resistance into acceptance and support. As you continue on your innovation journey, keep these strategies in mind, and you will be well-equipped to navigate the challenges of societal skepticism and ultimately achieve success.

Financial Constraints

Innovation requires resources, and financial constraints can be a significant barrier. Whether you're a startup seeking initial funding or an established company trying to allocate a budget for a new project, money often determines the feasibility of your ideas. I've encountered this challenge multiple times throughout my career, and I've learned that securing funding is not just about having a great idea; it's about presenting a compelling business case to potential investors.

Securing financial support begins with thorough preparation. You need to develop a detailed business plan that outlines the market potential, scalability, and expected return on investment (ROI). Investors want to see that you have done your homework and have a clear strategy for how their money will be used to generate returns. This means conducting market research, analyzing competitors, and identifying your unique value proposition.

One of the key components of a compelling business case is demonstrating the market potential. Investors need to be convinced that there is a significant demand for your product or service. This involves providing data on market size, growth trends, and customer demographics. Highlighting success stories or case studies from similar innovations can also be persuasive. For example, if you're developing a new tech gadget, showing how a similar product disrupted the market can help investors see the potential of your idea.

Scalability is another critical factor. Investors are more likely to support ideas that can grow and expand beyond the initial market. This means outlining a clear path for scaling your operations, whether it involves expanding to new geographic regions, reaching new customer segments, or developing additional features and services. Demonstrating that you have a scalable business model can reassure investors that their investment will lead to substantial growth.

Return on investment (ROI) is perhaps the most important metric for investors. They need to know that their money will generate returns, and they want to understand the timeline for those returns. This involves providing financial projections, including revenue forecasts, profit margins, and cash flow analysis. Be realistic and transparent in your projections. Investors appreciate honesty and a well-thought-out financial plan over overly-optimistic estimates.

Presenting a compelling business case also means effectively communicating your vision and passion. Investors need to believe in you as much as they believe in your idea. Your enthusiasm and commitment can be contagious, and they can make a significant difference in securing financial support. When you pitch your idea, tell your story. Share your journey, your challenges, and your dedication to making your innovation a reality. This personal touch can help build a connection with potential investors.

In addition to preparing a solid business case, it's crucial to explore various funding sources. Traditional avenues like venture capital and angel investors are common, but there are many other options available. Crowdfunding platforms, government grants, and corporate partnerships can provide alternative funding opportunities. Each funding source has its own criteria and expectations, so tailor your pitch accordingly.

Crowdfunding, for example, allows you to raise small amounts of money from a large number of people. This method not only provides funding but also helps validate your idea by showing that there is public interest and demand. Government grants, on the other hand, often require meeting specific criteria related to innovation, research, and development. These grants can be a valuable source of non-dilutive funding, meaning you don't have to give up equity in your company.

Corporate partnerships can also be a strategic way to secure funding. Partnering with a larger company can provide financial resources, industry expertise, and access to a broader customer base. These partnerships can be mutually beneficial, as the larger company can gain access to innovative ideas and technologies while you receive the support needed to bring your innovation to market.

Managing financial constraints also involves being resourceful and strategic with your budget. Prioritize your spending by focusing on critical areas that will have the most significant impact on your innovation's success. This might involve investing in product development, market research, or building a strong team. Look for cost-saving opportunities, such as leveraging open-source software, using shared workspaces, or outsourcing non-core tasks.

Finally, maintaining financial discipline is essential. Keep a close eye on your cash flow, monitor your expenses, and regularly review your financial performance. This will help you identify potential issues early and make necessary adjustments. Financial discipline not only ensures the sustainability of your innovation but also builds trust with investors, demonstrating that you are a responsible steward of their investment.

Financial constraints can be a significant barrier to innovation, but they are not insurmountable. By developing a compelling business case, exploring various funding sources, and managing your budget strategically, you can secure the financial support needed to bring your innovative ideas to life. Stay committed to your vision, be resourceful, and maintain financial discipline. These practices will help you navigate financial challenges and set the stage for successful innovation.

Importance of a Supportive Environment

A supportive environment is crucial for innovation to flourish. This includes having a leadership team that champions innovation, a culture that encourages experimentation, and a network of mentors and peers who provide guidance and support. Without this environment, even the most brilliant ideas can struggle to take off. I've seen firsthand how a lack of support can stifle creativity and innovation. Conversely, a nurturing environment can inspire individuals to take risks and pursue ambitious goals.

In the professional realm, the role of leadership in fostering a supportive environment cannot be overstated. Leaders who prioritize innovation create a culture where new ideas are welcomed, and experimentation is encouraged. They provide the resources and support necessary for innovation to thrive and recognize and reward creative thinking. This kind of leadership sets the tone for the entire organization. When employees see that their leaders value and invest in innovation, they are more likely to feel empowered to contribute their ideas and take risks.

A supportive professional environment also includes fostering a culture of collaboration and open communication. When team members feel safe to express their ideas without fear of criticism or failure, they are more likely to engage in creative problem-solving. Encouraging cross-functional teams and diverse perspectives can lead to breakthrough innovations. Regular brainstorming sessions, innovation workshops, and open forums for idea sharing can help create this kind of collaborative environment.

However, a supportive environment extends beyond the workplace. The environment at home and within one's friend circle also plays a significant role in nurturing innovation. If you want to achieve something different, you need to be surrounded by people who can create a fire in your belly. Your home environment should be a place where you feel encouraged and supported. Family members who believe in your vision and provide emotional support can be a tremendous asset. They can offer a sounding board for your ideas, celebrate your successes, and help you navigate setbacks.

Similarly, having friends who share your passion for innovation or who at least understand and support your ambitions can be incredibly motivating. These friends can provide different perspectives, offer constructive feedback, and serve as a source of inspiration. Surrounding yourself with individuals who challenge you to think differently and push you to achieve your best can help keep your innovative spirit alive.

Creating a supportive environment also involves seeking out mentors and peers who can guide and inspire you. Mentors can provide valuable insights and advice based on their own experiences, helping you navigate the challenges of innovation. They can also introduce you to networks and resources that you might not have access to otherwise. Peers who are on a similar journey can offer camaraderie and mutual support. Together, you can share experiences, exchange ideas, and motivate each other to keep pushing forward.

In my journey, I've witnessed the profound impact of a supportive environment. Early in my career, I was part of an organization that had a rigid, risk-averse culture. Innovation was not encouraged, and new ideas were often met with skepticism. This stifling environment made it difficult to pursue creative solutions or take bold steps. As a result, the organization struggled to stay competitive and adapt to changing market conditions.

In contrast, I later joined a company that prioritized innovation and fostered a supportive culture. Leadership actively encouraged experimentation and learning from failures. They provided the resources and autonomy needed to explore new ideas. The company also invested in continuous learning and development programs, ensuring that employees were equipped with the latest knowledge and skills. This nurturing environment led to a surge in creativity and productivity, and the company quickly became a leader in its industry.

Beyond the workplace, I've also experienced the importance of a supportive environment in my personal life. Having a family that believes in my vision and friends who encourage my pursuits has been instrumental in my success. Their support has given me the confidence to take risks and the resilience to persevere through challenges.

Building and maintaining a supportive environment requires intentional effort. In the professional setting, it means advocating for a culture that values innovation, providing the necessary resources, and recognizing and rewarding creative contributions. At home and among friends, it means fostering relationships that are based on mutual support, encouragement, and shared aspirations.

To truly thrive and achieve your innovative goals, you must be surrounded by people who inspire and motivate you. Seek out environments where creativity and experimentation are valued, and align yourself with individuals who ignite your passion and drive. Remember, even the most groundbreaking ideas need a nurturing environment to grow and succeed. By creating and sustaining a supportive environment, you can overcome obstacles, fuel your innovative spirit, and achieve extraordinary outcomes.

Fostering Resilience

Resilience is the backbone of innovation. The journey is fraught with setbacks and failures, and the ability to bounce back is crucial. I've found that fostering resilience involves cultivating a mindset that views failures as learning opportunities. Encouraging your team to embrace challenges and persist despite obstacles is essential. Sharing stories of past failures and how they led to eventual success can help reinforce this mindset.

In my experience, resilience starts with the right mindset. It's about viewing failures not as dead ends but as valuable lessons that bring you closer to success. This perspective shift can reshape how you and your team approach challenges. Instead of fearing failure, you learn to see it as an integral part of the innovation process. By reframing setbacks as opportunities for growth, you create a culture where resilience thrives.

One practical way to foster resilience is to openly discuss and analyze failures. Create an environment where team members feel safe to share their mistakes and learnings. This can be done through regular debriefing sessions where you dissect what went wrong in a project, identify the root causes, and brainstorm solutions to avoid similar pitfalls in the future. This practice not only helps in learning from mistakes but also normalizes the idea that failure is a natural part of the journey.

Sharing stories of resilience can be incredibly powerful. Highlight examples from your own experiences or from well-known innovators who faced significant setbacks before achieving success. For instance, Thomas Edison famously failed thousands of times before inventing the electric light bulb. Each failure brought him one step closer to the final breakthrough. These stories serve as reminders that perseverance and resilience are key to eventual success.

Encouraging a growth mindset within your team is another crucial aspect of fostering resilience. A growth mindset, as opposed to a fixed mindset, is the belief that abilities and intelligence can be developed through dedication and hard work. This mindset fosters resilience because it encourages individuals to view challenges as opportunities to develop their skills and knowledge. Provide opportunities for your team to develop this mindset through training and development programs that emphasize continuous learning and personal growth.

Building a supportive network is also vital for resilience. Surround yourself and your team with mentors, peers, and advisors who can provide guidance and encouragement during tough times. These relationships can offer different perspectives, help navigate obstacles, and provide a source of motivation when facing setbacks. Encourage team members to seek out mentors and build a network of support within and outside the organization.

Resilience is not just about bouncing back from failures but also about maintaining a positive outlook during challenging times. Encourage practices that promote mental and emotional well-being. This could include mindfulness exercises, regular breaks, and team-building activities that foster a sense of camaraderie and support. When team members feel valued and supported, they are more likely to stay resilient in the face of adversity.

Implementing flexible work practices can also contribute to resilience. Allowing team members to work in a way that suits their strengths and preferences can help them manage stress and stay motivated. Flexible schedules, remote work options, and the ability to take breaks when needed can all contribute to a more resilient workforce. By accommodating different working styles, you can help your team maintain their productivity and creativity, even during challenging times.

Encourage a culture of experimentation where trying new things and taking calculated risks are valued. This approach can help your team build resilience by learning to handle uncertainty and adapt to changing circumstances. When team members are encouraged to experiment, they become more comfortable with the idea of failure as a part of the learning process. This can lead to more innovative solutions and a stronger, more resilient team.

Another effective strategy is to set realistic expectations and celebrate small wins along the way. Acknowledge the effort and progress made, even if the ultimate goal has not yet been achieved. Celebrating small victories can boost morale and provide the motivation needed to keep pushing forward. It reinforces the idea that every step, no matter how small, is a part of the journey toward success.

Incorporating resilience training into your organization can also be beneficial. Provide workshops and resources that teach techniques for managing stress, staying motivated, and bouncing back from setbacks. These training sessions can equip your team with the tools they need to stay resilient in the face of challenges. By investing in resilience training, you demonstrate a commitment to your team's well-being and long-term success.

Regularly review and adjust your strategies to ensure they are effective in fostering resilience. Solicit feedback from your team on what is working and what needs improvement. This iterative approach allows you to continuously refine your methods and create an environment that supports resilience. By staying attuned to your team's needs and making necessary adjustments, you can maintain a resilient and motivated workforce.

In conclusion, fostering resilience is crucial for navigating the innovation journey. It involves cultivating a mindset that views failures as learning opportunities, encouraging open discussions about setbacks, and sharing stories of perseverance. Building a supportive network, promoting mental and emotional well-being, and implementing flexible work practices all contribute to a resilient culture. Encourage a culture of experimentation, set realistic expectations, and celebrate small wins. Invest in resilience training and regularly review your strategies to ensure they are effective. By fostering resilience, you equip your team with the ability to overcome challenges and persist in the pursuit of innovation.

Navigating the innovation journey is both exhilarating and challenging. As we've explored, societal skepticism, financial constraints, and the need for a supportive environment are all part of the landscape. But with resilience, strategic planning, and a strong support network, these challenges can be overcome. Embrace failures as stepping stones to success and foster an environment that encourages creativity and perseverance.

Remember, innovation isn't just about having a great idea—it's about having the determination to see it through, despite the obstacles. Surround yourself with people who believe in your vision and push you to keep going, even when the path seems difficult. Stay flexible and open to change, and never lose sight of the impact your innovation can have.

As you continue on this journey, take the lessons and strategies we've discussed to heart. Believe in your potential to make a difference, and don't be afraid to take risks. Your innovative spirit, combined with resilience and support, will lead you to extraordinary achievements. Keep pushing forward, and let your passion for innovation drive you toward a future filled with limitless possibilities.

"Resilience is the strength that turns every stumble into a step forward and every setback into a setup for a comeback. Embrace it, and life's challenges will help you succeed."

– Bob Philips –

Chapter 8

The Power of Me Time

- **Importance of self-renewal.**
- **The power of extended breaks.**
- **Benefits of "me time" in your innovation journey.**

The concept of “me time” is essential in our fast-paced world, where the constant hustle can easily lead to burnout, decreased creativity, and diminished productivity. Setting aside time for self-renewal isn’t just a luxury—it’s a necessity. It’s about taking a step back to recharge your physical, emotional, and mental batteries.

The Importance of Self-Renewal

Self-renewal is the practice of regularly taking time to disconnect from the daily grind and focus on yourself. It’s about replenishing your energy, clearing your mind, and gaining new insights. This practice can lead to improved focus, enhanced creativity, and better problem-solving abilities.

Daily "Me Time" Practices

Integrating “me time” into your daily routine can significantly enhance your ability to innovate and stay productive. Here are some strategies to help you incorporate self-renewal into your everyday life.

Morning Reflection

Start your day with a few minutes of quiet reflection. This can involve meditation, journaling, or simply sitting in silence. Reflecting on your goals and setting a positive intention for the day can help you stay focused and centered. Benjamin Franklin, one of America’s founding fathers and a renowned inventor, was known for his meticulous daily routine that included time for reflection and planning each morning. He would ask himself, “What good shall I do this day?” This practice set a positive tone for his day and allowed him to approach his tasks with clarity and purpose.

Meditation is an excellent way to begin your morning reflection. It helps clear the mind and prepares you to face the day with calm and focus. Techniques such as mindfulness meditation, where you concentrate on your breath, can be particularly effective. Studies have shown that regular meditation can reduce stress, improve concentration, and enhance overall well-being.

Journaling is another powerful tool for morning reflection. Writing down your thoughts, goals, and intentions helps solidify them in your mind. It provides a space for you to process your emotions and clarify your thinking. You can use your journal to plan your day, set goals, and reflect on what you are grateful for. This practice not only sets a positive tone for the day but also helps track your progress over time.

Simply sitting in silence can also be incredibly beneficial. In our constantly connected world, moments of silence can be rare. Taking time to just sit and be present with your thoughts can foster a sense of peace and clarity. This quiet time allows your mind to wander and can often lead to unexpected insights and ideas.

Scheduled Breaks

Throughout your day, schedule short breaks to step away from your work. Use these moments to stretch, breathe deeply, or take a brief walk. These breaks can help clear your mind and prevent burnout. Jeff Weiner, former CEO of LinkedIn, advocates for scheduling time to think. He blocks out 90 minutes to two hours each day for what he calls "buffers." These are moments he uses to reflect, strategize, and simply catch his breath.

Stretching is an excellent way to use your breaks. It helps relieve tension in your muscles, improves circulation, and can boost your energy levels. Simple stretches like reaching for the sky, touching your toes, or twisting your torso can make a big difference in how you feel physically and mentally.

Deep breathing exercises can also be incredibly effective. Techniques such as diaphragmatic breathing, where you breathe deeply into your abdomen, can help reduce stress and increase oxygen flow to your brain. Taking a few minutes to practice deep breathing can leave you feeling more relaxed and focused.

Taking a brief walk, especially if you can get outside, is another great way to recharge. Walking increases blood flow to your brain, which can improve cognitive function and creativity. It also provides a change of scenery, which can help break up the monotony of the workday and refresh your perspective.

Digital Detox

Allocate specific times during your day to disconnect from digital devices. Avoid checking emails, social media, or news during these periods. This practice can reduce stress and help you stay present and engaged in your tasks.

Constant connectivity can be overwhelming and distracting. Setting boundaries with your digital devices can help create a healthier relationship with technology. One strategy is to designate "no tech" times, such as during meals, in the first hour after waking up, or the last hour before bed. This can help you be more mindful and present in the moment.

During these digital detox periods, focus on activities that don't involve screens. Read a physical book, go for a walk, spend time with loved ones, or engage in a hobby. These activities can provide a welcome break from the constant influx of information and help you recharge.

Evening Unwind

End your day with a relaxing activity that helps you unwind. This could be reading a book, listening to music, or engaging in a hobby. Allowing yourself to relax before bed can improve your sleep quality and prepare you for the next day. Winston Churchill, the British Prime Minister during World War II, was known for his strict evening routine that included painting and building brick walls around his estate. These activities helped him relax and detach from the stresses of his leadership responsibilities.

Reading a book, whether it's fiction or non-fiction, can be a wonderful way to unwind. Fiction can transport you to another world, providing a mental escape from your daily worries. Non-fiction can inspire new ideas and perspectives. Choose something that interests you and allow yourself to get lost in the pages.

Listening to music is another great way to relax. Music has been shown to reduce stress and anxiety, improve mood, and even enhance cognitive function. Create a playlist of your favorite relaxing tunes and let the music help you wind down.

Engaging in a hobby, whether it's painting, knitting, gardening, or cooking, can also be very therapeutic. Hobbies provide a creative outlet and a sense of accomplishment. They allow you to focus on something enjoyable and take your mind off work-related stress.

The Benefits of Regular Self-Renewal Practices

Integrating "me time" into your daily routine offers numerous benefits that extend beyond the immediate sense of relaxation and rejuvenation. These practices can have a profound impact on your overall well-being and productivity.

First and foremost, self-renewal helps reduce stress. By taking time to relax and recharge, you can prevent burnout and maintain a healthier work-life balance. This is crucial for sustaining long-term productivity and creativity.

Regular self-renewal practices also improve focus and concentration. When you give your mind a break from constant stimulation, you return to your tasks with greater clarity and sharpness. This can lead to more efficient and effective work.

Moreover, self-renewal fosters creativity. Taking time to relax and reflect can lead to new insights and ideas. It allows your brain to process information in a different way, often leading to "aha" moments that wouldn't occur in the midst of a busy workday.

Incorporating Continuous Learning

Continuous learning is a vital aspect of self-renewal. By regularly expanding your knowledge and skills, you keep your mind sharp and stay relevant in your field. Here are some strategies to incorporate continuous learning into your daily routine.

Make a habit of reading regularly. Choose a mix of books that interest you, including both business-related and fictional works. Reading business books keeps you informed about the latest trends and strategies, while fiction can stimulate your imagination and provide new perspectives. Diversifying your reading material can spark creativity and offer fresh insights.

Writing is another powerful tool for continuous learning. Regularly writing blogs, articles, or even short journal entries can help clarify your thoughts and ideas. It also provides a platform to share your knowledge and insights with others. Writing forces you to organize your thoughts and can lead to new discoveries.

Consider recording podcasts to discuss topics related to your field or your personal interests. Podcasts offer a way to engage with a broader audience and share your expertise in a conversational format. They can also serve as a medium for continuous learning, as preparing for podcast episodes often involves research and reflection.

The Power of Extended Breaks

While daily "me time" practices are crucial, taking extended breaks away from your routine can provide even greater benefits. These longer breaks allow you to disconnect from the constant demands of work and daily life, giving you the opportunity to recharge and gain fresh perspectives. Let's explore how these extended breaks can significantly impact your innovation journey.

Planning a Retreat

Consider planning a personal retreat where you can spend a few days away from your usual environment. Choose a location that inspires you and allows you to disconnect from distractions. Whether it's a quiet cabin in the woods, a beachside cottage, or a mountain retreat, find a place where you can relax and reflect.

One inspiring example is Bill Gates, co-founder of Microsoft, who is known for his "Think Weeks." Twice a year, Gates retreats to a secluded location with a collection of books and articles. During these weeks, he disconnects from the outside world to read, reflect, and think deeply about the future of technology and his philanthropic efforts. These retreats have been pivotal in shaping his vision and strategy, providing him with the clarity and insights needed to drive innovation.

Similarly, you can plan your retreat by selecting a location that resonates with you. The key is to find a setting that allows you to break free from your usual routine and immerse yourself in an environment conducive to deep thinking and creativity.

Disconnecting from Distractions

During your retreat, commit to staying away from social media, email, and other digital distractions. The constant barrage of notifications and updates can be overwhelming and hinder your ability to think deeply. Use this time to immerse yourself in nature, engage in reflective practices, and focus on your personal and professional growth.

Consider setting boundaries for your digital detox. Inform your colleagues, friends, and family about your retreat and your intention to disconnect. This will help manage their expectations and allow you to fully engage in your time away. By disconnecting, you create a mental space that fosters creativity and introspection, free from the noise of daily life.

Engaging in Reflective Activities

Use your retreat to engage in activities that promote reflection and creativity. This could include journaling, painting, hiking, or simply sitting in silence. Allow yourself the freedom to explore new ideas and gain insights that can enhance your innovation journey.

Journaling can be a powerful tool during your retreat. Write about your thoughts, feelings, and reflections on your work and personal life. This practice helps clarify your thinking and can lead to valuable insights. Reflect on your successes and challenges, and consider how you can apply these lessons moving forward.

Engaging in creative activities such as painting or drawing can also stimulate your imagination. These activities provide a different way of expressing yourself and can lead to unexpected ideas and solutions. Hiking or spending time in nature can help you reconnect with yourself and the world around you, providing a sense of peace and inspiration.

Reconnecting with Your VisionExtended breaks provide the perfect opportunity to reconnect with your vision and goals. Reflect on your progress, reassess your objectives, and make any necessary adjustments to your plans. This time away can help you gain clarity and reignite your passion for your work.

During your retreat, take time to revisit your long-term vision. Consider where you started, where you are now, and where you want to go. Reflect on the impact you want to make and the legacy you wish to leave. This reflection can help you realign your actions with your overarching goals and ensure you are on the right path.

Reassess your objectives and identify any areas that may need adjustment. The fresh perspective gained from your retreat can provide valuable insights into how to refine your strategy and approach. Use this time to set new goals and create an action plan for the coming months.

The Benefits of Extended Breaks

Extended breaks offer numerous benefits that extend beyond immediate relaxation. They provide a chance to step back and view your work from a broader perspective, leading to deeper insights and more effective solutions. These breaks also enhance your creativity by giving your mind the space to wander and explore new ideas.

Moreover, extended breaks can improve your mental and emotional well-being. By disconnecting from the constant demands of work, you reduce stress and prevent burnout. This rejuvenation can lead to increased energy, motivation, and productivity when you return.

Taking time for yourself also reinforces the importance of self-care and balance. It sets a positive example for your team and encourages a culture that values well-being alongside hard work. This balance is crucial for sustaining long-term innovation and success.

Implementing Extended Breaks

To implement extended breaks effectively, plan them into your schedule well in advance. Treat them as essential components of your work routine, not as luxuries. Communicate with your team and stakeholders about the purpose and benefits of these breaks, ensuring they understand their importance.

Prepare for your retreat by setting clear intentions and goals. Decide what you want to achieve during this time and how you will use it to reflect, recharge, and gain new insights. This preparation ensures you make the most of your extended break.

Upon returning from your retreat, take time to integrate the insights and ideas you gained into your daily work. Share your experiences with your team and apply the new strategies and perspectives to your projects. This integration reinforces the value of extended breaks and maximizes their impact on your innovation journey.

The Benefits of "Me Time" in Your Innovation Journey

Taking regular breaks allows your mind to relax and wander, leading to new and creative ideas. When you're constantly working, your brain can become fatigued, stifling creativity. "Me time" gives your brain the space it needs to generate innovative solutions.

Self-renewal practices help you recharge, making you more focused and productive when you return to your tasks. By taking care of your mental and emotional well-being, you can approach your work with greater energy and efficiency.

Reflection and downtime enable you to process information more effectively, leading to better decision-making. When you're constantly busy, it's easy to make hasty decisions. "Me time" allows you to step back, consider all options, and make informed choices.

Regular self-renewal practices build your resilience, helping you navigate the ups and downs of the innovation journey. By taking time to care for yourself, you strengthen your ability to cope with challenges and setbacks.

Strategies for Maintaining a Renewal Practice

Consistency is Key

Make self-renewal a regular part of your routine. Consistency is crucial for reaping the benefits of "me time." Whether it's daily, weekly, or monthly, find a rhythm that works for you and stick to it.

Personalize Your Approach

Everyone's renewal needs are different. Find what works best for you and tailor your practices accordingly. Experiment with different activities and routines until you find what truly rejuvenates you.

Accountability Partners

Share your self-renewal goals with a friend or colleague who can help hold you accountable. Having someone to check in with can provide motivation and support in maintaining your renewal practices.

Reflect and Adjust

Regularly reflect on your self-renewal practices and their impact on your well-being and productivity. Adjust your approach as needed to ensure it continues to meet your needs.

The power of "me time" cannot be overstated. Taking time for self-renewal is not a luxury but a necessity for maintaining your well-being and sustaining your innovation efforts. By prioritizing self-care, you can enhance your clarity, creativity, and overall productivity. Whether it's through daily reflection, engaging in hobbies, spending time in nature, or taking extended breaks, find what rejuvenates you and make it an integral part of your routine.

Remember, the journey of innovation is a marathon, not a sprint. Taking time to renew yourself ensures that you can continue to push boundaries, generate new ideas, and achieve your goals. Embrace the power of "me time" and let it fuel your journey toward sustained innovation and success. By integrating these strategies into your life, you'll be better equipped to handle the challenges of innovation and maintain a steady flow of creative ideas. So, take a step back, recharge, and let the power of "me time" propel you forward. Your future self—and your innovative endeavors—will thank you.

"In the quiet moments of 'me time,' you find the seeds of your greatest ideas. Are you giving yourself enough time to grow?"

– Bob Philips –

Epilogue

Innovation is not just a cliché; it's a way of life. It's the magic that transmutes dreams into reality, the spark that ignites progress, and the seed that grows into something magnificent. When we talk about innovation, we're not just discussing new products or groundbreaking technologies. We're talking about a mindset—a way of thinking and living that embraces change, seeks out new possibilities, and continuously strives for improvement.

Throughout this book, we've explored the MAGIC formula—Mindset, Analyze, Generate, Implement, Change—to guide you on your innovation journey. This formula is more than a set of steps; it's a philosophy that empowers you to turn your ideas into tangible outcomes. Each component of the MAGIC formula plays a crucial role in helping you navigate the complexities of innovation, from developing the right mindset to effectively implementing and sustaining change.

Now, as we conclude, I want to remind you that everything is possible. There is nothing under the sun that is impossible. The universe waits for your instructions, and it will follow your orders 100%. What you think is exactly what will happen to you. Your thoughts shape your reality, and your mindset determines your success. Embrace the MAGIC formula, believe in your vision, and take bold steps towards your goals. The future of innovation is in your hands, and the possibilities are limitless. Go forth with confidence, and let your journey of innovation begin.

Let me share a story that beautifully illustrates the power of potential and the importance of the right environment and nurturing.

The Story of the Forgotten Seed

In a remote village, many years ago, a mason was busy constructing a house. As he was laying bricks and plastering walls, he noticed a small seed lying on the ground. For no particular reason other than amusement, he picked up the seed and placed it between the bricks, sealing it with cement. The seed was completely enclosed within the walls of the house, forgotten and left to its fate.

The house stood tall for a hundred years, sheltering generations of families. It witnessed countless stories, laughter, tears, and celebrations. Over the years, the seed remained dormant, waiting patiently for the right moment to awaken.

One day, the descendants of the original owners decided to demolish the old house and build a new one. As the walls came down and the rubble piled up, a young girl, part of the new generation, stumbled upon the seed. She was curious and fascinated by the tiny object that had been hidden away for so long. She picked it up and put it in her pocket, carrying it with her as she explored the ruins of her ancestral home.

Later that evening, while playing in the garden, she absentmindedly threw the seed into the soil. The seed, finally free from its confinement, embraced the warmth of the earth, the moisture of the rain, and the light of the sun. It began to sprout, grow, and reach for the sky. Over the years, it grew into one of the tallest and most magnificent trees in the neighborhood, providing shade, beauty, and shelter to many.

This story is a testament to the incredible potential that lies dormant within us, waiting for the right conditions to flourish. Just like that seed, you have a creative and innovative seed within you. This seed of yours needs the right environment and nurturing to grow into something extraordinary.

Nurturing Your Seed with the MAGIC Formula

The MAGIC formula is designed to provide you with the tools and techniques to nurture your seed of innovation.

Mindset: Cultivating Innovation from Within

Your journey begins with the right mindset. Believe in yourself and your ability to innovate. Embrace curiosity, foster resilience, and develop a growth mindset. The way you think sets the stage for everything that follows. Remember, the universe responds to your thoughts. What you focus on expands, so focus on possibilities, solutions, and growth.

Analyze: Understanding the Innovation Ecosystem

To innovate effectively, you need to understand the landscape. Analyze market trends, customer needs, and technological advancements. Use tools like NEWT to identify opportunities and threats. By staying informed and aware, you can make strategic decisions that position you for success.

Generate: Ideation and Concept Development

Generating ideas is the heart of innovation. Use techniques like brainstorming, mind mapping, reverse thinking, and the Six Thinking Hats to spark creativity. Collaborate with others, value diverse perspectives, and keep an idea journal to capture your thoughts. Remember, the more ideas you generate, the higher the chances of finding a truly groundbreaking one.

Implement: Turning Ideas into Reality

Execution is where dreams meet reality. Use the EXECUTE principles to guide your implementation efforts. Establish a clear vision, expand with a strategic plan, engage the right team, consolidate resources, utilize prototyping, test with phased implementation, and evaluate and adjust continuously. Turning ideas into reality requires meticulous planning, commitment, and adaptability.

Change: Leading and Sustaining Innovation

Leading innovation involves more than just starting new projects. It requires sustaining momentum and embedding innovation into your organizational culture. Use the OVERCOME principles to navigate challenges, foster a supportive environment, and build resilience. Measure success with clear metrics, celebrate achievements, and learn from failures to drive continuous improvement.

The Seed Within You

Now, there is a seed within you—a seed of creativity and innovation. This seed holds the potential to grow into something remarkable, but it needs the right environment and nurturing. Just like the seed in the story, your innovative ideas need to be planted in fertile soil, watered with knowledge, and exposed to the light of inspiration.

Your environment matters. The people you surround yourself with have a profound impact on your growth. Seek out those who inspire you, challenge you, and support your journey. These could be mentors who have walked the path before you, peers who share your vision, or communities that are passionate about innovation. The right network can provide invaluable insights, encouragement, and opportunities.

Creating a conducive environment for your seed of innovation involves more than just physical space. It's about cultivating a mental and emotional space where creativity can flourish. Designate a specific area for your creative pursuits, whether it's a home office, a quiet corner, or even a favorite café. This space should be free from distractions and filled with elements that spark joy and inspiration—art, books, plants, or anything else that stimulates your imagination.

Knowledge is the water that nurtures your seed. Make continuous learning a part of your daily routine. Read extensively in your field and beyond; both business and fictional books can provide new perspectives and ideas. Attend workshops, seminars, and webinars. Stay curious and open to new experiences. The more you know, the more connections you can make between seemingly unrelated ideas, leading to innovative solutions.

Disconnecting from distractions is crucial. In today's hyper-connected world, it's easy to get lost in the noise of social media, news, and constant notifications. Schedule regular digital detoxes where you unplug from your devices and focus on your thoughts. Use this time to reflect, meditate, and recharge. Quiet moments of introspection often lead to the most profound insights.

Self-renewal is essential for sustaining innovation. Take care of your physical, mental, and emotional well-being. Exercise regularly, eat healthily, and get enough sleep. Engage in activities that relax and rejuvenate you—whether it's hiking, painting, cooking, or simply spending time with loved ones. A well-rested and healthy mind is more capable of creative thinking and problem-solving.

Your seed of innovation also needs the light of inspiration. Expose yourself to different cultures, ideas, and experiences. Travel, meet new people, and explore new places. Inspiration often comes from the most unexpected sources. Sometimes, stepping out of your comfort zone and seeing the world from a different perspective can ignite a spark that leads to groundbreaking ideas.

Remember, nurturing your seed of innovation is an ongoing process. It requires patience, persistence, and a willingness to embrace uncertainty. There will be setbacks and challenges along the way, but these are opportunities to learn and grow. Every great innovation started as a small seed, nurtured over time with dedication and care.

Believe in Your Vision

As you embark on your innovation journey, believe in your vision. No matter how challenging the path may seem, remember that every great achievement starts with a single idea. The universe is waiting for your instructions, ready to follow your lead. What you think is exactly what will happen to you. So, think big, dream boldly, and take action.

The MAGIC formula is here to guide you, but the true magic lies within you. Your thoughts, actions, and persistence will determine the outcome. Trust in your abilities, stay committed to your goals, and keep moving forward. The future of innovation is yours to shape.

A Final Thought

I follow a guiding philosophy in my life (Mathew 5): to be like Salt and Light. Just like salt brings out the best flavors and preserves what's good, I strive to improve and protect the positive aspects around me in meaningful, yet often small, ways. And like light, I aim to display honesty and integrity, helping to light the way in difficult or unclear situations. This way of thinking influences all my actions and motivates me to leave a positive, enduring mark in my part of the world. It's more than just my actions; it's a part of who I am.

Imagine a world where every innovative idea is nurtured and allowed to flourish. Imagine the impact we can create, the problems we can solve, and the lives we can improve. It all starts with you and the seed of innovation within you. As you step into your role as a catalyst for change, remember that you are the salt and light in your world. Your unique ideas and innovative spirit have the power to enhance and preserve what is good, while also illuminating the path forward in challenging times.

Innovation is not just about grand, sweeping changes. Often, it's the small, thoughtful actions that lead to significant results. By being attentive to the needs around you and taking steps to address them, you are already contributing to a better, brighter future. Your efforts, no matter how modest they may seem, have the potential to create ripples of positive change that extend far beyond your immediate surroundings.

So, go on and do it. Plant your seed, nurture it, and watch it grow into something extraordinary. The world needs your creativity, your vision, and your determination. Every step you take towards nurturing your innovative ideas brings us closer to a world where innovation thrives and makes a meaningful difference. Whether it's developing a new product, improving a process, or finding a solution to a pressing problem, your contributions matter.

The future of innovation is bright, and it is in your hands. Believe in your vision, take action, and make it happen. The world is waiting for your innovation—let your journey begin. As you start on this path, remember to be the salt and light in every endeavor. Enhance and preserve the good, shine brightly in the face of challenges, and inspire others to do the same.

The journey of innovation is not always easy, but it is incredibly rewarding. There will be moments of doubt, setbacks, and obstacles, but these are all part of the process. View them as opportunities to learn and grow. Stay resilient and keep pushing forward. Your perseverance will pay off, and the results will be worth it.

As you move forward, continue to seek out new knowledge and experiences. Surround yourself with people who inspire and challenge you. Take time for self-renewal and reflection. These practices will help you stay focused, energized, and ready to tackle whatever comes your way.

In the end, innovation is about making a positive impact on the world. It's about solving problems, improving lives, and leaving a lasting legacy. Your innovative ideas have the power to do just that. So, go out there and be the salt and light the world needs. Let your creativity shine, and make your mark on the world. The future is yours to create, and it all starts with the seed of innovation within you.

Believe in yourself, take bold steps, and watch as your ideas grow and flourish. The world is waiting for your innovation—let your journey begin. You have the power to make a difference, and the time to start is now. Face the challenges, celebrate the successes, and never stop pushing the boundaries of what is possible. The future of innovation is yours, and the world is ready to see what you will achieve.

Bibliography

1. De Bono, Edward. *Six Thinking Hats*. Little, Brown, 1985.
2. Christensen, Clayton M. *The Innovator's Dilemma: When New Technologies Cause Great Firms to Fail.* Harvard Business Review Press, 1997.
3. Ries, Eric. *The Lean Startup: How Today's Entrepreneurs Use Continuous Innovation to Create Radically Successful Businesses.* Crown Business, 2011.
4. Kim, W. Chan, and Renée Mauborgne. *Blue Ocean Strategy: How to Create Uncontested Market Space and Make the Competition Irrelevant.* Harvard Business Review Press, 2005.
5. Osterwalder, Alexander, and Yves Pigneur. *Business Model Generation: A Handbook for Visionaries, Game Changers, and Challengers.* Wiley, 2010.
6. Robinson, Ken. *Out of Our Minds: Learning to Be Creative.* Capstone, 2011.
7. Brown, Tim. *Change by Design: How Design Thinking Transforms Organizations and Inspires Innovation.* Harper Business, 2009.
8. Goleman, Daniel. *Emotional Intelligence: Why It Can Matter More Than IQ.* Bantam Books, 1995.
9. Covey, Stephen R. *The 7 Habits of Highly Effective People: Powerful Lessons in Personal Change.* Free Press, 1989.
10. Dweck, Carol S. *Mindset: The New Psychology of Success.* Random House, 2006.

11. Gladwell, Malcolm. *Outliers: The Story of Success.* Little, Brown and Company, 2008.

12. Grant, Adam. *Originals: How Non-Conformists Move the World.* Viking, 2016.

13. Tidd, Joe, and John Bessant. *Managing Innovation: Integrating Technological, Market, and Organizational Change.* Wiley, 2018.

14. Schilling, Melissa A. *Strategic Management of Technological Innovation.* McGraw-Hill Education, 2016.

15. Christensen, Clayton M., and Michael E. Raynor. *The Innovator's Solution: Creating and Sustaining Successful Growth.* Harvard Business Review Press, 2003.

16. Gates, Bill. "Bill Gates's 'Think Week': A Blueprint for Taking a Break from the World." *The Atlantic*, 2012.

17. Hoffman, Reid, Ben Casnocha, and Chris Yeh. *The Alliance: Managing Talent in the Networked Age.* Harvard Business Review Press, 2014.

18. Feynman, Richard P. *Surely You're Joking, Mr. Feynman! Adventures of a Curious Character.* W. W. Norton & Company, 1985.

19. Edison, Thomas A. *The Diary and Sundry Observations of Thomas Alva Edison.* Omnigraphics, Inc., 1998.

20. Da Vinci, Leonardo. *The Notebooks of Leonardo Da Vinci.* Edited by Jean Paul Richter, Dover Publications, 1970.

These sources have informed and inspired the insights and strategies shared throughout this book. For those interested in further exploring the concepts discussed, these references provide a wealth of knowledge and practical wisdom.

About The Author

Bob Philips is an internationally recognized expert in behavioral training, innovation, and leadership. He is the co-founder of Skills Cafe, a pioneering game-based training company that has revolutionized the professional development landscape for thousands of leaders and organizations worldwide. With over two decades of experience, Bob has trained and mentored leaders across the globe, delivering impactful keynote speeches and workshops for Fortune 500 companies and diverse organizations.

Bob's approach to leadership and innovation is deeply rooted in his guiding philosophy from Mathew 5: to be like Salt and Light. Just as salt enhances and preserves, and light guides through darkness, Bob's work aims to bring out the best in people and illuminate the path to success. His passion for empowering individuals to lead with integrity and creativity has made him a sought-after speaker, coach, and mentor.

A USA national, Amazon and Kobo best-selling author, Bob has penned books and articles that explore into the intricacies of leadership, innovation, and personal development. His writings and teachings reflect his commitment to helping others unlock their potential and make a meaningful impact in their communities.

Residing in Dubai, Bob continues to inspire and mentor leaders through his dynamic speaking engagements and insightful publications. His dedication to fostering a culture of continuous learning and innovation has left an indelible mark on countless professionals, encouraging them to think boldly, act with purpose, and lead with compassion.

To learn more about Bob Philips and his groundbreaking work, visit bobphilips.com.

www.ingramcontent.com/pod-product-compliance
Lightning Source LLC
LaVergne TN
LVHW041009150826
845672LV00001B/29

* 9 7 8 9 3 6 0 0 6 8 9 7 4 *